Ant‹

MW01140195

The Capability Approach and Early Childhood Education Curricula
An Investigation into Teachers' Beliefs and Practices

Bibliographic Information published by the Deutsche Nationalbibliothek
The Deutsche Nationalbibliothek lists this publication in the Deutsche Nationalbibliografie; detailed bibliographic data is available in the internet at http://dnb.d-nb.de.

Library of Congress Cataloging-in-Publication Data
Names: Potsi, Antoanneta, 1985- author.
Title: The capability approach and early childhood education curricula : an investigation into teachers' beliefs and practices / Antoanneta Potsi.
Description: New York : Peter Lang, 2016. | Series: Labour, education & society ; volume 35 | Includes bibliographical references.
Identifiers: LCCN 2016010737 | ISBN 9783631665299
Subjects: LCSH: Early childhood education--Curricula.
Classification: LCC LB1139.4 .P68 2016 | DDC 372.21--dc23 LC record available at http://lccn.loc.gov/2016010737

ISSN 1861-647X
ISBN 978-3-631-66529-9 (Print)
E-ISBN 978-3-653-05855-0 (E-Book)
DOI 10.3726/ 978-3-653-05855-0

© Peter Lang GmbH
Internationaler Verlag der Wissenschaften
Frankfurt am Main 2016
All rights reserved.
PL Academic Research is an Imprint of Peter Lang GmbH.

Peter Lang – Frankfurt am Main · Bern · Bruxelles · New York · Oxford · Warszawa · Wien

This publication has been peer reviewed.

www.peterlang.com

Table of Contents

List of Tables

List of Figures

Introduction

Early childhood education and care has come to the forefront of social policies in the past decades due to the increasing interest of scientists, policymakers, politicians, and economists. Strengthening early childhood education and care are regarded not only as approaches that help reconcile work and family life, but also promote the socio-economic integration of vulnerable groups in society. A short look at the results of well-known intervention studies with cost-benefit analyses such as the "Chicago Child–Parent Centres" (Reynolds, 1997), "High Scope Perry Preschool Program" (Schweinhart & Weikart, 1997), or "Carolina Abecedarian Projects" (Campbell et al, 2002) leave no room for doubt regarding the positive long-term effects of preschool programs on children's cognitive and social development – especially for those living in poverty or at risk. The rationale behind public investment in such programmes is the expectation of a demonstrable and calculable return in the form of student performance, a quasi-contract in which preschools receive funding in exchange for delivering specified outcomes (Dahlberg & Moss, 2005). Influential international organizations such as UNESCO and the World Bank were also involved in public and academic discussions. Consequently, early childhood education and care programmes have grown more academically demanding over the last 20 years. As a bridge between the home and the school, early childhood education and care have come to be seen as serving a number of critical functions in chlidhood development, including preparation for academic learning, remediation for the effects of poverty, socialization, and academic training in itself.

The educational reports issued by the Organisation for Economic Cooperation & Development (OECD) have had a significant impact on policy measures for early childhood education and care in the European Union. At the Barcelona summit in 2002, EU member states adopted targets to provide childcare to at least 90 percent of children aged between 3 years and the nation's mandatory school age, as well as to at least 33 percent of children under the age of 3 years by 2010. Among the various EU benchmarks for 2020 that have been set for education, the goal is to have at least 95 percent of children (from the age of 4 to compulsory school age) participate in early childhood education. Ensuring suitable childcare arrangements is seen as an essential policy provision as an essential step towards achieving equal opportunities for women and men in the workplace, and accordingly, is explicitly included in the European Employment Strategy. In 2006, the issue of high-quality education became one of the predominant strategic objectives in the broader socio-political landscape of the European Union: "Pre-primary education has the highest returns in terms of the social adaptation of children. Member states should invest more in pre-primary education as an effective means to establish the basis for further learning, preventing school drop-out, increasing equity of outcomes and overall skill levels" (Education, Audiovisual and Culture Executive Agency, 2009).

As a member of the European Union, this broader sequence of transnational policy decisions had an impact on early childhood education in Greece. Among the multiple changes that have been occurred in the field of early childhood education and care in Greece, including the curriculum reform of 2001, have been the subject of considerable attention. The curriculum has been criticised as leading to the so-called 'schoolification' of pre-primary school by placing greater weight on performance-based academic objectives (Chrysafidis, 2006; Doliopoulou, 2002, 2003), rather than on capabilities objectives, which focus on the intrinsic value of children's abilities. Schoolification is defined as the move to shift primary school academic activities into pre-primary programs, which tends to makepre-primary school a kind of preparatory stage for children's success in primary school. Indeed, this trend of 'schoolifying' pre-primary education is stated clearly (Fragkos, 2002; Sofou, 2010; Tsafos & Sofou, 2010). The establishment of the all-day pre-primary school aiming at the upgrading of pre-primary education as well as the full preparation of children for primary school has been a government law (l. 2525) in Greece since 1997. Accordingly, aspects such as play-oriented experiences, social recognition, and socio-emotional growth have been ascribed less importance.

Evidence suggests, however, that the official curriculum may only be loosely connected to what teachers actually teach in the classroom (Cohen et al., 1990, cited in Lee Stevenson & Baker, 1991). According to Dahlberg and Moss (2005), although regulatory frameworks – such as standards, curricula, or guidelines – provide external norms that may be reinforced through processes of inspection, practitioners also create their own internal norms, and these are indeed more important in determining their implementation. It is worth mentioning here that within the Greek landscape of policy reform, those actually implementing the reforms in the classroom were the "bit players"[1] in the overall design and planning procedures.

---

1   A bit player is a role in which there is direct interaction with the principal actors and no more than five lines of dialogue.

The lack of research-based evidence and assessment process on the pre-primary curriculum that has been implemented thus far is what led me to examine pre-primary teachers' beliefs and practices regarding the actual curriculum approach dictated by current educational policy. I used the broad early childhood curricular approaches that have been identified within the literature on the subject as a theoretical background, namely, the social pedagogic (capabilities-based) and the pre-primary (performance-based) one. The aim of this study was to extend knowledge on how teachers' beliefs and their practises relate to the two sorts of curricular approach being followed in early childhood education. Antecedent personal and contextual factors (years of experience, administrative control, decision latitude, self-efficacy) were included in the model in order to gain a better understanding of the social structures that restrict teachers' freedom of agency. Within this framework, I investigated the relationship between teachers' beliefs and their respective practises, and the preference for a specific sort of belief that teachers may favour. Furthermore, I explored the potential of the Capability Approach as a normative framework that can shape a curriculum that goes above and beyond academic content alone.

Policymakers increasingly recognize that schools can be no better than the teachers and administrators who work in them (Guskey, 2002). Teachers' beliefs, thoughts, and decisions on educational matters make up a substantial and significant part of the teaching process, as a teacher's beliefs usually influence the actual instruction the teacher provides to students (Kagan, 1992). Beliefs, which are based on personal experiences, value systems and philosophies, have a direct impact on all aspects of human behavior, and individuals create a belief system for each major issue that concerns them. Beliefs need not be founded upon scientifically valid data – and rarely are. Most beliefs are related to deep-rooted, internalalized representations. Given this reality, it can be argued that teachers' beliefs shape the information received from formal teachers preparation and directly affect their classroom practices.

Over the past 25 years, researchers have shown increasing interest in studying teachers' beliefs and how these beliefs relate to teaching and learning practices (Fang, 1996; Kagan, 1992; Pajares, 1992) According to Fullan (1989), mastering practices and beliefs is the key to a pre-primary teacher's success. If effective use of the structure materials such as the curriculum is not achieved, particularly due to the beliefs and practices of front-line implementers, outcomes will not be achieved.

Although there has been global research conducted on early childhood teachers' beliefs, this work is mainly linked to examining the National Association for the Education of Young Children (NAEYC) guidelines (1991) regarding what are considered to be developmentally appropriate practices (DAP) and developmentally inappropriate practices (DIP) (Bredekamp & Copple, 1997).

ECEC services are largely depicted as local sites of disciplinary power (Foucault, 1977), characterized by the presence of regulatory controls that seemingly leading to normalized and privileged technical practices undertaken by disempowered early childhood teachers, who are burdened by the increasing regulatory accountabilities. Some critics (example.g. Grieshaber, 2002; Duncan, 2004) have suggested that under the weight of such regulatory accountabilities – along with the sanctions and enticements these regulations entail – early childhood teachers can become "docile yet productive" (Grieschaber, 2002, p. 162). Up until this point, there is a paucity of empirical research in Greece in the area of pre-primary teachers' beliefs. Furthermore, the issue of which aspects of the curriculum are endorsed and implemented by teachers has not been addressed.

This study uses the concept of the Capability Approach (CA), pioneered by the economist and philosopher Amartya Sen and further developed by the philosopher Martha Nussbaum, as an alternative critical lens through which to examine early childhood curricula. The CA is a broad normative framework for evaluating individual well being and social arrangements, policy design, and proposals regarding social change in society (Robeyns, 2003). The CA aims to assess the relative quality of human lives and societies by posing the question of "what are people actually able to do and to be?" (Nussbaum, 2011). As such, the framework provided by the CA serves as a counter narrative to the narrow instrumentalism that reduces education to a mere process of acquiring academic skills to be used in the workplace.

Focusing on the case of Greece, the central finding of the book is that the pedagogue's capability and responsibility to engage in curriculum development is a prerequisite for efficient early childhood pedagogy. Becoming involved in the process enables a sympbosis between the pedagogues' beliefs, their practical experience and their theoretical knowledge. Together, this ensures the representation of a variety of diverse viewpoints when it comes to defining what foundational based of knowledge is essential, and defining what skills are necessary for the highly unpredictable future. I believe that the issues discussed here are unlikely to be confined to this country alone and will have resonances on other national or international contexts.

Chapter 1 introduces the early childhood education in Greece and defines the critical vocabularly for the reader. A literature review of related fields and concepts is outlined in Chapter 2, which describes the current state of early childhood education and care from an international perspective as well as within the Greek context. Chapter 2 also presents the curriculum of 2001, its criticisms, and the debate that it has since generated. This chapter also presents the theoretical context and research conducted on teachers' beliefs and practices, attempting to embed the present research within a wider theoretical framework and to pinpoint its contribution to this field of research. This is followed by an in-depth analysis of the literature on the CA. Chapter 3 sums up the research problems identified in the literature review and presents research questions and hypotheses. It also introduces the research model constructs and research aims of this study. Chapter 4 develops the research methodology and delineates the research design, the instrument's development, population sample, the data collection process, and the tools used in the empirical investigation. Chapter 5 reports the research findings and explains the results of mean comparisons, correlation analyses, confirmatory factor analyses, and structural equation modelling. The discussion that follows in Chapter 6 bridges the gap between theoretical considerations and the evidence gleaned from research.

Chapter 1: Developing a common language

The school must be a spearhead into the future classless society.
(Olof Palme, 1968)

1.1 Greek educational system

In order to understand the dynamics of the development of early childhood education and specifically pre-primary school in Greece, it is important to be familiar with the essential information provided in this section. This book does not aim to describe the Greek education system. However, a brief overview of both the administrative organisation and the structure of this system is necessary before the debate on early childhood education can continue.

Greece's educational system is highly centralized and its administrative organization can be distinguished into four levels: national, regional, prefectural, and the single school unit. Education is divided into three levels of study: primary, secondary, and tertiary. Mandatory schooling lasts 10 years and consists of 1 year in pre-primary school (*nipiagogeio*), 6 years in primary school (*dimotiko*), and 3 years in lower secondary school (*gymnasio*). Primary education is composed of pre-primary schools (*nipiagogeia*) and primary schools (*dimotika scholeia*). Pre-primary school may optionally enrol children who reach the age of 4 on December 31st of the year of registering. Nevertheless, attendance of pre-primary school is mandatory for all children who reach the age of 5 on December 31st of the year of registering. Attendance of primary school (*dimotiko scholeio*) is also mandatory. Children who reach the age of 6 on December 31st of the year of registering have to enrol in primary school and attend for 6 years. Secondary education is composed of lower secondary schools (*Gymnasia*), unified upper secondary schools (*Eniaia Lykeia*), and technical vocational schools (*Technika Epaggelmatika Ekpaideftiria*). Primary school graduates enter 3 years of lower secondary school (*gymnasio*) up to the age of 15, before deciding to continue in either an upper secondary school (*eniaio lykeio*) or a technical vocational school (*TEE*). Tertiary education consists of universities (*AEI*) and technological educational institutes (*TEI*). Education in Greece is provided free of charge in public schools. The concept of free education includes the free supply of textbooks, state provision of financial aid to schools for their operation, and scholarships for high-performing young students. Figure 1.1 illustrates the education system structure as presented by Karras (2010).

Due to this study's focus on the first stage of primary education, namely, pre-primary education for which the Ministry of Education and Religious Affairs, Culture and Sports is responsible, the information provided on the Greek educational system is limited. Further information can be found in Eurydice/Eurybase (2010).

Figure 1.1. Structure of the Greek educational system

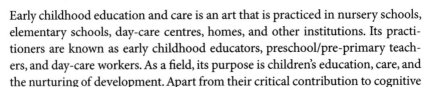

1.2 Early Childhood Services

Early childhood education and care is an art that is practiced in nursery schools, elementary schools, day-care centres, homes, and other institutions. Its practitioners are known as early childhood educators, preschool/pre-primary teachers, and day-care workers. As a field, its purpose is children's education, care, and the nurturing of development. Apart from their critical contribution to cognitive stimulation, socialization, child development, and early education, they are an essential service for employed parents (Kamerman, 2006).

The centre-based early childhood services in Europe date back to the end of the 19th century and are the twofold outcome of: (a) preschool institutions, pioneered by the French and Belgians and known as *l'école maternelle*, initially providing part-time education for children aged 3 to school age and (b) nursery institutions of the welfare sector to be found in Germany and Scandinavia. The former were created by the middle-classes to prepare young children for primary schooling, whereas the latter emerged as charitable activities or as health or welfare centres for the children of working parents or families at risk (Bennett & Kagan, 2010). The distinct historical roots of these institutions, although blurred over time, are still preserved. The diverse standpoints on children's childhood can be traced in their programme goals, contents, and approaches.

Although, today "childcare" and "early education" are regarded as being for all families, and nurseries increasingly emphasize developmental or educational aims (UNESCO, 2004), they differ in their types of service, workforce, access criteria, funding, and regulation (including curriculum). UNESCO (2004) highlights:

> The dual origins have left a legacy in many countries: divided systems of early childhood services, with differences in administration, access, cost to parents, funding, regulation – and in the structure and education of the workforce. Typically one system has "childcare" or "nursery workers", the other "teachers". Typically, too, the latter have higher levels of basic education, better pay and other employment conditions and greater social status.

However, subsequent developments were slow, with some expansion occurring during World War II and some following that. Kamerman (2006) argues that except for the eastern European socialist countries, in which extensive developments occurred right after World War II, and in France, with the integration of preschool into the education system in 1886 and the expansion of the *école maternelle* in the 1950s, the most significant developments date from the 1960s: the end of colonialism, the establishment of independent states in Africa, the dramatic increase in female labour force participation rates, the extensive developments in child and family policies in Europe and the United States, and the debate between care versus development as the critical issue in the ECEC field.

Several countries such as the UK follow a divided approach in ECEC by providing public education in nursery schools and market-provision services. This approach retains its class-related characteristics.

Greece clearly adopted a bifurcated approach to early childhood reception structures because there is an administrative division with two forms of publicly funded childcare facilities for pre-school children: one within the framework of the education system which falls under the Ministry of Education and Religious Affairs, Culture and Sports (from now on referred to as the Ministry of Education); and the other within the framework of the social welfare system under the supervision of municipalities, which fall under the Ministry of Interior.

Sims-Schouten (2000) explains that there are three types of childcare centres within the Greek welfare system, namely, infants' centres (for babies from 1–30 months), children's centres (for children from 2.5–6 years) and infant–toddler centres (for children from 40 days–6 years). In contrast, within the education system, pre-primary schooling is provided for children from 3.5 years to compulsory school age, which is 6 years.

Greece's early childhood education and care sector is underfunded and underdeveloped despite the proven benefits to the child, economy and society. Access to early childhood education and care is constrained by the low number of opening hours and limited number of services. Subsidised provision is offered only on a part-time basis (European Commission, 2009). The public childcare centres and pre-primary school supply is unable to meet demand and serves only a proportion of those who would like to use such facilities. The rest are obliged to turn to private sector providers. Private pre-primary schools also come under the responsibility of the Ministry of Education, which regulates staffing, building requirements, and staff–child ratios. The number of public pre-primary schools far outweighs the number of private, because according to the Hellenic Statistic Authority for the school year 2011/2012, only 474 out of a total of 5,921 pre-primary schools were private. The lack of places in public care has a social impact on specific families contributing to their vulnerability and creating greater inequalities. Although eligibility criteria such as the socio-economic situation of the family (poor) or the type of family (single parent family) are supposed to be taken into account and priority should be given to those with a low income, better-off families know how to "play the system" and ensure a place for their child. It should be noted that private sector providers can be of two sorts, namely, private non-subsidized childcare and childcare offered by relatives and/or friends. The role of the private for-profit sector in the provision of certain social services such as childcare has increased greatly in Greece over the last decade. It appears that parents who can afford to pay prefer private to public childcare for reasons of quality. However, due to the financial crisis and economic recession, a shift towards publicly funded childcare facilities and a decline in the parents' willingness to pay for a place in a private institution can be observed. The lack of national official records on the demand and availability of childcare facilities is indicative of the marginal role early childhood education and care plays in Greek politics, making it hard to estimate the level on which ECCE needs to catch up in order to meet the needs of society.

Resources devoted to education are modest. Participation in early childhood education and care is particularly low, influencing education outcomes in later years, the child care sector is poorly regulated and under-developed, and the separate administration of pre-school and childcare has led to inefficiencies. (Koutsogeorgopoulou, 2009) Notably, trying to get a childcare place for a child under the age of 3 years is like running a marathon. Koutsogeorgopoulou (2009) highlights that only 7 percent of 3- and under 3-year-old children were enrolled in childcare in 2003 compared to an average of 22 percent in the OECD area. These children are usually cared for by grandparents; or, in some cases, parents employ immigrant women as nannies who are often working illegally in Greece. The existence of the black economy makes it hard to gain an overview of child-care arrangements organised by families.

Certainly, the Greek situation needs to be regarded through the lens of the prevalent family model. Carlos and Maratou-Alipranti (2000) argue that Greece, being a Southern European country, has a traditional family model dominated by marriage – usually the married two-parent family – and child-rearing values. As they characteristically note, the incidence of divorce, cohabitation, and births out of wedlock is low, and fertility rates are also low. Further, although the nuclear family is the usual household form, the family unit is part of a larger, close network of kin relationships. Relatives in Greece constitute a support network providing economic and social functions for the family. Traditionally, grandparents and other extended family members contribute to the care of the children in their family network (Oberheumer, Schreyer, & Neuman, 2010). Solidarity between the generations continues to fulfil valuable economic and social support functions, and to provide family members with a pool of resources in areas such as health care, nursing, employment opportunities, and care of children and the elderly (Carlos & Maratou-Alipranti, 2000). Furthermore, the role of the woman within the family but also within the labour force should be taken into account. Oberhuemer, Schreyer, and Neuman (2010) explain that despite a significant increase in recent years, the female employment rate in Greece is fairly low by EU standards, because less than one-half of the female population (48.7 percent) was officially employed outside the home in 2008, compared with an EU average of 59.1 per cent.

1.3 Pre-primary school (nipiagogeio)

Following the trend in other European countries, pre-school education was established by law in Greece at the end of the 19th century. The organization, duration, and content of the training of pre-primary teachers, was last defined by law in 1985, along with the structure and, generally, the operation of primary and especially pre-primary education; the legal regulations on the structure and operation of the latter are still in force today with additional detailed regulations on more specific subjects.

Pre-primary school is, after the family, the first level of education in which children are confronted with arrangement issues, procedures, practices, and activities associated with the implementation and operation of school rules in the educational process. Pre-primary school is part of the Greek educational system within the framework of primary education. Its purpose according to Law 1566/85 is "to help the infants to develop physically, emotionally, mentally, and socially within the framework of the broader purpose of primary and secondary education". The objective of the *Nipiagogeio* is to give an equal opportunity to all young children to develop physically, emotionally, mentally and socially within the framework defined by the broader objectives of Primary and Secondary education. Specifically, *Nipiagogeio* helps young children to:

– develop their senses and organize their motor and cognitive abilities
– enrich and enable each child to make sense of the experiences deriving from their physical and social environment
– acquire the ability to distinguish the relationships and interactions existing in it
– develop the ability to understand and express themselves through symbols generally and especially in the fields of language, mathematics, and the arts
– create interpersonal relations that will assist their gradual and harmonious integration into the life of the community
– develop initiatives freely and easily within the framework of the organized environment and to become accustomed to the give-and-take relationship between the individual and the group.

Pre-primary school is free of charge based on Article 16 of the Greek Constitution, according to which free education is a fundamental right for all Greeks. However, according to Doliopoulou (2006), it is well known that significant burdens – regarding mainly operational costs – are often laid on the parents unofficially. Since 2006, pre-primary school has become compulsory for one year. Children can begin this stage of their education at the age of 4 years and stay until they are old enough to attend the first stage of primary school. There are two types of pre-primary schools - half-day pre-primary schools with hours from 8.30 a.m. to 12.15 p.m. and all-day pre-primary (*Oloimero Nipiagogeio*) operating from 7.45 till 16.00. Generally speaking, the morning pre-primary schools employ one teacher, who could be male or female. This teacher will have between 7 and 30 children aged 4–5.5 years. The children are together in the same class but the pace and degree of difficulty of activities is differentiated according to each child's ability. All-day pre-primary schools employ two teachers and can expect to have 31–60 children. The school year for *Nipiagogeio* begins on September 1st and ends on June 21st.

The pre-primary sector has undoubtedly been influenced by developments in school education. The thrust of educational policy has been to improve the quality of education and promote learning in the classroom. In order to monitor the standards of school education services provided, the Directorates of Education in each prefecture oversee the registration, operation, and inspection of all schools including pre-primary ones. The Government's early reluctance to become involved more directly in pre-primary education is reflected in a number of policy documents. There is evidence for the emphasis given in recent years to pre-primary education in the legislative barrage on the organization and operation of pre-primary schools and in a number of weighty changes such as the significant increase in pre-primary school units, the upgrade of pre-primary teachers' training, and their grade and salary equalization with primary teachers. Through its reports and resultant recommendations, the Ministry of Education has made some efforts to tackle several important issues and barriers to high-quality pre-school education. Nevertheless, pre-primary education has been and continues to be somewhat neglected, because it receives comparatively low priority from the Ministry of Education compared to primary, secondary, and tertiary education. The Government is not committed to continue the further training of pre-primary teachers. In the literature, it is claimed that the equalization of salaries between preschool teachers and teachers of older students as well as equal accreditation will contribute to improving preschool teachers' status and professionalization (Jalongo et al., 2004; Lindsay & Lindsay, 1987). However, in Greece despite the apparent "universification" (Arreman & Weiner, 2007) of educators within the educational system with regard to standards of training and salaries, it is clear that preschool teachers face low prestige within society but also within the educational system in comparison with primary and secondary school teachers.

The situation could be illustrated by paraphrasing Opper (1993) and adjusting his argumentation to fit the Greek context: Pre-school education continues, as in the past, to be the Cinderella of the education system. As her two elder sisters,

Primary and Secondary, prepare themselves to go to the ball organised by the Ministry of Education, she remains in the kitchen, neglected and despised, gleaning the meagre droppings that fall from the Ministry's table.

1.4 Qualifications of pre-primary teachers

Pre-primary teachers in Greece are pedagogues. The pedagogue is a professional working with the theory and practice of pedagogy. Pedagogy is a long-established tradition in Continental Europe but virtually unknown in, for example, the English-speaking world in which "pedagogy" is often translated, incorrectly, as "education" and the "pedagogue" as "teacher". The approach is relational and holistic: "The pedagogue sets out to address the whole child, the child with body, mind, emotions, creativity, history and social identity" (Moss & Petrie, 2002, cited in UNESCO, 2004).

Pre-primary teachers' basic training has undergone many changes during the past years. As a result of these changes, Zografou (cited in Doliopoulou, 2006) identified the following categories depending on teachers' age and educational background:

i)   older teachers who had undergone a 1-year training;
ii) middle-aged (or slightly younger) 2-year training teachers;
iii) graduates of a 4-year pre-school education course; and
iv) the youngest teachers with the strongest academic background, postgraduate studies, further training, and so forth.

The first two categories may cover a minor number of the teachers in pre-primary schools because most of them – if not all – have now retired. According to Vrinioti, Kyridis, Sivropoulou-Theodosiadou, and Chrysafidis (2012), a significant percentage (approximately 90 percent) of pre-primary school staff has university training, a standard unmatched in several highly developed countries in Europe. Greek universities have nine departments of pre-primary education offering an eight-semester full course of studies for a bachelor degree including practical training in pre-primary schools and offering potential graduate pre-primary teachers high levels of educational attainment. This degree enables prospective teachers to enter the national pedagogical examination: If they pass this examination, they are eligible to apply for a position as a public servant working for the Ministry of Education. Every department has its own syllabus with compulsory and free selection courses and each syllabus department may vary significantly from another. The department graduates are mainly women, because, as in many Western countries, pre-primary education is in principle a gender-skewed profession saturated by females who are primarily interested in getting jobs as regular or supply teachers in public pre-primary schools.

In its effort to increase and disseminate knowledge of developments in the field of in-service education and to reform the education system, the Greek Ministry of Education established a network of in-service teacher education centres (PEK) in 1985. *PEKs* offer a 100-teaching-hour programme in three sequential phases. These phases are structured around three main dimensions: cognitive, practical, and reflective. The attendance of the programme is mandatory and varies according to a teacher's length of service. The first phase lasts 60 hours for newly appointed teachers and 30 hours for substitute teachers. The second and third phases are attended by newly appointed teachers who, when entering the PEK, have less than 8 months of teaching experience in schools and have completed the first phase of introductory training. The introductory training programme addresses newly appointed primary and secondary school teachers as well as those hired as substitutes. The programme addresses an adult population that varies in terms of gender, age, basic university education, educational training and, most importantly, in terms of teaching experience.

In particular, one large group is teachers who have just graduated from university and whose teaching experience is limited only to placements completed during their studies. Another group consists of teachers from either public or private schools who have worked for a long time in other kinds of occupational field – unrelated to ECEC – before being assigned to schools. These teachers already have teaching experience, but are likely to have developed vocational and educational approaches different to those required for the classroom – in some cases better, but in others, worse. A third group is the teachers who have graduated several years ago, have work experience in other business areas, and will now have to meet the requirements of their new role. Hence, the training needs of participants are significantly diverse.

Another opportunity for further training is offered to pre-primary teachers in Didaskaleia. The purpose of **Didaskaleio** is to retrain and qualify preschool educators. In this context, the Didaskaleio of pre-primary educators seeks to monitor developments in educational science and educational technology in order to promote research, the production and transmission of knowledge, and experiences contributing to the educational development of the country in order to provide the necessary additional, general and specific, knowledge and skills that ensure free and fair academic and professional careers for teachers in pre-primary education. Under the law, a pre-primary school teacher in either the public or private sector who has completed no less than 5 and no more than 25 years of educational service has the right to participate in the selection process for postgraduate studies at Didaskaleio (this also includes the years as substitute teacher in public education). The selection of teachers attending Didaskaleio is made by the Ministry of Education via written examinations. Attendance at a Didaskaleio is compulsory and teachers are released from their teaching duties. Those who successfully finish the biennial cycle of retraining in Didaskaleio are given a diploma in retraining in educational science.

However, all in-service training types have been formulated by the state; the available education is under the control of the Ministry, and any other initiatives directly or indirectly involving in-service training activities have not been supported by the Ministry. Within this administrative context, teachers' unions have criticized the state monopolization of in-service activities due to the lack of any active teacher participation in their formulation and implementation. Moreover, both the initial and in-service teacher education courses require a mixture of theoretical and practical training, whereas both types of course offered by the state emphasize training in only theoretical knowledge.

1.5 The gender loop in the profession

Educators in Greece, irrespective of the level they are teaching, fall under one single unified payroll (the same payment structure) and they all need to have high levels of educational attainment (the vast majority is holding at least a BA degree from a university or equivalent), which means obtaining at least an eight-semester bachelor degree. Though, despite the "Universification" (term borrowed by Arreman & Weiner, 2007) resemblances of the educators within the educational system with regard to standards of training and their salaries, pre-primary teachers face a low prestige within the society but also within the educational system in comparison with the primary and secondary school teachers.

According to the statistical data of the Greek National Statistical Service, for the year 2014–2015, in a total of 13.106 pre-primary teachers only 210 were men, i.e., about 1,6 percent. In contrast, the percentage of male in the other educational levels is relatively high; for the same year at the primary schools was 29,7 percent, while at the lower secondary level schools 33,9 percent and upper secondary school the percentage was raised to 46,1 percent. These numbers reflect the view of the profession as an extension of the female-mother role. For the Greek society, the profession of pre-primary teacher is defined as a woman's natural task and more often than not it is presented as a job that anyone could easily do. The occupation itself is often identified as so familiar and ordinary and it lucks a specified form and content.

Apple (1982) argues that in every occupational category, women are more apt to be proletarianized than men. As women, the pre-school teachers thus found themselves in subordinate positions and, since their clients were the youngest children, they were placed at the bottom of the ladder of the teaching profession (Holmlund, 1996, p. 319, cited in: Weiner & Kallos, 2000).

In the last decades, efforts have been made to remove gender discrimination in education, which included the abolition of single-sex secondary schools, the abolition of a school pinafore for girls, the removal of gender stereotypic images from textbooks, and the possibility for males to enter pre-school (kindergarten) teacher education (since 1983). Nevertheless, there is still a clear distinction of the specific stereotypic roles of males and females in the various family and work roles in the textbooks (Kantartzi, 1991, cited in Hopf & Hatzichristou, 1999).

In the literature it is highlighted that the career paths of men and women differ along gender lines as male teachers are likely to benefit from higher wages and better opportunities than their female counterparts (Kauppinen et al. 1989; Cameron, 2001).

The contribution and the value of this educational level are diminished by the Ministry of Education as well as by the Educators' Federation by devoting the least resources to pre-primary in comparison with the other educational levels. With regard to the Educators' Federation, it is worth mentioning that since its foundation there was none preschool teacher member of its administrative board where the decisions are being taken for the whole sector of educators. Preschool teachers are always represented by educators from greater educational levels and normally by men, since the Board is male-dominated. In general, the situation could be illustrated by using Opper's (1993: 88) argumentation and adjusting them into the Greek context: Pre-school education continues, as in the past, to be the Cinderella of the education system. As her two elder sisters, Primary and Secondary, prepare themselves to go to the ball organised by the Ministry of Education, she remains in the kitchen, neglected and despised, gleaning the meagre droppings that fall from the Ministry's table.

Pre-primary teacher is a profession which demands a high level of personal commitment. The teacher involves her own personality to a large extends in order to carry out her work successfully. Lindsay and Lindsay (1987) argue that when society values the service and gives prestige to those who offer it, the practitioner's own belief in the worth of the work is reinforced. How individual teachers view themselves as contributors to the whole school appears to be important to their level of satisfaction beyond the classroom, and the formation of this view of teachers is related to their school cultural environment (Ma & MacMillan, 1999).

1.6 Glossary of terms

A wide range of terminology is used in the field and across agencies. In order to avoid misinterpretations, this section presents and defines the operational terms used in this study.

Pre-primary schools refer to public schools responsible for the provision of education and care of 4- to 6-year-old children.

Pre-primary school teachers refer to tertiary education pedagogues who are working in pre-primary schools.

Beliefs are "the implicitly held assumptions about people and events that individuals bring to a particular knowledge domain" (Kagan, 1992, p. 75). These assumptions influence one's values, decisions, and behaviours. Beliefs often "involve moods, feelings, emotions, and subjective evaluations" (Nespor, 1987, p. 323).

Practices "actions taken ....hich may reflect beliefs of teachers as well as other facets of the situation such as school and district policies" (Smith & Shepard, 1988, p. 309).

Children's capabilities refer to actions/activities that children are able and have the opportunity to do and to be.

Capability of emotions can be defined as the emotional competence (resilience) of the children (any strong agitation (diegersi) of the feelings of the children actuated by experiencing love, hate, fear, etc.).

Capability of imagination can be defined as the ability of the children to form mental images or concepts of what is not actually present to their senses.

Capability of senses can be defined as feelings or perceptions of the children produced through the organs of touch, taste, and so forth.

Capability of thought can be defined as the products of mental activity of the children (ideas, notions).

Capability of play can be defined as the involvement of the children in several types of activity (such as dramatic play, free play, play with games, or puzzles) for amusement or recreation.

Capability of affiliation can be defined as children's social associations (social competence) with peers and adults (cooperation, communication, etc.).

Classroom environment "refers to the social and physical context of the classroom" (Shavelson & Stern, 1981, p. 465).

Early childhood education is the schooling of children from birth to age 8.

Chapter 2: Literature Review

Doing justice to thought, listening to our interlocutors, means
trying to hear that which cannot be said but that which tries to make itself heard.
Bill Readings

2.1 Evolution of Early Childhood Education

Early childhood education has its roots in Europe where the field was fertilized through the seeds of great thinkers such as Plato and Aristotle in ancient Greece, John Comenius (1592–1670), John Locke (1632–1704), Jean-Jacques Rousseau (1712–1778), Johann Heinrich Pestalozzi (1746–1827), Friedrich Fröbel (1782–1852) – the father of *kindergarten* – and also Maria Montessori (1879–1952) – the founder of the *casa dei bambini*. However, we cannot discard contributors such as John Dewey (1859–1952), the American philosopher and educator who interlinked education and democracy and perceived schools as sites for transforming society. All of these thinkers have influenced the history of early childhood education, and their ideas continue to be present in current debates.

Lascarides and Hinitz (2000) argue that Comenius recognized the importance of early childhood education and saw it as a key to equality of opportunity. They quote the following statement by Comenius: "there is nothing in the intellect that has not first existed in the senses," and interpret his words as follows: the material of knowledge is derived through the senses, therefore training the senses is fundamental to learning and knowledge acquired through the senses becomes permanent (Lascarides & Hinitz, 2000, p. 42). Comenius emphasized the value of active learning and the involvement of parents in their children's education. His publication *The World of Pictures* (1658) is viewed as the first picture book for children.

For John Locke, experience would determine what a child would become, because he claimed that children are born as a *tabula rasa* (blank slate) that is filled gradually with ideas, concepts, and knowledge from experiences in the world. He concluded that the quality of early experiences, particularly how children are raised and educated, would shape the direction of a child's life.

The French philosopher Jean-Jacques Rousseau claimed that children at birth are innately good and that their natural tendencies should be protected against the corrupting influences of society. He also recognized that children's way of thinking and learning is different from that of adults.

Johann Heinrich Pestalozzi claimed that all people, even the poorest, had the right to an education as a way of helping them develop their moral and intellectual potential. He stressed the importance of the mother in children's earliest experiences. Unlike Rousseau, Pestalozzi actually worked with children and developed educational methods that are still in use today.

Friedrich Fröbel is known as the father of Kindergarten, because he was the first to establish training for teachers and contributed to areas in learning, curriculum, and methodology. He is widely known from the Fröbelian gifts, the first educational toys providing creative activities for children. He stressed that nature and the child's developing mind were connected, he regarded play as a pure and natural mode of learning, and he stressed the importance of play in young children's development.

Maria Montessori was a true feminist of her time. She was the first female doctor in Italy, and she worked with children with cognitive disabilities, because she regarded their problems as being more educational than medical. In 1907, she opened the *Casa dei Bambini* in which she introduced her didactic teaching materials. She used the term *prepared environment* to describe the match of right materials to the child's stages of development.

John Dewey is known as the father of progressive education. He saw the classroom as the ideal setting for a democratic citizen's development. His work attacked the teacher- and subject-centred approach by developing a child-centred approach. He also opposed the harsh punishments and rote learning (memorization through repetition) that were the norm in schools at that time.

Pestalozzi, Fröbel, and Dewey saw early childhood pre-primary schools as an extension of the ideal home environment and stressed the importance of emotionally secure, loving relationships – meaning that a teacher should not exert strict discipline and should guide children in discovering the world instead of teaching them (Education, Audiovisual and Culture Executive Agency, 2009).

Moreover, early childhood education, in its current form, has been greatly influenced by Sigmund Freud's (1846–1924) psychoanalytic theory, Erik Erikson's (1902–1994) theory of psychosocial development, Jean Piaget's (1896–1980) age–stage theory of cognitive development, and Lev Vygotsky's (1899–1934) socio-cultural approach to understanding cognition. Through different conceptions of knowledge and development, the aforementioned theories have shaped curriculum model development in the field. One of the internationally renowned approaches in early childhood education, based on the aforementioned scholars, is the *Reggio Emilia* (Hertzog, 2001; Nutbrown & Abbot, 2001; Soler & Miller, 2003; Vakil, Freeman, & Swim, 2003). This approach emerged in the homonymous city in Italy, where, in 1945, the first preschool "was built literally by the hands of the parents using proceeds from the sale of a war tank, three trucks and six horses" left over from the Second World War. Nutbrown and Abbot (2001) argue that the respect given to the potential of children, the organization and quality of centre and preschool environments, the promotion of collegiality, and the ethos of co-participation with families in the educational project are the characteristics that impress visitors to Reggio Emilia from around the globe every year. Reggio Emilia is "a cultural and political project of the local commune" that constitutes a source of inspiration for progressive educational reform and "provides a vivid example of foregrounding ethics and politics, without discarding technical practice" (Dahlberg & Moss, 2005, p. 15).

2.2 Recent Developments in Early Childhood Education

Early childhood education and care nowadays attracts the attention of social policymakers at the national and international level and have been subject to comparative educational and social policy analyses by international institutions. Nowadays, it is regarded as a way to reconciliate work and family life, increase women's labour participation, and promote the socio-economic integration of vulnerable groups in society. As a result, recent years have seen an intensification of the systematic organisation of child care and education services.

The results of well-known intervention studies with cost-benefit analyses such as "The Chicago Child-Parent Centres" (Reynolds, 1997), "High Scope Perry Preschool Program" (Schweinhart & Weikart, 1997), "Carolina Abecedarian Projects" (Campbell, Ramey, Pungello, Sparling, & Miller-Johnson, 2002), the Syracuse Family Development Research Project, the Yale Child Welfare Project, the project CARE, the Infant Health and Development Program, the Chicago Child–Parent Centers Programme, the Turkish Early Enrichment Programme (Education, Audiovisual and Culture Executive Agency, 2009) "Sure Start" and "Neighbourhood Nurseries Initiative" (Roberts, Mathers, Joshi, Sylva, & Jones, 2010) are highlighting the long-term effects of preschool programmes on children's cognitive and social development – especially for those living in poverty or at risk. These have all contributed to a view of early childhood education and care as an instrument to deliver predefined outcomes. These programmes involve intensive, early-starting, child-focused, centre-based education together with strong parent involvement, parent education, programmed educational home activities, and measures of family support (Education, Audiovisual and Culture Executive Agency, 2009, p. 23). Despite the significance of these interventions' results, it remains a matter of debate whether the positive effects of high-quality childcare model interventions can be generalized to the different sorts of high-quality childcare offered in the real world nowadays.

The rationale for public investment in such programmes is the expectation of a demonstrable and calculable return, a quasi-contract in which preschools receive funding in return for delivering certain outcomes (Dahlberg & Moss, 2005). The RAND research brief (2005) identifies three features associated with more effective interventions based on experimental and quasi-experimental evaluations of programme design features:

- Programmes with better-trained caregivers appear to be more effective. In the context of centre-based programmes, this may take the form of a lead teacher with a college degree as opposed to no degree. In the context of home visiting programmes, researchers have found stronger impacts when services are provided by nurse home visitors as opposed to a paraprofessional or lay professional home visitor.
- In the context of centre-based programmes, there is evidence to suggest that programmes are more successful when they have smaller child-to-staff ratios.
- There is some evidence that more intensive programmes are associated with better outcomes, but not enough evidence to indicate the optimal number of programme hours or how they might vary with child risk characteristics.

RAND research briefing (2005) illustrates the conceptualization of such an investment:

> Notably, many of the benefits from early childhood interventions can be translated into dollar figures and compared with program costs. For example, if school outcomes improve, fewer resources may be spent on grade repetition or special education classes. If improvements in school performance lead to higher educational attainment and subsequent economic success in adulthood, the government may benefit from higher tax revenues and reduced outlays for social welfare programs and the criminal justice system. As a result of improved economic outcomes, participants themselves benefit from higher lifetime incomes, and other members of society gain from reduced levels of delinquency and crime.

> Because not all benefits can be translated into dollar values, these benefit-cost estimates for effective programs are likely to be conservative. Moreover, such analyses do not incorporate some of the other potential benefits that were not measured in the studies. These might include improved labour market performance for the parents of participating children, as well as stronger national economic competitiveness as a result of improvements in educational attainment of the future workforce. It is important to note that these findings represent the potential effects of well-designed and well-implemented interventions. They do not necessarily imply that all such early childhood interventions, delivered for any given amount of time, would generate benefits that offset costs.

For decision-makers considering investments in early childhood interventions, these findings indicate that a body of sound research exists that can guide resource allocation decisions. This evidence base sheds light on the types of programs that have been demonstrated to be effective, the features associated with effective programs, and the potential for returns to society that exceed the resources invested in program delivery. These proven results signal the future promise of investing early in the lives of disadvantaged children. Researchers have conducted benefit-cost analyses, using accepted methodologies, for a subset of the programs we identified as having favorable effects. For those programs with benefits that could readily be expressed in dollar terms and those that served more disadvantaged children and families, the estimates of benefits per child served, net of program costs, range from about $1,400 per child to nearly $240,000 per child. Viewed another way, the returns to society for each dollar invested extend from $1.80 to $17.07. Some of the largest estimates of net benefits were found for programs with the longest follow-up, because those studies measured the impact for outcomes that most readily translate into dollar benefits (e.g., employment benefits, crime reduction). Large economic returns were found for programs that required a large investment (over $40,000 per child), but returns were also positive for programs that cost considerably less (under $2,000 per child). (pp. 2–3)

Influential international organizations such as UNESCO, and the World Bank were involved in the discussions. Penn (2002) provides the World Bank's conceptualization of early childhood by quoting Mary Eming Young, a senior public health specialist at the World Bank responsible for much of the justificatory literature on the Bank's early childhood development policies and programmes across the world and concluded that:

Evidence suggests that [Early Childhood Development] programmes are effective in addressing such vital human development issues as malnutrition among children under five, stunted cognitive development and unpreparedness for primary education ….arly childhood interventions can increase the efficiency of primary and secondary education, contribute to further productivity and income, and reduce the cost of health care and public services…. Deficits in individuals caused by early malnutrition and inadequate care can affect labour productivity and economic development throughout society. Properly designed and implemented interventions in the early childhood years can have multidimensional benefits. (Young, 1998, pp. 209–210, as cited in Penn, 2002, p. 123)

The United Nations Educational, Scientific and Cultural Organisation (UNESCO) has an active programme of publications on early childhood policy (see www.unesco.org), whereas the World Bank has loaned over £1 billion to support a range of ECEC programmes in the Majority World, maintains a website on Early Childhood Development (see www.worldbank.org/children), commissions publications, and organizes regional and global conferences (Dahlberg & Moss, 2005; Penn, 2002).

The United Nations International Children's Emergency Fund (UNICEF) concludes that there is increasing government interest in early childhood services because they offer an apparent opportunity to break into the cycle by which disadvantage tends to reproduce itself, and because no nation today can afford to ignore opportunities for maximizing investments in education in a competitive economic environment increasingly based on knowledge, flexibility, and lifelong learning skills (Dahlberg & Moss, 2005).

Consequently, early childhood education and care programmes appear to have grown more academically demanding over the last 20 years. A significant number of curricula have been planned and carried out in many countries all over the world, and these have been accompanied by numerous discussions on their effectiveness as well as their implementation in the pre-primary setting. A significant number of references related to the preparation as well as the formulation of early childhood curricula can be found in the current bibliography. In addition, it is notable that since 1996, there has been a tendency for Ministries of Education within the member states of the European Union to reform their early childhood curricula on a national level (Norway: 1996; Sweden: 1998; UK/Scotland: 1999; UK/England: 2000; Greece: 2001, 2003, 2011; France: 2002; Finland, Denmark, and Germany: 2003). Early childhood education and care has been viewed as a bridge between home and school, as a preparation for academics, as remediation for the effects of poverty, as a way of socializing children, and as academic training in itself.

On the EU level, the OECD reports have impacted significantly on policy measures with respect to early childhood education and care. Article 27 of the Council of Europe's revised Social Charter refers to the need "to take appropriate measures ….o develop or promote ….hild day-care services and other childcare arrangements" (Council of Europe, 1996, as cited in Dahlberg & Moss, 2005, p. 4). In 2002, at the Barcelona summit, Member States adopted targets to provide childcare by 2010 to at least 90 percent of children between 3 years old and the mandatory school age and to at least 33 percent of children under 3 years of age. The importance of ensuring suitable childcare provision as an essential step towards achieving equal opportunities in employment between women and men is recognized explicitly in the European Employment Strategy. In 2006, the question of high-quality education became one of the predominant strategic objectives in the broader socio-political environment of the European Union. "Pre-primary education has the highest returns in terms of the social adaptation of children. Member states should invest more in pre-primary education as an effective means to establish the basis for further learning, preventing school drop-out, increasing equity of outcomes and overall skill levels" (Education, Audiovisual and Culture Executive Agency, 2009, p. 3).

Early childhood, in accordance with modern scientific data derived from the discipline of developmental psychology, is a critical and essential period for the all-round development of the child. This evidence has fuelled the political interest and the great research interest in the field of early childhood education (ECE) on a worldwide level. Within the past 20 years, there have been radical shifts in education and higher education. Within the field of ECE, politicians and researchers have scrutinized issues such as teaching and learning methods, the curriculum and assessment, the quality of the early childhood setting, management and funding, the training and retraining of professionals, as well as the role of the parents within the educational process.

In addition, one can observe a growing trend to improve the quality of services provided to children of preschool age. Numerous researchers in early childhood education highlight the importance of quality in early childhood programmes, and their surveys indicate the short- and long-term results of attending a high quality preschool programme (Barnett, 1992; Howes et al., 2008; Nores, Belfield, Barnett, & Schweinhart, 2005; Vandell, 2004). Christopher Ball (1994) points out the importance of early learning and the benefits from preschool education for the children as future adults as well as for society as a whole. This is a study of the objects of numerous investigations in various countries: the curricula implemented in preschools, educational innovations in the field of early childhood education, and appropriate practical methodology for children of preschool age. There has been a general move to restructure all levels of education, which, in many countries, took place in the 1990s – with the implementation of national curricula; the setting of teaching and learning targets, national assessment tests, and new inspection procedures; along with the whole discourse on performativity (Tsatsaroni, Ravanis, & Falagas, 2003).

The expansion of early childhood education has been dominated by a discourse mainly informed by the discipline of developmental psychology. According to Dahlberg and Moss (2005), this discourse, usually discussed as if it was natural and inevitable, offers a regime of truth about early childhood education and care as a technology for ensuring social regulation and economic success, in which the young child is constructed as a redemptive agent who can be programmed to become the future solution to our current problems. The results of such projects as High Scope, the Perry Preschool Program, and the Carolina Abecedarian project stoked public concern, and had considerable influence on ECE policies. The Head Start and Perry/High Scope programmes were particularly influential, because they demonstrated that high-quality pre-school provision experience for children from poor families, combined with home visiting, led to long-lasting benefits in terms of employment, crime, and teenage pregnancy. Clarke (2006) argues that one extensively cited finding from Perry/ High Scope was that for every \$1 invested by the state in the programme, \$7 was saved to society, in particular through savings in the criminal justice system.

Nonetheless, Clarke (2006) juxtaposes:

> This conceptualization of the problem of inter-generational reproduction of social exclusion draws strongly on certain traditions within Anglo-American developmental psychology and quantitative sociology that demonstrate statistical associations between a large number of variables, labelled as "risk factors", and particular negative outcomes. Such empirical findings do not form the basis for an explicit causal theory of the associations observed; rather, what is proposed is a complex mesh of interrelated factors operating at several different levels and in different contexts that together result in particular outcomes by means of processes that are largely untheorized (p. 706)

Moss and Dahlberg (2005) argue that, so far, the rationale for public investment in such programmes is the expectation of a demonstrable and calculable return, a quasi-contract in which preschools receive funding in return for delivering certain outputs. The implicit assumption is that poverty and related social ills derive from individual failures – of children /or parents – that interventions through preschools can rectify. The following quote from the Education, Audiovisual and Culture Executive Agency (2009) illustrates the dominant discourse:

> Maturation and constructivist theories have continued to inspire child-centred approaches, in which play, peer-play, self-initiated exploration, discovery learning, and cooperative work with peers are seen as the prime mechanisms of development stimulation resulting in school readiness by the age of 6 or 7 years for most children.... Learning theories ....ave stressed the importance of teacher-directed transmission of language & cognitive skills that directly relate to the primary school curriculum, resulting in a more didactic approach with even very young children – using direct instruction and rewards to reinforce the learning processes within a highly structured and planned "academic" curriculum. Pre-primary education programmes for low income and ethnic minority children working according to the learning approach, using direct academic instruction, have been reported to be rather effective in obtaining the cognitive and academic goals (e.g. Gersten et al., 1988; Schweinhart & Weikart, 1997). Nonetheless, the approach has been criticized for having negative effects in the social-emotional domain (see for instance Burts et al., 1992; Haskins, 1985; Stipek et al., 1995). (p. 29)

Andersen and Hansen (2012) refer to Bourdieu's theorizing on cultural capital, according to which the culture of the most powerful classes serves as a legitimate culture that can be mastered to varying extents. Students who have been inculcated in these cultural forms from childhood will have the greatest probability of academic success, whereas students with working-class origins will have disadvantages in the educational system because of the distance between their class culture and the "legitimate" culture that dominates the school system (Andersen & Hansen, 2012). Apple (1982) argues that the curriculum needs to be linked to a whole array of proposals for centralization of cultural and economic control and accountability that extend well beyond the school. For Apple (1988), a curriculum takes particular social forms and embodies certain interests that are themselves the outcomes of continuous struggles within and among dominant and subordinate groups; and it is certainly not the result of some abstract process, but comes about through the conflicts, compromises, and alliances of identifiable social movements and groups. For Kessler (1991) the "academic" nature of the curriculum in many pre-primary classrooms stands out as one of the major issues in early childhood education. She quotes Spodek (1982):

> The emphasis in some programmes for 4- and 5-year-old children has moved away from children's development and moved toward a concern with the teaching of specific academic skills, many of which were formerly taught in the first grade. (cited in: Kessler, 1991, p. 183).

Within this discourse, Tsatsaroni et al. (2003) point to the tendency to intensify the focus on academic knowledge in early childhood institutions:

> The emerging "learning society" discourse might ….ffect educational provision in nursery classes. At the level of rhetoric, at least, there is already a call for intensifying learning processes at all levels of the education system, including or rather paying particular attention to early ages of schooling. Thus in Greece, for example, there is talk about the need for compulsory nursery attendance (and/or provision) and more systematic ways of organizing knowledge, demands which in fact create a lot of confusion. Therefore, one can hypothesise that the more emphasis is put on systematic provision in nursery classes, the more nursery school teachers will be pressed to introduce activities with more specialised content, especially from science, mathematics, and possibly computer science, which arguably underpin "the knowledge society" in the "information age" (pp. 389–390).

To counter this academic emphasis, in 1987, the National Association for the Education of Young Children – NAEYC, the largest professional organization representing early childhood educators at the USA, coined the NAEYC guidelines as to what it considered developmentally appropriate practices (DAP) and developmentally inappropriate practices (DIP). This document was based on the perception that "programs designed *for* young children [should] be based on what is known *about* young children" (Bredekamp & Copple, 1997). This approach to education regards the child as a developing human and lifelong learner and aims to help teachers and parents to develop more appropriate learning experiences, curricula, teaching strategies, and assessment for their children.

Developmentally appropriate practices (DAP) had a great impact on the theory, research, and practice of early childhood education, and have resulted in a voluminous body of scientific papers (Benson McMullen, 1997, 1999; Bredekamp, 1993; Burts, Hart, Charlesworth, & Kirk, 1990; Fowell & Lawton, 1992; Kessler, 1991; Wien, 1996). Mahon (2010) agrees with Bennett that DAP was initially advanced as a counter to the "schoolification" of early childhood education and care. The concept of schoolification will be discussed in more depth in a later section. At the moment, it is worth focusing on the debate over developmentally appropriate practices.

The discourse over developmentally appropriate curricula interweaves three distinct discursive threads. It appeals to developmental psychology for its scientific base, it inscribes assumptions of progressive efficiency, and it assumes a behaviourist approach to establish educational objectives (Fendler, 2001).

Kessler continues with a valid critique of the NAEYC guidelines:

....he NAEYC position statement claims that the application of knowledge about child development determines the degree to which a program is developmentally appropriate and is the major criterion for determining program quality. Furthermore, the position paper maintains that the inappropriate formal teaching techniques observed in programs for young children are largely the result of misconceptions about how children learn (Elkind, 1986). Therefore, some early childhood professionals are holding workshops to inform practitioners and administrators of the latest knowledge in the field of child development, assuming that education as to how children develop will bring desirable practices. Following a similar logic, some colleges of education are requiring of their graduates more courses in child development, again assuming that greater knowledge about how children develop would lead to appropriate practices (p. 185).

Ryan and Grieshaber (2005) add:

In the world of early education, postmodern examinations of the developmental knowledge base have shown that the research being used to frame practice has been conducted predominantly on homogenous student populations (White, middle class) with little attention to the ways culture and class mediate patterns of growth (Lubeck, 1994). Similarly, critical analyses of developmentally appropriate practice (Mallory & New, 1994) demonstrate that the use of a set of guidelines grounded in hierarchical theories of growth that view children's development as moving towards adulthood, results in teachers overlooking childhood agency (Silin, 1995) and regulating children's learning to what is considered to be "normal" development (Atwater, Carta, Schwartz, & McConnell, 1994; Polakow, 1989; Williams, 1994).... Although the incorporation of other knowledges about children's learning is important, this additive approach has resulted in child development retaining its prominent position in the curricurum (Isen-berg, 2000). A continuing reliance on child development knowledge raises concerns, however…. There is an additional concern that has been catalyzed by the current policy focus on "harnessing" early education as means to ensure children's ongoing educational success (pp. 35–36).

Fendler (2001) and Dahlberg and Moss (2005) depict the issue of the normality or better naturality (naturalness) of the findings of developmental psychology. Dahlberg and Moss (2005) argue against the natural and inevitable way the discourse in this field is taking place "seeking the best methods and procedures for delivering predetermined outcomes – a stable, defined and transmittable body of knowledge, but also implicitly a particular subject, today the autonomous and flexible child." *Developmentality*, as Fendler (2001), and Dahlberg and Moss (2005) refer to it, is the technology of normalization that connects developmental psychology, efficiency, and behaviourism in educational curricula and becomes a means by which the self disciplines the self. Fendler (2001) argues that the findings of developmental psychology are not treated as objects of science to be questioned or tested, but rather they are deployed as rationalistic, a priori truths upon which a curriculum can be designed or evaluated according to its degree of "appropriateness."

Kessler (1991) summarizes the issues emerging from the NAEYC response to the problem of inappropriate practices and the academic curriculum.

….he NAEYC position does not address the major question curriculum theorists must answer: What knowledge is of most worth? It is the illumination and articulation of this basic problem that a theory of curriculum emerges…. Without the knowledge component, the call for developmentally appropriate practices lacks a strong theoretical foundation, which results in the inability on the part of early childhood educators to thoroughly explain or justify what they believe are good programs for young children…. What schools have done is to implement a curriculum which maximizes the achievement of a few students, while minimizing the chances of success for many. Seen in this light, the problem of an academic curriculum and inappropriate practices is identified as a matter of priorities, not appropriateness (pp. 185–186).

Kessler's valid critique of NAEYC's misrepresentation of the academic curriculum problem addresses it in terms of (in-) appropriateness and a prioritization of academic knowledge at the expense of other equally significant elements such as socialization per se. The "academic" nature of the curriculum filters down to pre-primary schools and in many pre-primary classrooms stands out as one of the major issues in ECE. It is obvious nowadays that the emphasis in pre-primary education has moved away from children's development and socialization towards a matter of teaching specific academic skills.

2.3 Cross-Thematic Curriculum Framework and the Phenomenon of Schoolification of the Pre-Primary School

A curriculum reflects the political and ideological values of a society. Its philosophy is inseparable from the socio-political system that education is called to serve. Factors such as religion, political regime, culture, history, economy, technology, research, and tradition influence the curriculum directly or indirectly. Curriculum analysis is political in essence, and the curriculum is not a neutral document but a cultural artefact (Sofou, 2010). Kessler (1991) claims that all curriculum decisions depend on what the community believes is important and involve assumptions about the nature of knowledge, about what is valued and considered important, as well as answers to the question of how to live "the good life" – philosophical analysis is central to all discussions about the curriculum. The interests of students are not legitimate until they are compared with what is desirable.

PISA scores as well as the OECD reports on Greece have influenced the Greek educational policy measures that have been initiated with respect to the entire spectrum of educational levels including pre-primary education. Among these measures, the curriculum reform (2002) and its outcome have been criticized intensively (Bikos, 2005; Chrysafidis, 2004, 2006; Doliopoulou, 2002, 2003; Fragkos, 2002, 2005; Kiprianos, 2007; Kitsaras, 2004; Koutsouvanou, 2006). Broström (2009) argues that the international political focus on learning in early childhood care and education – primarily on language and social competencies – aims to bring preschool closer to school, using as tools transition activities, strategies such as coherence in curricula, and closer collaboration between preschool teachers and school teachers in order to realize the idea of early learning.

The Cross-Thematic Curriculum Framework (CTCF), a 36-page text, was introduced in pre-primary as well as in primary school as a realization of the aim that Broström refers to, namely, bringing preschool closer to school. Four years later, in 2006, it was accompanied by the "Pre-primary Teacher's Guide." The aim of this guide is to give the basic methodological and theoretical support to the teacher. This attempt triggered confusion and insecurity among the educationalists who are called to apply it in daily educational praxis. The CTCF is based on subjects such as those from Europe, America, New Zealand, Australia, the English National Curriculum, and the National Curriculum in Scotland. The CTCF embraces fundamental values and goals as well as guidelines, but it does not lay down the means by which these goals should be attained. Under this scope, the pre-primary education offered in Greece would fit the characteristics of invisible pedagogy originating in the new middle class described so marvellously by Basil Bernstein (1975): The control of the teacher over the child is implicit rather than explicit. Ideally, the teacher arranges the context that the child is expected to rearrange and explore. Within the arranged context, the child apparently has wide powers over what she or he selects, over how she or he structures, and over the time scale of her or his activities. The child apparently regulates her or his own movements and social relationships. There is a reduced emphasis upon the transmission and acquisition of specific skills. The criteria for evaluating the pedagogy are multiple and diffuse.

According to Fragkos (2002), the Cross-Thematic Curriculum Framework (CTCF) completely ignores the importance and the role of play as a learning bearer, and it directs the lower grades to adjust, no matter whether they can or cannot, towards what prevails in higher school classes (primary school) (p. 64). Kiprianos (2007) further agrees that the curriculum outlines the directions for

Schoolification of pre-primary development of activities in the context Make inclusive education matics, environmental studies, creamore challenging. ama, music, physical education), and

at there is a tendency to "schoolify" the pre-primary institutions, a fact which (is a matter of concern for) a number of educators and academics who are worried about the schoolification of the early childhood curriculum. (Fragkos, 2002; Sofou, 2010; Tsafos & Sofou, 2010). The challenge is illustrated succinctly by Moss and Bennett (2006):

> Globally, there is a tendency to treat early childhood services as junior partners, preparing children for the demands of formal schooling; this threatens what the Swedes call 'schoolification', the school imposing its demands and practices on other services, making them school-like (p. 2).

Tsatsaroni et al. (2003) claim that, for many decades now, a basic characteristic of pre-school organization in many western societies has been play-like activity. This has required teachers to structure the experiences of young children by acting upon the contexts of learning rather than the content. However, current policy initiatives and developments in a number of countries since the 1990s, including Greece, demand that teachers make systematic use of specialized content from science, mathematics, and other subjects to structure pre-school curriculum activities.

Fragkos (2002) points out that

> The structure, the way of writing, and the volume of these curricula should not give the impression that they are the new curricula because nomologically, as far as I know, they

should have been issued as new Presidential Decrees instead of Ministerial Decisions. Interdisciplinarity in the Curriculum is being referred only at the end of the section, as a "passive, transient and insignificant component" and not as the basis and substance of the curriculum (p. 63).

Doliopoulou (2002) argues:

> The most important element of this new program is that it incorporates the pre-school in the united design of education. This (development) trend is very positive because it recognizes the educative role of the preschool, and its connection with the other educational levels of education. However, if you move in the direction of schoolification of the pre-school it may be a negative development (p. 72).

Doliopoulou (2002) goes on to wonder:

> Why so little attention ....n Social Education, particularly, if we consider that socialization is perhaps the most important goal of kindergarten? Is it because, ignoring this important sector, is highlighted indirectly, again the intellectual or cognitive area, so, again indirectly, pre-school is being pushed to schoolification? (p. 74)

Doliopoulou (2003) argues that although they criticized this curriculum, the authors did show significant concern for this. She moves a step further by acknowledging that the integration of pre-primary school into the unified educational design is a positive evolution, because the educational role of pre-primary school and its connection with higher educational grades is recognized. However, she stresses the danger of moving towards the schoolification of pre-primary school, which may have a negative impact.

For Chrysafidis (2006), it sounds quite paradoxical that *the intonation of the absence of distinct scientific disciplines is achieved through the strong presence of these subjects.... It could have been avoided, thus, getting rid of all that noise created around DEPPS, and the risks to make once more the pre-school a misprint of primary school. Rather sacrificed the peace of mind and childishness on the altar of the intensification of knowledge. Obsessions for reading and writing have plagued so much the educational world in preschool education* (p. 109). As Diehm (2011) stresses, this phase, so dominated by play, should not be misunderstood as a purely preliminary stage of schooling. However, nobody would deny that this is an important phase of cognitive and social development.

Doliopoulou (2002) notes that ignoring the field of socialization once again emphasizes the mental or cognitive domain, thereby indirectly pushing the Kindergarten towards schoolification. A proper intervention requires effort, knowledge, and a high degree of sensitivity. But due to the demanding task of understanding the capacity of young children, most Kindergarten staff turn to ideas and techniques from elementary school.

It should be considered seriously that if early childhood education sticks to the curricula of different disciplines, there is a need for more guidance and suggestions for teachers to avoid a situation in which the physiognomy of the Kindergarten will be distorted. It would be criminal if the Kindergarten staff in the pursuit of scientific knowledge, were to sacrifice all those arts and creative activities and simply mimic the tactics of teachers in primary education.

Empirical evidence from Tsatsaroni et al. (2003) is indicative of the existing tendency.

> In nursery classrooms, usually, there are texts (and most usually, non-specialised oral pedagogical communications in the classroom) with activities related to science topics, integrating different kinds of school and out-of-school knowledge .... Evaluation of taught content is the prevalent aspect or element of instructional discourse, and given that this activity has been chosen by the teacher in advance, there is no doubt that power relations are, indeed, in place in this classroom (p. 394).

Koutsouvanou (2006) points out that DEPPS has no progressive structure of the content and the skills. The skills and content listed in the mathematical concepts are not understood and are rather confusing and problematic for the teacher as they do not help her to create situations of reflection which will facilitate the child to explore and discover basic types of relationships that are necessary e.g. for classification and ordering.

Tsafos and Sofou (2010, p. 148) conclude from a qualitative study using in-depth interviews with 11 Greek preschool teachers that "the introduction of the school-like learning areas is considered by some teachers legitimate as it improves their professional status whereas others emphasize that it could lead to the schoolification of preschool education." This tendency provokes a controversy as regards the role and the purpose of the kindergarten and its functional place within society.

Schoolification is named the phenomenon of pushing down primary school academic activities into pre-primary programmes, perceiving pre-primary school as a preparation stage for children's success in primary school mainly, and putting too much emphasis on formal learning in areas such as the three R's – reading, writing, arithmetic. In the French context, Garnier (2011, p. 13) refers to the phenomenon of "scolarisation" of the *école maternelle* that "may thus be analysed as a transformation of its objectives and curriculum to favour cognitive and language learning". She argues:

> In other words, the *école maternelle* is truly becoming a school as its programme and practices increasingly subscribe to what has become, in France at least, a manifest cultural truth: "school is the place where language is learned (p. 13).

er to Bernstein's models of the curricu- ...mpetence model. According to Bern- stein (1996), ...the other category, and performance models of the curriculum are the most dominant around the world. The *performance model* has its origin in the behavioural objectives movement, and it clearly emphasizes marked subject boundaries, traditional forms of knowledge, explicit realization and recognition rules for pedagogic practice, as well as the designation and establishment of strong boundaries between different types of students. Implicit in this model is the sense that explicit criteria would save teachers and ...achlan et al. (2010) identify the Cana- ...undation Stage curriculum as indica- ...use the former is quite explicit about ...uring the year before starting school ...m outcomes for very young children. ...the competence model suggests that learners have some control over the selection, pacing, and sequencing of the curriculum. Although competence models have been more common in early childhood education, their dominance in early childhood education is changing in several countries. According to McLachlan et al. (2010), New Zealand's early childhood curriculum, TE Wariki (Ministry of Education, 1996), is a good example of this sort of curriculum.

One significant distinction between the two models is the *temporal modality*. Competence models select the present tense as the temporal modality in which *time is not explicitly or finely punctuated as a marker of different activities; as a consequence the punctuation of time does not construct future* (Bernstein, 1996, p. 46). Bernstein (1996) stresses that in the case of performance models, *the future is made visible, but that which has constructed this future is a past invisible to the acquirer* whereas in the case of the competence models *it is the future which is invisible to the acquirer and the present which is continuously visible* (Bernstein, 1996, p. 48). In addition, competence models are less susceptible to public scrutiny and accountability, as their products are more difficult to evaluate objectively, while their transmission costs are likely to be higher relative in comparison to performance models.

Moore (2008) presents another dimension on which approaches to early childhood services can be placed. This is identified through the OECD thematic review of early childhood education and care policy (Bennett, 2005; OECD, 2006). This described two broad curricula approaches: the social pedagogic approach and the pre-primary approach. As summarized by Bertrand (2007), social pedagogic practices, common in Scandinavian countries, New Zealand, and Italy, combine a broad developmental framework with local curriculum development. The focus is on developmental goals, interactivity with educators and peers, and a high quality of life in the early childhood setting. The curriculum has broad orientations for children rather than prescribed outcomes, and the acquisition of developmental skills is perceived as a by-product rather than as the driver of the curriculum. This approach is in contrast to the pre-primary practices common in France, the United Kingdom, and the United States that are characterized by centralized development of the curriculum – often with detailed goals and outcomes that determine or influence curriculum decisions about what and how children learn. The goals and outcomes are often stated as learning standards or learning expectations and are related to school readiness tasks and skills. Educators tend to interact with children around activities related to the identified learning expectations and rely more on direct instruction strategies. This approach, known as pre-primary approach because the content of the curriculum mirrors what might be seen in primary school, is often referred to as the "schoolification" of the early years (OECD, 2006). McLachlan et al. (2010) note that the design of the pre-primary approach curriculum is underpinned by the scholarly academic ideology, as being presented by Schiro, and it is based on the notion that our culture has accumulated knowledge over the centuries that has been organized into academic disciplines within universities. As they argue:

> Followers of this ideology believe that the academic disciplines, the world of the intellect and the world of knowledge are loosely equivalent. The central task of education is to extend this equivalence on both the cultural and individual planes; to discover new truths for the former and to acculturate individuals into their civilisation in the latter.... The vision of the child in this ideology is of the child as incomplete, a "neophyte", an immature member of the discipline, who is capable of developing intellect, memory and reasoning, shaped by the discipline (Shiro, 2008). This view sees the child as a "blank state" or "empty" needing to be filled with knowledge. Learning is viewed as a function of teaching: the teacher is a transmitter and the child is a receiver. Although no formal theory of learning using this model is espoused by most curriculum developers, there is an understanding of readiness which supports Jerome Bruner's statement that "any subject can be taught effectively in some intellectually honest form to any child at any stage of development". (p. 14)

Bertrand (2007) defines schoolification as the usually required assessment of children's achievements in meeting the learning expectations. She goes on by stating that this approach is in contrast to other jurisdictions that are developing curricula based on ideas and values about childhood and the purpose of preschool programmes. According to her, in practice, most jurisdictions use approaches that blend elements of both, but lean towards either a pre-primary approach or a social pedagogic approach.

Grieshaber (2009) argues that where "school readiness" is the focus of transition to the compulsory years of schooling as it is in France and many English-speaking countries, the onus is on children being ready for school and the tendency is for cognitive development to be emphasized through the acquisition of a range of knowledge, skills, and dispositions (OECD, 2006). In such approaches, there is a risk of "schoolifying" (OECD, 2006, p. 59) programmes in the year before compulsory schooling by orienting them towards cognitive development. Schoolification sits in contrast to the Nordic countries in which the preference is for early childhood pedagogy to form the basis of early primary education (OECD, 2006). In Denmark for instance, the pedagogical approaches of the pre-school learning environment are continued into the first and second grades with great success (OECD, 2006). This type of pedagogical continuity can only enhance the move from the non-compulsory to the compulsory years of schooling.

Fleer, Anning & Cullen (2009) argue that *we have little empirical evidence about the effectiveness of different curriculum models* (p. 192). In Greece, insofar, it cannot be estimated which aspects of the curriculum are implemented, because of the lack of assessments of teachers' practices. A carefully planned curriculum does not necessarily lead to a high-quality programme. The absence of an institution or a foundation responsible for assessing the quality of the education provided makes it impossible to acknowledge what kind of education is delivered to the children. The lack of a national framework for setting quality standards for early childhood education and care influences the quality of services (Koutsogeorgopoulou, 2009). As Kitsaras (2004) points out, Greece is not suffering from arrangements, counter-reforms, deregulations, and changes to improve its educational system, but from the implementation of education laws. He argues:

> It is established that there is a portion of kindergarten teachers, who do not implement the curriculum, even if it is law of the State, but are negatively disposed. Beyond this, there is another portion of kindergarten, who either due to a lack of information or due to conviction, either for ideological reasons – even a small percentage – enter a partial, incomplete, or misapplication. The lack of consistent and uniform implementation of the curriculum makes it difficult or impossible for a meaningful assessment of results. Of course, the implementation of the curriculum requires the fulfilment of certain conditions. It's not enough to be suitable for this age, to whom it addresses to, and be written by experts but it is needed to participate in its compilation everyone involved in the process of development of the infant. The processes during the preparation of a curriculum

should be transparent and respect of parents is necessary. More, it is required the prior consent of those who will be called to implement it. This can be ensured, taking into account their views, especially if a frank dialogue with the concept of exchange arguments and not compliments or party positions. When teachers are asked to play the role of spectator in an ostensibly democratic process of making important decisions, such as writing curriculum, and when information is incomplete, then the poor implementation of the program is assured. (p. 89)

Apple and Teitelbaum (1986) also recognize that many teachers experience this loss of control over their programme.

> At the local, state, and federal levels, movements for strict accountability systems, competency-based education and testing, systems management, a truncated vision of the "basics," mandated curricular content and goals, and so on are clear and growing. Increasingly, teaching methods, texts, tests, and outcomes are being taken out of the hands of the people who must put them into practice. Instead, they are being legislated by state departments of education or in state legislatures, and are being either supported or stimulated by many of the national reports (p. 179).

Bevanot and Resh (2003) report that the translation of official curricular policies into actual school or classroom activities is rarely a smooth or complete process, because, more often than not, "slippages" or discontinuities are apparent. For them, undoubtedly, gaps between the officially intended curriculum and the actually implemented curriculum occur in various degrees in all national educational systems. Evidence suggests that the official curriculum may be connected only loosely to what teachers teach in the classroom (Cohen et al., 1990, as cited in Lee Stevenson & Baker, 1991). Moreover, although research shows that early childhood care and education has a positive impact on children's learning and development (Sammons, Melhuish, Siraj-Blatchford, Taggart, & Elliot, 2002, 2003), yet, as Hirsh-Pasek, Hyson, and Rescorla (1990) showed in their study, the provision of an early highly academic environment does not result in academic advantages for children, but rather in potential disadvantages in creative expression and emotional well-being. In addition, Hirsh-Pasek (1991) finding shows that academic orientations provide no advantage to children's scholastic or intellectual development. Phillips and Stipek (1993) conclude that *the modest short-term benefits that might be achieved through programs that attempt to accelerate children's acquisition of basic skills and concepts are overshadowed by substantial costs. The negative consequences that have been reported encompass children's attitudes toward school, self-perceptions of their abilities, anxiety about achievement and stress behaviours, challenge-seeking, peer interactions, creativity, and independent achievement-striving. These results apply to minority and non-minority children of all social classes, thereby lending support to arguments that highly structured curricula are stressful, rather than supportive, even for children who enter school having experienced more authoritarian and less academically oriented home environments* (Phillips & Stipek, 1993, p. 147). Howes, Burchinal, Pianta, Bryant, Early, Clifford, Barbarin (2008) in their study results on standardized measures of language, literacy, and math of children attending prekindergarten programs made small gains from instructional and social activities with the intention of increasing school-related achievement skills. Therefore, it is necessary to be cautious about rushing to conclusions. Furthermore, Schlotter, Schwerdt, and Woessmann (2009) doubt that the well-known and multi-cited Perry Preschool Program Project results, as indicative proof of early childhood intervention's benefits, can be generalized. As they argue, while the assignment of children to the groups was random, the choice of the underlying sample targeted explicitly at-risk children, limiting the "external validity" of the study to this sample. As a result, the causal inference was limited to the specific group of African-American children from disadvantaged backgrounds. If the selection process had been completely random, effects might have differed.

2.4 Teachers Beliefs

Teachers live at the centre of the maelstrom of rhetoric, vilification, and conflict over making our educational system better. They have been expected to "shape up" and implement the reforms that others have developed. They have been treated more like uninformed hired hands than professionals to whom we entrust our most precious asset. They have been the last to be consulted when we consider what is broken and how to fix it. Their voices have not and still do not inform the actions taken to rectify what reformers believe to be the matter with education (in the United States). The absence of teachers from the dialogue and decision-making on reform has been a serious omission. It has yielded faulty definitions of the problem, solutions that compound rather than confront the problem, and a demeaned and demoralized teaching force. Efforts to improve education are doomed to failure until teachers become respected partners in the process. If reform is to be successful, their voices and views must be included in any attempts to improve and alter their work. Although their involvement cannot insure success, their absence will guarantee continued failure. (Cohn & Kottkamp, 1993, pp. xv–xvi)

This quote clearly delivers the message that although parents and policymakers expect teachers to demonstrate high skills and knowledge, teachers still remain the missing voice in education. As Apple and Jungck (1990) point out, despite all the rhetoric about teaching and professionalism, about enhancing teachers' power, and about raising pay and respect, the reality of many teachers' lives bears little resemblance because, rather than moving in the direction of increased autonomy, their daily lives in classrooms in many nations are becoming ever more controlled, ever more subject to an administrative logic that seeks to tighten the reins on the processes of teaching and curriculum. As they claim, teacher development, cooperation, and "empowerment" may be the talk, but centralization, standardization, and rationalization are the tendencies (Apple & Jungck, 1990, p. 228).

However, policy developers keep constantly ignoring the teachers' views and beliefs, and they continue to plan curricula without taking into account the front-line implementers. It seems as if they simply ignore the fact that teachers make myriad decisions in everyday practice that are highly influenced by their beliefs. This implicit neglect and disregard of teachers' positioning into the educational frame downplays their influential role on the formulation of children's learning experiences. Educational procedure develops largely on two levels: the personal level and the systemic level on which the interrelation between the participants, their interaction, dramatizes an intrinsic role in the whole procedure. Crucial factors of the pedagogical procedure constitute the former personal experience of the educator, her or his knowledge, attitudes and beliefs, teaching, and the cultural environment.

In the last 15 years, the study of teachers' beliefs has emerged as a major area of enquiry. Teachers' thought processes have been categorized into three fundamental types: (1) teacher planning, (2) teachers' interactive thoughts and decisions and (3) teachers' theories and beliefs (Clark & Peterson, 1986). Kagan (1992) argues that teachers filter new information through their personal beliefs. The literature reveals a variety of terms used to define what the current study calls teachers' beliefs. Richardson (2003) reports that beliefs have been explored by philosophers, social psychologists, anthropologists, sociologists, and researchers in the "derivative" fields of study such as education, organizational theory, business, and nursing. Pajares (1992) acknowledges that despite the remaining conceptual confusion over the term belief, researchers have made considerable attempts to clarify this terminological discussion. As a result, a plethora of terminologies has emerged to describe teachers' beliefs, among them: attitudes, values, judgements, axioms, opinions, ideology, perceptions, conceptions, conceptual systems, preconceptions, dispositions, implicit theories, internal mental processes, action strategies, rules of practice, practical principles, perspectives, repertoires of understanding, and social strategy (Pajares, 1992, p. 309). According to him, the terms attitude, values, perceptions, theories, and images have been used in the literature. However, these consist of beliefs in disguise.

Before offering a profound discussion on the dominant discourse literature of teachers' beliefs, it is important to examine the sociological view on teachers' "philosophy and/or ideology." In the eyes of the author, these are additional disguised terms for the concept of beliefs. Green (2000, p. 110) quotes the two main traditions in the study of human knowledge drawn from Elias' (1978) and Wilterdink's (1977) works. He distinguishes two traditions: the philosophical tradition, which Elias (1978) referred to as a classical theory of knowledge that centres conceptually upon the notion of a "solitary individual" who "thinks, perceives, and performs" in isolation in pursuit of "definite and certain knowledge"; and the sociological tradition, wherein "all knowledge is regarded as culture-bound, socially determined, and therefore ideological." He adds that from the perspective of figurational sociology, it is more accurate as well as more productive to view knowledge as lying along a continuum of greater or lesser adequacy due to the conception that one cannot escape the fact that knowledge – or rather what people believe to be true – is inherently social and needs to be understood as such.

Price (1969) defines beliefs as what an individual holds to be true and sees them as guidelines to actions and practical decisions. Further he claims that a person can believe a proposition without realizing it, and that there are unconscious or repressed beliefs (Einarsdottir & Gardarsdottir, 2009).

In the psychology camp, Richardson (2003) argues that although there is considerable agreement on the definition of beliefs as psychologically held understandings, premises, or propositions about the world that are felt to be true, there is a lack of conventional agreement among researchers on the definition of teachers' beliefs. Fishbein and Azjek (1975, pp. 11–12) offer their definition on beliefs, and draw on the difference between an attitude and a belief. "Belief is a subjective probability of a relation between the object of the belief and some other object, value, concept, or attribute. Thus a person may believe that he possesses certain attributes that a given behaviour will lead to certain consequences that certain events occur contiguously, etc." For them, whereas an attitude refers to a person's favourable or unfavourable evaluation of an object, beliefs represent the information he or she has about the object, because a belief links an object to some attribute. The object of the belief may be a person, a group of people, an institution, behaviour, a policy, an event, and so forth and the associated attribute may be any object, trait, property, quality, characteristic, outcome, or event. They argue:

> With respect to any object-attribute association, people may differ in their belief strength. In other words, they may differ in terms of the perceived likelihood that the object has (or is associated with) the attribute in question. Thus we recommend that "belief strength" or more simply, "belief," be measured by a procedure which places the subject along a dimension of subjective probability involving an in object and some related attribute (p. 12)....hree different processes may underlie belief formation. Belief:

descriptive, inferential, informational. A person's beliefs are directly tied to the stimulus situation, and at the inferential end, beliefs are formed on the basis of these stimuli as well as residues of the person's past experiences.... Many of our beliefs are formed neither on the basis of direct experience with the object of the belief nor by way of some inference process. Instead, we often accept information about some object provided by an outside source (p. 133).... Beliefs formed by accepting the information provided by an outside source may be termed informational beliefs.... A belief is formed as soon as an object is linked to an attribute, irrespective of the subjective probability associated with the link. When the person has little information on which to base the inference, his subjective probability may be at chance level, indicating a high degree of uncertainty. (pp. 12–133)

For Kagan (1992), a teacher's belief is a particularly provocative form of personal knowledge that is generally defined, as pre- or in-service teachers' assumptions about students, learning, classrooms, and the subject matter to be taught. As Fang (1996) points out, beliefs act as a filter through which a host of instructional judgments and decisions are made. Pajares (1992) has collected a number of belief definitions that are cited below:

Brown and Cooney (1982) explained that beliefs are dispositions to action and major determinants of behaviour, although the dispositions are time- and context-specific qualities that have important implications for the research and measurement. Sigel (1985) defined beliefs as "mental constructions of experience – often condensed and integrated into schemata or concepts" (p. 351) that are held to be true and that guide behaviour. Harvey (1986) defined belief as an individual's representation of reality that has enough validity, truth, or credibility to guide thought and behaviour.... Dewey (1933) described belief as the third meaning of thought, "something beyond itself by which its value is tested; it makes an assertion about some matter of fact or some principle or law (p. 6). He added that the importance of belief is crucial, for "it covers all the matters of which we have no sure knowledge and yet which we are sufficiently confident of to act upon and also the matters that we now accept as certainly true, as knowledge, but which nevertheless may be questioned in the future" (p. 6). (p. 313)

Richardson (2003) is concerned with the confusing and ambivalent conceptual question raised in teacher cognition studies, namely, the differentiation (or lack thereof) between the concepts of beliefs and knowledge. She argues:

In the traditional philosophical literature, knowledge is thought to depend on a "truth cognition" or warrant that compels its acceptance as true by a community (Green, 1971; Lehrer, 1990). Propositional knowledge, then, requires epistemic standing; that is, some evidence to back up the claim. Beliefs, however, do not require a truth cognition. Feiman-Nemser and Floden (1986) agree with this differentiation between beliefs and knowledge. "It does not follow that everything a teacher believes or is willing to act on merits the label 'knowledge'" (p. 3).

On the other hand, within the educational psychological literature that examines teachers' knowledge and beliefs, there is often no distinction made. For example, Alexander, Schallert, and Hare (1991) equated beliefs and knowledge: "Knowledge encompasses all that a person knows or believes to be true, whether or not it is verified as true in some sort of objective or external way" (p. 317). In a review of the literature on preservice teacher learning, Kagan (1990) agreed. She suggested that since teachers' knowledge is subjective, it is much like beliefs. (p. 3)

For Pajares (1992), the difference lies in the fact that knowledge systems are open to evaluation and critical examination whereas beliefs are not. He refers to Nespor's argument that belief systems are unbounded in that their relevance to reality defies logic, whereas knowledge systems are better defined and receptive to reason. Accordingly, beliefs for Nespor are far more influential than knowledge in determining how individuals organize and define tasks and problems, and they are stronger predictors of behaviour. Woolley et al. (2004) distinguish between "traditional teaching" beliefs versus "constructivist teaching" beliefs of elementary teachers (that mirror teacher-centred to student-centred approaches). These beliefs are tied directly to teaching practices (Berry, 2006; Graham, Harris, MacArthur, & Fink, 2002). The practices teachers use in their classroom with children are not based on explicit theories alone. Teachers' professionally derived curriculum beliefs (formal or explicit) come from education and professional training, whereas their personally derived curriculum beliefs (their informal or implicit beliefs) may be based more on childhood experiences and/or classroom teaching experiences (Charlesworth et al., 1993; McMullen, 1997; Wang et al., 2008). Although explicit knowledge of how children learn and develop is important, many education researchers are beginning to recognize that beliefs greatly influence a teacher's practice (Fang, 1996; Pajares, 1992). Scholars argue that beliefs impact strongly on classroom decisions (Fang, 1996; Pajares, 1992; Vartuli, 1999). Fang (1996) argues that teachers' implicit theories can influence teacher behaviour and ultimately student learning.

Pajares (1992) refers to Nespor's identification of four belief characteristics, namely, the existential presumption, alternativity, affective and evaluative loading, and episodic structure. He follows Nespor's suggestion that beliefs have stronger affective and evaluative components than knowledge, and that affect typically operates independently of the cognition associated with knowledge, because beliefs draw their power from previous episodes or events that colour the comprehension of subsequent events.

Teachers' beliefs are important for understanding and improving educational processes because they are related to teachers' strategies for coping with challenges in the educational environment. Prevalent beliefs are considered to be a crucial factor for educational practices. A person's reasons to establish a belief are

54

subjective, and most of the times subconscious. Based on personal experience, value systems, and/or philosophy, a person creates a belief system for each major issue of concern. These beliefs rarely rest on scientifically valid data, because, most of the time, beliefs are related to internal deep-rooted representations that influence how an individual characterizes phenomena and makes sense of the world. Beliefs tempered by personal experience often remain unconscious, in a latent form, not allowing the teacher to control the content and confront them as may be the case with scientific knowledge.

Richardson (2003) argues that there is also considerable agreement that these systems are not necessarily logically structured. He quotes Rokeach's (1968) suggestion that some beliefs are more central than others, and that the central beliefs are more difficult to change. Furthermore, he refers to Green's (1971) philosophical treatise on the nature of teaching in which Green proposed that an individual may hold beliefs that are incompatible or inconsistent due to the fact that beliefs are held in clusters and there is little cross-fertilization among belief systems. Thus, incompatible beliefs may be held in different clusters. Therefore, Green proposed to set beliefs side by side and examine them for consistency. This process of investigation has become a component in teacher education and professional development programmes that attempt to develop and change beliefs.

According to Wang et al. (2008), teachers in different cultures presumably have varying informal and formal belief-forming experiences guided by different cultural norms. Einarsdottir and Gardarsdottir (2009) offer a valuable pathway on the links between beliefs and culture:

Van Fleet (1979) builds on Herskovits' (1963) idea of cultural transmission and suggests that teachers acquire knowledge and beliefs about teaching through three different processes: enculturation, education and schooling. This means that teachers' socio-cultural backgrounds affect their beliefs and interactions and how the process of parent and family is constructed. The school culture and school's attitude towards parents and cooperation with them also influence teachers' practices and become the accepted standard (Souto-Manning & Swick, 2006). Further, teachers' beliefs and actions cannot be understood without considering the social, cultural and historical contexts within and into which they grow (Kagitcibasi, 1996; Kitayama & Markus, 1999a; Rogoff, 2003; Shweder et al., 1998). Bruner (1996) proposed that culture is central in shaping human life and the human mind. He used the term *folk psychology* for the underlying beliefs in a culture about human tendencies and how minds work. Along the same lines, Rogoff (2003) talks about how people follow cultural processes to organise their lives. She argues against treating individuals as entities separate from cultural processes, existing independently of their cultural communities. Further, she states that culture is not merely an entity that influences individuals. Instead, people contribute to the creation of cultural processes, while at the same time cultural processes contribute to the creation of people. (p. 198)

Vartulli (2008) notes the following:

> When classroom problems occur, teachers often make guesses or assumptions, based on their beliefs, to solve the problems (Abelson, 1979; Nespor, 1987). Teachers' implicit theories about the nature of knowledge acquisition can affect teacher behaviour and ultimately student learning (Fang, 1996). In early childhood, teacher pedagogical beliefs and practices fall along a continuum of philosophical principles from child-initiated or child-centered to teacher-initiated, didactic, or academically directed; or somewhere in-between (middle-of-the road or intermediate) (Marcon, 1988, 1999; Stipek, Daniels, Galluzo, & Milburn, 1992) ....iversity of teacher beliefs could be due to teacher preparation (certification), variations in program/school sponsorship, the personal nature of teaching, or isolation of teachers from colleagues (Spodek, 1988). Beliefs about classroom pedagogy often are derived from experiences in place before teachers begin undergraduate courses. (pp. 489–490)

Kagan (1992) argued that researchers have little direct information about how a teacher's personal pedagogy evolves over the course of her or his career, resulting in a crucial gap in our understanding of teaching. However, a significant strand of the work being done on beliefs has focused on the relationship between teachers' beliefs and their practices. According to Clark and Peterson (1986, as cited in Wang, Elicker, McMullen, & Mao, 2008), beliefs make up an important part of teachers' general knowledge, through which teachers perceive, process, and act upon information in the classroom to make decisions.

Teachers are an important source of motivation and learning in the preschool and have an important role in developing and delivering the curriculum. The early childhood education literature stresses that better qualified teachers and recognition of the importance of continuing professional education will undoubtedly further improve the quality of early childhood education and care in years to come. Pre-primary teachers play a very important role in a child's early development. What children experience and learn during their very early years often helps build their views of the world and themselves. A pre-primary teacher has the power to influence a child's failure or success through school and even into their personal lives because they significantly influence the cognitive and emotional development of each child, depending on how they treat the profession. Pre-primary teachers require a variety of aptitudes and skills, including the natural ability to work with children and the power to create effective teaching methods in a suitable learning environment. To a major extent, this depends directly on the beliefs that guide them. It is based on these beliefs that educators conceive their educational procedure and their actions – especially when problem situations occur. The beliefs of a rational subject are not static but change over time as new information is added.

Charlesworth et al. (1993) stress that although it has been recognized increasingly that the psychological context of teaching, particularly teachers' thought processes, is critical to understanding teachers' actions in planning, teaching, and assessment, conventional research on teaching has focused on practice while ignoring the thought process of teachers. *Isenberg (1990) believes that an important task for researchers is to collaborate with practitioners in identifying their beliefs and translating them into standards of practice. She point out that research on teacher thinking indicates that there are inconsistencies between teachers' beliefs and practices. These need to be identified so that teachers can be supported in reflecting upon analysing their beliefs and how they relate to teaching practice* (cited in Charlesworth et al., 1993, p. 257). Information is needed not only on reported practice; it is also important to observe teachers in their classrooms to note how reported beliefs relate to actual practice (Charlesworth et al., 1993; Pajares, 1992).

Shulman (cited in Gess-Newsome, 2002, p. 3) has argued that the study of "teachers' cognitive understanding of subject matter content and the relationships between such understanding and the instruction teachers provide for students" may be the "missing programme" in educational research. Beliefs are the best indicators of the decisions individuals make throughout their lives (Bandura, 1986; Dewey, 1933; Nisbett & Ross, 1980; Rokeach, 1968), an assumption that can be traced back to human beings' earliest philosophical contemplations (Pajares, 1992). Teachers' pedagogical beliefs are important to study because beliefs are a major determinant of behaviour through being the basis of teachers' classroom decisions (Vartuli, 1999). Thus, it is important to investigate how teachers make sense out of their teaching world. An understanding of what beliefs influence teacher behaviour is critical to the understanding of the complexities of teaching.

Fullan (1989) recognized the significant role of beliefs and their crucial role in pedagogical praxis and the realization of the curriculum. As he stressed, beliefs and practices, together with the structure and the materials used in an institution, are the key to success in a sense that they represent the means for achieving desired outcomes on policy implementation. As he characteristically points out: if effective use does not occur, especially with respect to practices and beliefs on the part of the front-line implementers, outcomes will not be achieved.

The association between teachers' beliefs and their practices has attracted much research attention, and a substantial number of empirical studies – mainly from the field of educational psychology – have been conducted. The following section sketches the state of the art in research on teachers' beliefs and practices.

2.5 Research on Teachers' Beliefs and Practices

Through the shift in research on teaching from the product–process approach to the teachers' cognitive processing, teachers' beliefs became a matter of investigation in empirical studies, and many researchers recognized the need to understand teachers' beliefs in relation to their practices. Specifically, over the last two decades, numerous studies have been conducted to address this very issue. Many studies have been conducted that examine the relationship between the beliefs and practices of early childhood teachers, including pre-school, kindergarten, and primary teachers (e.g. Buchanan, et al., 1998, Charlesworth, et al., 1991; Charlesworth, et al., 1993b; Smith & Shepard, 1988).

Vartulli (1999) distinguishes the following categories in research on beliefs in early childhood:

(1) the relationship between teacher self-reported beliefs and practices (Bryant, Clifford, & Peisner, 1991; Hyson & Lee, 1996; Smith & Shepard, 1988);
(2) self-reported beliefs and observed practices (Charlesworth, Hart, Burts, & Hernandez, 1990; Charlesworth et al., 1993; Kagan & Smith, 1988; Stipek & Byler, 1997; Stipek et al., 1992);
(3) the association between teacher and principal beliefs (Butterfield & Johnston, 1995; Spidell-Rusher, McGrevin, & Lambiotte, 1992); and
(4) beliefs associated with child outcomes (Burts et al., 1998; Marcon 1992a, 1994, 1999; Spodek, 1987; Verma & Peters, 1975); the kindergarten classroom (Bryant et al., 1991; Charlesworth et al., 1990, 1993; Hatch & Freeman, 1988; Kagan & Smith, 1988; Marcon, 1993, 1994); the primary grades (Buchanan, Burts, Binder, White, & Charlesworth, 1998; Bussis, Chittenden, & Amarel, 1976; Marcon, 1992b; Smith, 1992, 1993); and teachers from all three age levels (Mc Mullen, 1999; Spodek, 1988; Stipek & Byler, 1997).

Pajares (1992, p. 316) highlights the importance of exploring a teacher's educational beliefs as opposed to her beliefs in general. These beliefs may include teacher efficacy beliefs, epistemological beliefs, locus of control, motivation, writing comprehension, math anxiety beliefs, self-concept, and/or self-esteem beliefs, reading instruction, the nature of reading, and whole language beliefs. Kagan (1992, p. 73) refers to researchers who have found that a teacher's beliefs usually reflect the actual nature of the instruction the teacher provides to students and may be mediated by epistemological differences inherent in respective content areas or by the kinds of instructional materials that happen to be available.

According to Kagan (1992), empirical studies have yielded quite consistent findings in regard to two generalizations. First, teachers' beliefs appear to be relatively stable and resistant to change (e.g. Brousseau, Book, & Byers, 1988; Herrmann & Duffy, 1989). Second, a teacher's beliefs tend to be associated with a congruent style of teaching that is often evident across different classes and grade levels (e.g. Evertson & Weade, 1989; Martin, 1989). Stipek and Byler (1997) referred to previous research indicating that teachers' practices are associated with their beliefs (Charlesworth, Hart, Burts, & Hernandez, 1991; Charlesworth, Hart, Burts, Thomasson, Mosley, & Fleege, 1993; Smith & Shepart, 1988; Stipek, Daniels, Galluzzo, & Milburn, 1992), and that teachers filter new information through their personal beliefs (Kagan, 1992).

Westwood, Knight, and Redden (1997) highlight the broad investigation of teachers' belief systems and their impact on learning (e.g. Agne, Greewood, & Miller, 1994; Fang, 1996; Jordan, Kircaali-Iftar, & Diamond, 1993; Schuum et al., 1994). According to them, this literature reveals that teachers' beliefs are frequently so strongly held that (a) they can cause resistance to changes in curriculum and methods (Allington & Lie, 1990; Smith & Shepherd, 1988), (b) they can lead to resistance to advice and support from resource staff (Fields, 1995), and (c) they can influence the degree to which teachers are willing or not willing to adapt their teaching approach for students with learning problems.

According to Wang et al. (2008), some scholars suggest that the belief–action relationship may differ for teachers with varying amount of experience or professional training (Peters & Sutton, 1984; Rosenthal, 1991). However, one recent study found no moderating effect of teacher expertise (novice vs experienced teachers) in the training–beliefs relationship (Wilcox-Herzog, 1999).

In early childhood education, a remarkable amount of attention has been given to the investigation of teachers' developmentally appropriate or inappropriate beliefs and practices. Wang et al. (2008) add that in the United States, recent research on early childhood teachers' beliefs and practices focuses on principles derived from "developmentally appropriate practice" (DAP) (Bredekamp & Copple, 1997; National Association of Education for Young Children [NAEYC], 1990). Accordingly, measures to assess beliefs and practices have been developed based on DAP constructs (e.g., Charlesworth et al., 1991, 1993; Hoot et al., 1996; Hyson et al., 1996). These measures have been used to investigate the extent to which developmentally "appropriate" or "inappropriate" beliefs and/or practices were reported or observed (e.g., Charlesworth et al., 1993; McMullen, 1997, 1998; Sherman & Mueller, 1996; Stipek & Byler, 1997), and whether teachers' beliefs about DAP are congruent with their classroom teaching behaviours (e.g., Charlesworth et al., 1993; Dunn & Kontos, 1997; Hatch & Freeman, 1988).

Research indicates that teachers' practices are associated with their beliefs (Charlesworth, Hart, Burts, & Hernandez, 1991; Charlesworth, Hart, Burts, Thomasson, Mosley, & Fleege, 1993; Smith & Shepart, 1988; Stipek, Daniels, Galluzzo, & Milburn, 1992), and that teachers filter new information through their personal beliefs (Kagan, 1992). Charlesworth et al. (1993) have found a moderate correlation between teachers' developmentally appropriate beliefs and their respective practices. Stipek and Byler (1997) found that for preschool and kindergarten teachers, but not for first-grade teachers, the beliefs they espoused about appropriate and effective practices for young children correlated significantly with the practices they implemented in their classrooms. Studies revealed that self-reported beliefs correlated highly with observed practices (e.g. McMullen, 1999; Stipek & Byler, 1997), whereas others have found a discrepancy between the teachers' self-reported beliefs and their actual classroom practices (e.g. Charlesworth et al., 1991; Charlesworth et al., 1993).

Kagan (1992) refers to a variety of empirical studies that testify consistently that preservice teachers tend to leave their university programmes with the same beliefs they brought to them rather than modifying their initial biases (Feiman-Nemser & Buchman, 1986; Tabachnick & Zeichner, 1984; Zeichner, 1989).

McMullen (1999) asserts that personality factors such as self-efficacy, locus of control, and trait anxiety in addition to education and professional experiences influence beliefs and practices. New teachers may lack the necessary resources and coping skills to implement what they have been taught and what they may truly believe are best practices with young children (Buchanan, Burts, Bidner, White, & Charlesworth, 1997). Although McMullen (1999) provided evidence that personal beliefs are good determinants of practice, many studies indicate that other environmental factors may have a greater impact on teachers' practices (such as parental or administrative pressures – Charlesworth et al., 1991; Charlesworth et al., 1993; McMullen, 1999; Smith & Shepard, 1988).

Fang (1996) stresses that contextual factors such as administrative support and collegial attitudes, school climate, children's abilities and backgrounds, and government regulations can have powerful influences on teachers beliefs' and influence classroom practice. Snider and Fu (1990) identified the teachers' education/academic degree, the number of content areas covered in child development/early childhood education courses taken, and the interaction of child development/early childhood education content and supervised practical experience as factors that have the most impact on teacher's developmentally appropriate classroom practices. Smith and Shepard (1988) examined kindergarten teachers' beliefs and practices regarding readiness and retention and found that formal rules from the district regulating curriculum and instructional time seemed to force teachers to "push" academic subjects and "conform to the pace of the school" (Smith & Shepard, 1988, p. 324). Informal pressures also impacted on the classroom structure, including parental pressure and first-grade entrance expectations, because many teachers felt pressured to prepare their children academically for the first year.

For the empirical elicitation of teachers' beliefs, a variety of indirect methods has emerged such as semi-structured interviews videotaping practices that teachers are then asked to comment on (Kagan, 1992), and Likert-type rating scales (e.g. Deci, Schwartz, Sheinman, & Ryan, 1981).

In Greece, research on teachers' beliefs and practices in early childhood education is limited. Doliopoulou (1996) attempted to investigate the beliefs and practices of 67 pre-primary school teachers with regards to their developmentally appropriateness based on the guidelines of the National Association of Young Children (NAEYC). Almost a decade and a half later, Sofou and Tsafos (2010) published the results of their qualitative study on preschool teachers' understandings of the Greek national preschool curriculum. The scarce evidence in the field led to the development of this empirical study. Kagan's (1992) argument incorporates the essence and significance of research on teachers' beliefs and practices that is shared by the present study. As she points out:

> The more one reads studies of teacher belief, the more strongly one suspects that this piebald form of personal knowledge lies at the very heart of teaching. Teacher belief appears to arise out of the exigencies inherent in classroom teaching, it may be the clearest measure of a teacher's professional growth, and it appears to be instrumental in determining the quality of interaction one finds among the teachers in a given school. As we learn more about the forms and functions of teacher belief, we are likely to come a great deal closer to understanding how good teachers are made. (Kagan, 1992, 85)

2.6 The Capability Approach

A major part of the theoretical framework of this project consists of the Capability Approach, an influential freedom-based metric on quality of life and social justice pioneered by Nobel Laureate Amartya Sen and further developed by a number of scholars, most widely recognised being the philosopher Martha Nussbaum. Walker and Unterhalter (2007) write that Amartya Sen is one of the key thinkers and commentators of the late twentieth and early twenty-first century who is as influential as a Nobel prize-winning economist and a political philosopher. Sen is a key contributor to identifying, detailing, and campaigning against forms of global inequality. The first basic articulation of the approach was unfolded in Amartya Sen's Tanner Lecture paper entitled *Equality of What?* in 1979. The Capability Approach rests on a critique of other approaches to thinking about human well-being in welfare economics and political philosophy that are concerned with commodities, a standard of living, and justice as fairness (Walker & Unterhalter, 2007). It provides an alternative to the utility assessment of well-being that has prevailed in economics. The core assertion of the Capability Approach is simultaneously simplistic and complex, because it suggests that instead of focusing on GNP per capita or income, one should shed light on what beings are capable of being and doing. GNP per capita and income dramatically fail to illustrate the actual conditions of society members' being and doing; and, in many cases, these kinds of measures can be highly misleading. Nussbaum (2006) argues that the Capability Approach was originally designed above all as an alternative to the economic-Utilitarian approaches that dominated, and to some degree still dominate, discussions on quality of life in international development and policy circles, especially approaches that understand the point of development in narrowly economic terms (Nussbaum, 2006, p. 70).

Alkire (2003) argues that a number of people have found that the Capability Approach better articulates the goal towards which they wish to work than the goals prevalent in some settings. She characterizes the Capability Approach as a normative proposition suggesting that social arrangements should be evaluated primarily according to the extent of freedom people have with which to promote or achieve the functionings they value. Robeyns (2003) defines the Capability Approach as a broad normative framework for the evaluation of individual well-being and social arrangements, the design of policies, and social change in society. The term *capability* represents the alternative combinations of things a person is able to do or be – the various "*functionings*" he or she can achieve (Sen, 1993). The term refers not simply to what people are able to do but to their freedom to lead the kind of lives they value, and have reason to value (Dean, 2009, p. 262). The difference between a functioning and a capability is similar to the difference between an achievement and the freedom to achieve something, or between an outcome and opportunity. Functionings are people's beings and doings, whereas capabilities are the real or effective opportunities to achieve functionings. According to Dean (2009), *capabilities represent the essential fulcrum between material resources* (commodities) *and human achievements* (p. 262).

In both Sen's and Nussbaum's works, education is in itself a basic capability that influences the development and expansion of other capabilities. Sen emphasizes the importance of schooling to nurture future capabilities (Saito, 2003). However, scholars disagree over whether education itself can be a basic capability (Terzi, 2007).

The Capability Approach does not give very precise guidelines on how these evaluative exercises should be conducted; instead it is an open and underdeveloped framework (Robeyns 2000, 2005; Sen, 1993).

Furthermore, Sen and Nussbaum take a different stance on selecting capabilities. Sen does not specify valuable capabilities because he considers the capabilities people have reason to choose and value to be a matter of public debate through democratic processes. For Sen, a list of capabilities in education or any other area cannot simply be pre-specified without public consultation (Walker & Unterhalter, 2007). Walker and Unterhalter (2007) argue:

> So Sen (1992, 1999, 2004a, 2004b, 2002) has consistently argued for the importance of public participation and dialogue in arriving at valued capabilities for each situation and context. His capability approach is deliberately incomplete; he does not seek a complete ordering of nonnegotiable options. He does not stipulate which capabilities should count, not how different capabilities should be combined into an overall indicator of well-being and quality of life. For him a "workable solution" is possible without complete social unanimity. He argues that all the members of any collective or society "should be able to be active in the decisions regarding what to preserve and what to let go" (1999, p. 242). There is a real social justice need, Sen says, "for people to be able to take part in these social decisions if they so choose" (1999, p. 242). The process of public discussion is crucial, so that the public as much as the individual is seen to be an active participant in change, as citizens whose voices count.... Those affected by any policy or practice should be the ones to decide on what will count as valuable capabilities. (pp. 11–12)

Yet, Martha Nussbaum claims that the Capability Approach should endorse a theory of social justice, and she stresses the need to adopt an Aristotelian political conception of the person that views the person from the start as both capable and needy. Alkire (2008) writes that Nussbaum argues, as do others, that specification of one "list" of domains or central capabilities is necessary to make sure that the content of the Capability Approach carries critical force. If the approach is too open-ended, then there is a real, practical possibility that the wrong freedoms will be prioritized and expanded. According to Walker and Unterhalter (2007), Nussbaum seeks to give a specific content to capabilities, arguing that Sen's reluctance to make commitments about what capabilities a society ought centrally to pursue means that guidance in thinking about social justice is too limited. They quote her words that the list constitutes "a minimum account of social justice" (2003a, p. 40) and is humble, open-ended, and revisable, although it is not clear who will revise it. As Nussbaum (2006a) argues:

> The basic intuitive idea of my version of the capabilities approach is that we begin with a conception of the dignity of the human being, and of a life that is worthy of that dignity

– a life that has available in it "truly human functioning", in the sense described by Marx in his 1844 *Economic and Philosophical Manuscripts*. (I use the Marxian idea for political purposes only, not as the source of a comprehensive doctrine of human life; Marx makes no such distinction) (p. 74)

The list in itself is open-ended and has undergone modification over time; no doubt it will undergo further modification in the light of criticism. (p. 76)

Due to its interdisciplinary nature, one can see a growing volume of literature on the Capability Approach because it serves quite different epistemological goals, spanning a wide range of traditional academic disciplines (Andresen, Otto, & Ziegler, 2006, 2009; Alkire, 2003, 2005, 2008; Clark, 2005, 2006; DiTommaso, 2006; Gasper, 2004; Kuklys & Robeyns, 2004; Osmani, 2000; Papadopoulos & Tsakloglou, 2005; Robeyns, 2000, 2003, 2005, 2006; Saito, 2003). This has led to the development of the approach in a variety of directions such as poverty or inequality assessment, quality of life measurement, and so forth. The Capability Approach has received substantial attention from philosophers, ethicists, economists, and other social scientists.

Wolff and De-Shalit (2007) argue that policies should be evaluated according to what extent people have the freedom (negative or positive) to achieve doings and beings that they (have reason to) value. Nussbaum (2007) notes:

Sen's use of the approach focuses on the comparative measurement of quality of life, although he is also interested in issues of social justice. I, by contrast, have used the approach to provide the philosophical underpinning for an account of core human entitlements that should be respected and implemented by the governments of all nations, as a bare minimum of what respect for human dignity requires.... I argue that the best approach to this idea of a basic social minimum is provided by an approach that focuses on *human capabilities*, that is, what people are actually able to do and to be, in a way informed by an intuitive idea of a life that is worthy of the dignity of the human being. I identify a list of central human capabilities, arguing that all of them are implicit in the idea of a life worthy of human dignity. (p. 70)

According to Alkire (2003, p. 6), Nussbaum distinguishes three kinds of capabilities: basic, internal, and combined. Basic capabilities are "the innate equipment of individuals that is the necessary basis for developing the more advanced capabilities and a ground of moral concern"; internal capabilities are "developed states of the person herself that are, so far as the person herself is concerned, sufficient conditions for the exercise of requisite functions ....ature conditions of readiness"; and combined capabilities are "internal capabilities combined with suitable external conditions for the exercise of the function." Nussbaum's approach (2006) uses the idea of a threshold level of each capability, beneath which it is held that truly human functioning is not available to citizens; the social goal should be understood in terms of getting citizens above this capability threshold. For Nussbaum (2011, pp. 33–34), the following combined capabilities are central for human flourishing and a life of dignity and need to be present for a fully human good life:

1. *Life.* Being able to live to the end of a human life of normal length; not dying prematurely, or before one's life is so reduced as to be not worth living.
2. *Bodily health.* Being able to have good health, including reproductive health; to be adequately nourished; to have adequate shelter.
3. *Bodily integrity.* Being able to move freely from place to place; to be secure against violent assault, including sexual assault and domestic violence; having opportunities for sexual satisfaction and for choice in matters of reproduction.
4. *Senses, imagination, thought.* Being able to use the senses; being able to imagine, to think, and to reason – and to do these things in a "truly human" way, a way informed and cultivated by an adequate education, including, but by no means limited to, literacy and basic mathematical and scientific training. Being able to use imagination and thought in connection with experiencing, and producing expressive works and events of one's own choice, religious, literacy, musical, and so forth. Being able to use one's mind in ways protected by guarantees of freedom of expression with respect to both political and artistic speech and freedom of religious exercise; being able to have pleasurable experiences and to avoid nonbeneficial pain.
5. *Emotions.* Being able to have attachments to things and persons outside ourselves; being able to love those who love and care for us, to grieve at their absence; in general to love, to grieve, to experience longing, gratitude, and justified anger. Not having one's emotional developing blighted by fear or anxiety. (Supporting this capability means supporting forms of human association that can be shown to be crucial in their development.)
6. *Practical reason.* Being able to form a conception of the good and to engage in critical reflection about the planning of one's life. (This entails protection for liberty of conscience and religious observance.)
7. *Affiliation.* (A) Being able to live for and in relation to others, to recognize and show concern for other human beings, to engage in various forms of social interaction; being able to imagine the situation of another. (B) Having the social bases of self-respect and nonhumiliation; being able to be treated as a dignified being whose worth is equal to that of others. This entails provisions of non-discrimination on the basis of race, sex, sexual orientation, ethnicity, caste, religion, national origin.

8. **Other species.** Being able to live with concern for and in relation to animals, plants, and the world of nature.
9. **Play.** Being able to laugh, to play, to enjoy recreational activities.
10. **Control over one's environment.** (A) **Political.** Being able to participate effectively in political choices that govern one's life; having the rights of political participation, free speech and freedom of association. (B) **Material:** being able to hold property (both land and movable goods); having the right to seek employment on an equal basis with others.

The capabilities are considered to be equally fundamental without any hierarchy, although they exist at different levels. However, Nussbaum, considers "practical reason" as one of the central capabilities for functioning and suggests that practical reason and affiliation have special importance since they both "organize and suffuse" all other capabilities (Nussbaum 2000, p. 82, as cited in Flores-Crespo, 2007, p. 48).

As Nussbaum (2006a) notes:

> These ten capabilities are supposed to be general goals that can be further specified by the society in question as it works on the account of fundamental entitlements it wishes to endorse. But in some form all are held to be part of a minimum account of social justice: a society that does not guarantee these to all its citizens, at some appropriate threshold level, falls short of being a fully just society, whatever its opulence. And although in practical terms priorities may have to be set temporarily, the capabilities are understood as both mutually supportive and all of central relevance to social justice. Thus a society that neglects one of them to promote the others has shortchanged its citizens, and there is a failure of justice in the shortchanging. (p. 75)

Nussbaum's effort to define specific capabilities has been a subject of criticism and controversy. Salais (2011) argued that *it is not up to theoreticians to define the list of valuable functionings through exterior knowledge, but rather society itself through democratic deliberation* (Salais, 2011, p. 2). Furthermore, this effort has led to the development or the expansion of the potential lists suitable for the measuring capabilities. Biggeri, Libanora, Mariani, and Menchini (2004), Ingrid Robeyns (2003), Lorella Terzi (2007), Wolff and De-Shalit (2007) belong to the followers of Nussbaum's effort to define and or extract core capabilities. Di Tomasso (2003) works with Nussbaum's list and takes out seven out of ten capabilities. In contrast, Biggeri (2003) proposes an *ad hoc* non-definitive and open-ended list of 14 children's capabilities selected following the method suggested by Robeyns (2003). Although all these efforts are interesting to review, it cannot be disputed that all lists end up with similar capabilities to the ones Nussbaum has on her list. Considering the minor differentiations, the aforementioned studies constitute a verification of Nussbaum's core capabilities list. Wolff's and DeShalit's (2007) view on the selection of Nussbaum's list as a starting point is shared in this study:

> We shall take as our starting point Martha Nussbaum's well-known list. While Alkire finds Nussbaum's list in some respects unsuitable for her purposes, and while scholars of the capability approach have distinguished between Sen's and Nussbaum's approaches, we find it intuitively very powerful, building on related ideas from Aristotle and early Marx concerning what it is that makes a life fully human. In addition, Nussbaum's list is a good starting point because it is meant to be a part of a policy oriented research project – in her case the "formulation of basic political principles of the short that can play a role in fundamental constitutional guarantees" – and because of its grounding in cross-cultural empirical and theoretical work. The latter, in part, leads Nussbaum to claim that even people who otherwise have very different comprehensive conceptions of the good can reach the same conclusion about what functionings are included in this list as an "overlapping consensus. (p. 38)

> But for the moment we side with Nussbaum who claims that a life that lacks any of these functionings is in some important sense deprived, when we define lacking them, or even finding one of them insecure involuntarily (we explain this idea in the next chapter), as a form of disadvantage. (p. 40)

Alkire (2003) notes that the capability approach is deliberately incomplete, both foundationally and in practice. Diehm and Magyar-Haas (2010, p. 105) praise the speciality of Nussbaum's accomplishment, the formulation of "a vague, open, arbitrarily extendable, politically relevant list of functionings that is, on the one hand, non-detached, but, on the other hand, objective." They argue:

> By postulating that capabilities must be supported and made possible, and that the individual's capabilities are indispensable for political and state task so while leaving the achieved functionings to the individual himself or herself, Nussbaum (1990, p. 224) formulates a universalistic approach that is able to take both pluralism and cultural differences into account to the same degree. (p. 105)

Education plays a central role in the enhancement and development of capabilities. Nussbaum (2006) perceives public education as a crucial element to the health of democracy and opposes the recent educational initiatives in many countries that focus narrowly on science and technology while neglecting the arts and humanities; that emphasize internalization of information rather than the formation of the student's critical and imaginative capacities. Such a narrow focus is, for Nussbaum, a danger for democracy's future. She identifies three key capabilities associated with education: first, critical thinking or "the examined life"; second, the ideal of the world citizen; and third, the development of the narrative imagination. One of the specificities of the Capability Approach is that it "leaves space for human diversity" (Alkire, 2003, p. 15), a fact that should be a prerequisite in an educational setting. As "a universal theory of the good" (Robeyns, 2003, p. 36), the Capability Approach applies to all social justice issues, including education; and by being sensitive to local culture and context, it is transferable and applicable in diverse structures. Sen (1992, p. 44) identifies education as one of "a relatively small number of centrally important beings and doings that are crucial to well-being" (as cited in Walker & Unterhalter, 2007, p. 8). Walker and Unterhalter (2007) report:

> Education, argues Sen (1999), fulfils an *instrumental social role* in that critical literacy, for example, fosters public debate and dialogue about social and political arrangements. It has an *instrumental process role* by expanding the people one comes into contact with, broadening our horizons. Finally, it has an empowering and distributive role in facilitating the ability of the disadvantaged, marginalized, and excluded to organize politically. It has redistributive effects between social groups, households, and within families. Overall, education contributes to interpersonal effects where people are able to use the benefits of education to help others and hence contribute to the social good and democratic freedoms. In short, for Sen, "education" is an unqualified good for human capability expansion and human freedom. (p. 8)

Nussbaum (2011) argues that the importance of education has been at the heart of the capabilities approach since its inception.

> Education (in schools, in the family, in programs for both child and adult development run by nongovernmental organizations) forms people's existing capacities into developed internal capabilities of many kinds. (p. 152)

> Heckman understands "capabilities" as skills or potentials for achievement. Heckman's central contention (drawing on a wide range of psychological research and other empirical studies) is that human capabilities are shaped decisively at a very early age by environmental influences of a wide variety, beginning with prenatal influences on later development, and continuing through early life in the family and early schooling. Heckman is interested in both cognitive and what he calls "noncognitive" skills, by which he means emotional and characterological abilities (attentiveness, self-control, and so on) that strongly influence adult success…. Empirical studies show that early intervention is crucial, building the case for preschool interventions and programs that partner with families seeking to develop potential in a society riven by inequality. Indeed, Heckman contends that a great deal of human potential is being wasted by the failure to intervene early, both through programs designed to enhance the future human being's health *in utero* and through programs after birth. Although research shows that most central human abilities are decisively affected by what happens at a very young age, Heckman also argues that some key emotional abilities, such as self-control, develop later, up through adolescence, thus giving reasons to devise supportive programs for those ages as well. (pp. 193–194)

Saito (2003) scrutinizes the strong relationship between Sen's capability approach and education. He points out:

> Few would deny that children need support from parents, teachers or societies in choosing what is best for their lives. When it comes to education also, the same argument can be made. Despite the fact that neither parents nor the State have a right to complete authority over the education of children, as Gutmann argues, it seems appropriate to say that a child remains in the care of others in the choice of what to learn, so that the child's interests can be facilitated. Therefore, although I agree that functionings, the set of things that a person can do in life in Sen's sense, are of course important for children, when it comes to capabilities in children, the matter appears complicated and problematic. To the question I posed, "How can we apply the capability approach to children, since children are not mature enough to make decisions by themselves?" Sen answered by showing this applicability in two respects. First, he emphasises the importance not of the freedom a child has now, but of the freedom the child will have in the future: If the child does not want to be inoculated, and you nevertheless think it is a good idea for him/her to be inoculated, then the argument may be connected with the freedom that this person will have in the future by having the measles shot now. The child when it grows up must have more freedom. So when you are considering a child, you have to consider not only the child's freedom now, but also the child's freedom in the future. This is well articulated in what John White argues in relation to education. He claims that adopting an extreme libertarian position vis-à-vis the child is irrational. In other words, making no effort to teach a child anything, since we do not know what is good or bad for the child, does not lead the child to improve his/her well-being. (p. 25)

The capabilities that adults enjoy are deeply conditional on their experience as children. All capabilities together correspond to the overall freedom to lead the life that a person has reason to value (Robeyns, 2003a, p. 63). Having the opportunity for education and the development of an education capability expands human freedoms. Not having education harms human development and impedes choosing and having a full life (Walker & Unterhalter, 2007). *Sen's argument has been that equal inputs do not necessarily give rise to equal outputs because human capabilities – the real freedoms that people have to fashion their own way of living – may be objectively constrained* (Dean, 2009, p. 262).

Specifically, Sen (1999) states that a fuller understanding of the extensive reach and critical importance of investing in early childhood can be obtained through seeing investment in children as a part of the overall process of development,. For him, the process of development can be seen as expansion of human freedom, and with the use of the example of Robert Myers book *The twelve who survive*, he stresses that we cannot be concerned only with the prevention of mortality in children, but must also focus on "strengthening programmes of early childhood development" for a fuller life of the children (Sen, 1999, p. 4).

Enhancing the quality of life of children, influenced by education, security, prevention of trauma, and so forth, can be crucially significant as a part of development. The quality of childhood is important not only for what happens in childhood but also for future life. Therefore, investment in education and other features of childhood opportunities can enhance future capabilities in quite different ways, because a securely preparatory childhood can directly make adult lives richer and less problematic by augmenting our skill in living a good life.

Although the Capability Approach offers a way of engaging with questions of educational equality, it should be a matter of concern that the absence or lack of a critical consideration of children's positioning within the approach as well as on intergenerational relationships may place the Capability Approach at risk of reproducing and reinforcing the material and knowledge-based power inequalities that are at the heart of the institutionalized educational system instead of combating the conditions of inequality. The controversy lies in the duality in the way of regarding children. Some researchers within the Capability Approach regard children as social actors who have values, make meaning, and need opportunities, whereas others see them as humans to be who need to be prepared for the adult life in which opportunities will come to fruition rather than seeing this as a reasonable situation for children to be accorded in the here and now of their lives. The Capability Approach focuses implicitly on measuring the well-being of adults whose freedom to choose a life they have reason to value is central to the notion of capabilities (Klasen, 2010; Sen, 1998). But to what extent can the capability approach be brought to bear on the analysis of well-being of children (Klasen, 2010)?

Walker and Unterhalter (2007) bring to the fore the issue that, according to Nussbaum, occurs as a necessity: that of promoting a relevant capability "by requiring the functioning that nourishes it" (Nussbaum, 2000, p. 91). They quote Nussbaum who gives the example of requiring children to spend time in play, storytelling, and art activities as a way to promote the general capability of "play" that is important for adults. Their claim is that in children's and young people's education, it makes sense to consider people's functionings (what we manage to achieve) and not just capabilities. As a result, teachers need to know if and how capability is being developed, by whom, and under what conditions, as well as how this relates to capabilities. They argue:

> It is clear that addressing the problem of children, capabilities, and functioning raises issues about the content of education capabilities. Brighouse and Swift (2003, p. 367) point out that education is not a neutral activity; it always embodies a view about what is good in human life, otherwise it might "seem vapid, even pointless." But are there education capabilities that we might argue are objectively good for an individual's educational

development? We might not wish to describe as education a process that tolerates, ignores, or even encourages prejudice, exclusion, marginalization, or harassment of any student on the basis of difference, or that limits their access to knowledge or critical and confident participation in learning. Education that contributes to *un*freedoms would be deeply compatible with the capability approach. (p. 15)

Biggeri, Libanora, Mariani, and Menchini (2004) acknowledge the influence of the adults (parents, guardians, teachers) on child development and capabilities (Biggeri, Libanora, Mariani, & Menchini, 2004): According to them, the capability of parents to function may directly or indirectly influence the capabilities of child because there may be a sort of intergenerational transfer of capabilities. As they characteristically state, the child's capabilities are at least partially influenced by the capability set and achieved functionings (and also by the means, i.e., assets, disposable income) of their parents (Biggeri et al., 2006, p. 63). They regard the possibility of converting capabilities into functionings to be dependant purely on parents', guardians' and teachers' decisions – thereby implying that the child's conversion factors are subject to further "constraints." As Alkire (2003) points out, capabilities interact with one another. Some may be intrinsically valued and also instrumental to further capabilities; some may crowd out or undermine other capabilities. Moreover, a potential form of capability failure may constrain the realization of another capability and/or functioning, and vice versa.

> A child could have different relevant capabilities to those of adults and it suggests that the relevance of these capabilities can vary according to the age and even to gender.... Childhood is complex and constituted by different sensitive periods and, as a consequence, careful timing of interventions for children's well-being is required. (Biggeri et al., 2006, p. 64)

Alkire (2003) suggests that rather than focusing attention on "mental" metrics such as utility, which may not adequately reflect a person's achievements; or on commodities, whose primary value is instrumental, the Capability Approach draws attention to "beings and doings" that may be valued as ends.

> "The life of money-making," as Aristotle noted, "is one undertaken under compulsion, and wealth is evidently not the good we are seeking; for it is merely useful and for the sake of something else." This is not to say that many capabilities are not also instrumentally valuable. Still, some care is taken to make sure that the instrumental and intrinsic values of different activities and policies are clearly identified, and that the objectives of activities are intrinsically valued ends. As the 1990 Human Development Report put it, "The end of development must be the human being." (p. 14)

2.7 The Capability Approach in Early Childhood Education

Atkinson claims that there is more than one way in which an idea such as the Capability Approach can be operationally effective (Atkinson, 1999, pp. 185–186). Saito (2003) highlights the potentially strong and mutually enhancing relationship between the Capability Approach and education – an interrelationship and interaction that could be crucial and groundbreaking. He calls for serious attention and research from educationists in order to realize the implications of the approach. Although efforts have been made to operationalize the Capability Approach within the field of education (e.g. Terzi, 2007; Walker & Unterhalter, 2007), to date, the context of early childhood education has not been a matter of thorough debate. This study partially responds to Saito's call because this section stresses the potential linkages and applicability of the Capability Approach in early childhood education.

Although it is tending increasingly to become formal and to be unified and integrated in the educational system, early childhood education still constitutes the space within education where more freedom is offered in comparison with the other educational levels. This by no means implies that within early childhood settings, power relations and the imposition of values and practices by the dominant discourse do not have a significant share in the process. However, the structure, the settings, and the actors involved experience a unique way of interacting, learning, and liberation that is not met in other educational settings.

Every early childhood curriculum sketches the concept of the good start in life based on the positioning of the agreed norms and values of a specific cultural setting. Furthermore, from this political work, one can derive the perspective or "resemblance" aims set for the next generation of this specific culture. If we consider Martha Nussbaum's list of central human capabilities as the minimum entitlements a person should have and compare this with the principles that govern early childhood education, one could easily realize that this normative evaluative framework is highly applicable in early childhood education. Undoubtedly, the central capabilities list would require a sort of minor modification when it is to be used in early childhood education, but the essence of the approach would remain the same. Many of the basic human capabilities have been scrutinized by scholars such as Montessori, Piaget, Vygotsky, Freud, or Fröbel, and these have produced an eminent argumentation on their indisputable value that continues to influence and shape early childhood education until today. Nussbaum Furthermore, a great number of early childhood curricula explicitly or implicitly endorse most of the central human capabilities. Some of them are considered in the Greek Cross-Thematic Curriculum Framework (CTCF) as well as in other curricula (e.g. Te Wariki, High Scope, Experimental Education, the Swedish curriculum, or the Reggio Emilia approach). With regard to the CTCF, the capabilities of play, senses–imagination–thought, emotions, and affiliation compose the essential means for the child's development and learning.

Another example of the wide use of the basic capabilities in early childhood curricula is the Finnish national curriculum guidelines on ECEC (2003) that illustrate their priorities and highlight which children's rights are embodied. Here, one can trace the children's right to "warm personal relationships" and to "their own culture, language, and beliefs" – aspects that could be linked with the capability of affiliation, whereas "secured growth, development and learning," and "secure, and healthy environments that allow play and a wide range of activities" could be linked to the capabilities of bodily health and bodily integrity. Furthermore, the following quotes from the national curriculum guidelines on early childhood education and care in Finnland (2003) offer a sense of the common language used.

> A good combination of care, education and teaching can promote the child's positive self-image, expressive and **interactive skills**, and the **development of thinking**…. An activity that children find meaningful also gives an **expression to their thoughts** and **feelings** …. Children play for the sake of playing, and at best, **play can give them deep satisfaction**. Although children do not play in order to learn, they learn through play… .s playing is social by nature, peer groups have a significant effect on the way the playing situation develops …. At an early age, children also start to actively explore their object environment, which prepares them to a **transition to imaginary play**. Imaginary games mean detachment from here and now, and the **onset of imagination and abstract thinking**…. When they play, they imitate and create new things. They pick up things that are meaningful for them from the sphere of both the real world and that of fantasy and fiction, translating them into a language of play….rtistic activities and experiences introduce the child to an aesthetic world: the joy of learning, artistic drama, forms, sounds, colours, scents, **sentiments** and combinations of experiences **based on the different senses**. Art gives the child an opportunity to experience an imaginary world where everything is possible and true and in a make-believe way. (pp. 15–22)

An additional example could be the well-known and highly appreciated Te Wariki curriculum of New Zealand (1996) that reveals a similar approach to the interrelation among these aspects:

> Cognitive, social, cultural, physical, emotional, and spiritual dimensions of human development are integrally interwoven. The early childhood curriculum takes up a model of learning that weaves together intricate patterns of linked experience and meaning rather than emphasising the acquisition of discrete skills. The child's whole context, the physical surroundings, the emotional context, relationships with others, and the child's immediate needs at any moment will affect and modify how a particular experience

contributes to the child's development. This integrated view of learning sees the child as a person who wants to learn, sees the task as a meaningful whole, and sees the whole as greater than the sum of its individual tasks or experiences. Learning and development will be integrated through: tasks, activities, and contexts that have meaning for the child, including practices and activities not always associated with the word "curriculum," such as care routines, mealtimes, and child management strategies; opportunities for open-ended exploration and play; consistent, warm relationships that connect everything together; recognition of the spiritual dimension of children's lives in culturally, socially, and individually appropriate ways; recognition of the significance and contribution of previous generations to the child's concept of self. (p. 41)

The present study emphasizes the capabilities affiliation, senses–imagination–thought, play, and emotions. These four out of the ten basic human capabilities referred to in Martha Nussbaum's list form the cornerstone of early childhood education, because they are of great relevance and significance for early childhood educational praxis and are commonly met in an early childhood education curriculum. The debate over these aspects of childhood is timely yet timeless. It starts with the ancient Greeks through the works of Plato and Aristotle and goes on till our days, revealing their interrelation as well as their instrumentality in child's development. Early childhood education literature praises their intrinsic and instrumental value. Saito (2003) argues that education involves both instrumental and intrinsic values. However, the dominant case is that in early childhood curricula, these capabilities play an instrumental role in serving academic knowledge acquisition. Wood (2010) stresses:

> The concept of integrated pedagogical approaches is supported in many different curriculum frameworks in ECE within and beyond the UK (Wood and Attfield, 2005; Wood, 2009; 2010a, 2010b), and is strongly endorsed in national policy frameworks for the pre-school and primary phases. The recommendations in Aistear (NCCA, 2009) reflect the subtle and complex combination of structure and flexibility in provision. There is broad agreement in research and policy frameworks that effective teachers plan play-learning environments in ways that enable children to exercise choice and autonomy in their self-initiated activities. Practitioners also plan adult-directed activities that focus on teaching specific content and skills that are related to the curriculum, as well as to children's interests and patterns of learning that emerge from their self-initiated activities. So teachers can combine play-led curriculum, and curriculum-led play. However, curriculum frameworks should not be seen as straitjackets. They provide guidance and advice, but it is up to skilled practitioners to develop their provision and practice in ways that are responsive to children, their interests and their home/family backgrounds. (pp. 3–4)

Major theorists such as Piaget, Vygotsky, and Freud, but even more recent researchers as well, have been concerned with the meaning and the role of these components of human existence for the development of the child. Piaget and Vygotsky highlighted the importance of play, imagination, thinking, and socialization (part of which is the notion of affiliation). There is a strong interaction between emotional, social, and cognitive development in early childhood, which depends upon environment and opportunity. Children can develop social-emotional competence through both planned and unplanned interactions with adults and peers. The child's free movement in space, his or her mental, creative, emotional, and imaginary expression and participation outside school in the present, or future established social frameworks of work constitute an axis for every present or future scheme pertaining to any preschool education strategy (Frangos, 1993).

The Capability of Play

Play is an important aspect of the human life pattern that is important for a healthy growth and well-being of the personality. The introduction of play in the curriculum indicates that we acknowledge its educational value (Kitsaras, 2004). Moreover, the incorporation of engagement in play as a right for every child in the UN Human Rights Convention on the Rights of the Child (Article 31) reinforces its significance. Hughes (2003) argues that this development is more important than its current credit given. He argues that "*the UN, even with all of the world's current and future problems to contend with, have given play the time of day, concluding that it is a vitally important experience for the world's current and future generations of children and giving it the status of a human right*" (Hughes, 2003: 16). Ginsburg (2007) points out:

> Play allows children to use their creativity while developing their imagination, dexterity and physical, cognitive and emotional strength. Play is important to healthy brain development. It is through play that children at a very early age engage and interact in the world around them.... Undirected play allows children to learn how to work in groups, to share, to negotiate, to resolve conflicts and to learn self-advocacy skills. (p. 183)

Wehman and Abramson (1976) argue that play helps children to communicate with their feelings. Singer and Singer (1990) highlight that play promotes the mental and social development of children, whereas for Pepler and Ross (1981), play enhances children's imagination and creativity. Piaget in his book *Play, Dreams and Imitation* (1962) succinctly unfolds his ideas concerning play. He classified play from the perspective of developmental stages of the child and considered play not only as a reflection of the cognitive skills but also of children's daily lives and problems. Lev S. Vygotsky (1896–1934) stated that play influences more than the children's cognitive development. For Vygotsky (1931), play has an important role in the development of children the child by enabling them to expand their zone of proximal development. In his views, symbolic or dramatic play fosters the children's abstract thinking. He also claimed that imagination begins to develop through play, and that before play there is no imagination.

A plethora of theorists approve play for its cathartic role in the child's emotional empowerment. According to Goelman, Andersen, Anderson, Gouzouasis, Kendrick, Kindler, Porath, and Koh, (2003), Freud (1938) noted that children use play as a tool to overcome their own hidden thoughts related to their perceived actions. Children's active involvement or inactive observation dominates their internalized thought processes and their conscious physical movements. Activity, the second role of play, is associated with the individual's social relationships or interpersonal dialogues. Play activities and explorations help children to better understand distressing events and search for alternative meanings that embrace pleasurable feelings and forego unpleasant ones. Play helps children to construe an event and link symbolic properties of people and objects in the present and past (Goelman et al., 2003).

Brown (2012) challenged the idea that the quality of play may be negatively affected by a child's material deprivation. In contrast to the assumption that children who are not able to access the play experiences of their wealthier counterparts will suffer a form of play deprivation he uses Hughes argument suggesting that *if children n the more prosperous western economies are not able to access the basic elemental experiences of their predecessors (such as digging holes and making dens) then they will experience play deprivation, with dangerous consequences for both the individual and human society as a whole* (Brown, 2012: 72). In his empirical study with materially deprived Roma children he concluded that the link between poverty and play is tenuous at best. He showed that those children, being among the most deprived children – poor and disadvantaged – enjoyed rich and healthy play experiences.

Despite its widely accepted significance, defining play has proven problematic within the literature because the ambiguity of the various definitions reflects the conceptualization struggle of play. Wood and Attfield (2005) stress the problematic positioning of play both in theory and practice through it being infinitely varied and complex. As they argue, play cannot be defined or categorized easily because it is always context-dependent and the contexts vary. Definitions of play should take into account different contexts as well as the needs, interests, affective states, and preferences of children at different ages: what counts as play will vary according to who is playing and the choice of play activity (Wood & Attfield, 2005, p. 7). Wood and Attfield (2005) quote Garvey (1991) who regards play as an attitude or orientation that can manifest itself in numerous kinds of behaviour. Furthermore, they refer to Meckley who has drawn on Garvey's definition of play characteristics in order to forge links between what play is, what it does for the child, and how children make links between their inner and outer worlds. According to them, the characteristics of play are that it is child-chosen, is child-invented, pretend but done as if the activity were real, focused on the doing (process not product), done by the players (children) and not the adults (teachers or parents), requires active involvement, and is fun. Wood and Attfield (2005) argue:

> Merkley's framework captures some of the complexities diversity and unpredictability of play, and provides "ideal" conceptions of what play and what it does for the child. The purposes and goals of play often shift as children manipulate play and non-play situations because are permitted, whereas others, such as mock aggression and play-fighting, are often banned. Play does not take place in a vacuum: everything that children play at, or play with, is influenced by wider social, historical and cultural factors, so that understanding what play is and learning how to play are culturally situated processes. (p. 5)

The OECD's 2004 report states:

> In documents and curricula about ECEC, little is said about play, although researchers sometimes claim that play is what distinguish ECEC from formal schooling. Play is often referred to in a non reflective and taken for granted way – as something allowed to children outside the curriculum. This is surprising as play, as a field of research, has developed greatly since Froebel, 150 years ago, established play as a main feature of preschool education (Fröbel, 1995). If ECEC should have a curriculum with goals, and play is a central to the child's development, then the challenge is raised to question and problematise what play means in the context of young children's learning. Is play an activity by itself, or is it a means to learning? In what way is it different from learning? These are questions that should be raised in curriculum work. (pp. 28–29)

As a verification of the vague and fuzzy interpretation of play in early childhood curricula, the Swedish curriculum Lpfö 98 (2010) states:

> Play is important for the child's development and learning. Conscious use of play to promote the development and learning of each individual child should always be present in preschool activities. Play and enjoyment in learning in all its various forms stimulate the imagination, insight, communication and the ability to think symbolically, as well as the ability to co-operate and solve problems. Through creative and gestalt play, the child is given opportunities to express and work through his or her experiences and feelings. (p. 6)

Wood and Attfield (2005) argue that in spite of continuing enthusiastic endorsements of play, its place in the curriculum remains problematic, particularly beyond the early years of school because its role, purposes, and value in the early years curriculum continue to be debated. They argue:

77

What counts as play is contested, and there are ongoing debates about the relationship between playing, learning and teaching. These issues have been particularly relevant for early years practitioners since the implementation of Education Reform Act in 1988, and the subsequent flow of educational policies which have see-sawed between an anti- and pro-play ethos. These debates have had a positive outcome because they have kept play high on educational agendas in policy, research and practice. Play continues to be taken seriously in the academic community, as evidenced by extensive research that is providing new theoretical frameworks and guidance for practice. Play is also being taken much more seriously by policy-makers, as evidenced by the endorsement for a pedagogy of play in the British Government's framework Birth to Three Matters, and the Foundation Stage for three- to five-year-old children. These trends can also be seen in many other countries, in a thriving international play scholarship, and ongoing debates about the role and value of play and its contribution to effective teaching and learning. Play also continues to fascinate and challenge practitioners who are concerned with improving the quality of their provision, understanding the meaning and value of play, and providing evidence of learning through play. However, play remains problematic both in theory and in practice. (p. 1)

Furthermore, Wood (2010) argued that although current policy documents for early childhood education (ECE) in the four UK countries (England, Northern Ireland, Scotland, Wales) and in Eire provide strong validation for play in pre-school and primary school settings, within these national policy frameworks, the model of play that has been developed is distinctly "educational play." As she stresses, play is seen as contributing to children's learning and development, and as one of many means through which they progress. In the CTCF (2003) it is stated on play:

> Play should be highlighted as the core of the entire program. (p. 587)

> Play feels the greater part of the child's life at this age. It is the means by which the child gets to know itself, learns about people, and the world around it, understands its possibilities and limits. It contributes to the socialization of the child. Children through play learn to cooperate, to take responsibilities and roles, learn to follow and respect rules. (p. 589)

The Capability of Senses

Beings receive a great deal of information on a daily basis through their senses, and this influences their behaviour and supports them in interacting with the world. Through sight, hearing, touch, taste, and smell, children discover and interact with the environment around them. Senses are the source of any knowledge one possesses on the material external reality. Senses should not be confused with emotions, because the former are effects of the external environment, whereas the latter are created from the body itself.

Te Wäriki (1996) incorporates children's active exploration with all senses as a priority. Within the Te Wäriki curriculum it is noted:

> Children develop ....trategies for actively exploring and making sense of the world by using their bodies, including active exploration with all the senses, and the use of tools, materials, and equipment to extend skills (p. 86); ....he confidence to choose and experiment with materials, to play around with ideas, and to explore actively with all the senses. (p. 88)

The national curriculum guidelines on ECEC in Finland (2003) mention that children practice and learn various skills, and when encountering new things, they make use of all their senses in the process of learning. Along the same lines, the CTCF (2003) points out:

> Children in a safe and rich in stimuli environment explore with their senses, create ideas and construct knowledge (p. 586).
> They use initially their senses, make assumptions, and try to explore the world (p. 588).
> By using different materials to realize that senses help us understand the external environment; to name and describe the sensory organs and senses (p. 604)
> Children are encouraged to observe their surroundings, to use their senses to handle various materials to find specific features, to compare them, to study their properties and to classify them. (p. 605)

The Capability of Imagination

Vygotsky (1967) defined imagination as the human combinatorial or creative activity that makes the human being a creature oriented towards the future and who thus alters her or his own present. This creative activity, based on the ability of our brain to combine elements, is called imagination or fantasy in psychology. Imagination, as the basis of all creative activity, is an important component of absolutely all aspects of cultural life, enabling artistic, scientific, and technical creativity alike. Child (1973) considers the inability of conventional tests to distinguish the potentially creative from the not so creative, the insufficiency of conventional learning and teaching modes, and the interaction between cognitive and non-cognitive variables (personality, motivation) on creativity as the factors that have contributed to the enthusiasm for on in creative thinking among psychologists. Valkenburg (2001) refers to the three related but distinguishable imaginal processes in which imagination has been operationalized, namely imaginative play, daydreaming, and creativity. House (2002) argues:

> Fantasy has a special place in infancy: it "takes hold of any kind of material, movements as well as ideas, for activating itself; ....and] fantasy without play and play without fantasy are almost unthinkable .... play enlivens fantasy....and] fantasy kindles and diversifies play" (Konig, 1998, p. 64). Moreover, "Real experiences have their sources only in

the child's fantasy....[T]he child can grasp his environment only as interpretation of his fantasy, and existence gains its true meaning and becomes experience in this way alone" (p. 64, emphasis added). As Konig graphically puts it, "Without [fantasy] all ideas stagnate.... Concepts remain rigid and dead, sensations raw and sensuous" (Konig, 1998, p. 66). And here is one of the last century's greatest minds, Albert Einstein: "I have come to the conclusion that the gift of fantasy has meant more to me than any talent for abstract, positive thinking" (quoted in Rawson & Rose, 2002, p. 21)

Udwin (1983) conducted an experimental study on imaginative play training as an intervention method with institutionalized preschool children from disadvantaged family backgrounds in which she found that the experimental group showed post-training advancement on imaginative play, positive emotionality, prosocial behaviours as well as on measures of divergent thinking and storytelling skills. She also found a decline in children's overt aggression.

Richards and Sanderson (1999) investigated the instrumental use of imagination to solve deductive reasoning problems in 2-, 3- and 4-year-olds. They found that when children in this age range were encouraged to use their imagination, they were able to reach logically correct conclusions, even though the content of the premises contradicted their knowledge about the real world. As they argue, high levels of imagination encouraged the children to create an alternate reality in which outcomes incongruent with their everyday experience were possible, so that they could set aside their real world knowledge. Furthermore, Singer and Singer (2005, 2007) stress that children's play and the growth of imagination may be seen as a critical opportunity of school readiness enhancement and personal growth enrichment. Saracho (2002) argues that teachers need to provide children with the opportunity to extend their imagination and assume these make-believe roles in an encouraging learning environment.

Te Wāriki (1996) supports the idea that children learn through a combination of imagination and logic.

Young children use their imaginations to explore their own and others' identities. (p. 25)
Children moving from early childhood settings to the early years of school are likely to ... be able to use discovery, invention, innovation, imagination, experimentation, and exploration as means of learning. (p. 83)
Children try out original and innovative ideas and exercise their imaginations to solve problems. (p. 97)

In the Swedish curriculum Lpfö 98 (2011), the role of imagination is presented as being interwoven with play, because "play and enjoyment in learning in all its various forms stimulate the imagination, insight, communication and the ability to think symbolically, as well as the ability to co-operate and solve problems" (p. 6).

Moreover, "preschool should provide scope for the child's own plans, imagination and creativity in play, and learning, both indoors and outdoors" (p. 7).

The CTCF (2003) emphasizes that the visual arts, theatre drama, and music "activate the physical abilities of children, excite, enchant, awaken their curiosity, motivate their imagination, encourage expression, foster creativity and provide opportunities for experimentation with materials and techniques" (p. 589). It is noted that the diversity of colours and materials stimulate the imagination and ingenuity of children and lead them on to new paths (p. 589). The teacher is involved in the process, plays roles, inspires children, provokes their imagination with questions, and reinforces their initiative (p. 589).

The Capability of Thought

According to Vygotsky (1962), symbolic or dramatic play fosters children's abstract thinking (Goelman et al., 2003). Brighouse (2002) argues that it is crucial for children and young adults to practice critical thinking and reflection, and for us to evaluate their functioning in these areas in order for them to develop and enhance this capability through education (Walker & Unterhalter, 2007). The thinking process permits individuals to model their world and represent it according to their aims, plans, and ends. Davydov (2006) considers human thought to be a specific mode of activity, a search for necessary conditions of actions by making changes (real or ideal) to the given situations, generally by modelling (e.g. problem-solving activities).

The encyclopaedia of early childhood education edited by Williams and Pronin Fromberg (1992) states that symbolic thinking, imagination, and fantasy are interrelated because each is a form of non-literal thinking. "Symbolic thinking or semiotics is a general ability to use and interpret signs. Imagination is mental imagery that takes a "what if" stance. Fantasy is the ultimate in non-literal thinking because it moves beyond reality and direct experience to products of the imagination" (p. 219).

Wood and Attfield (2005) quote Rawson and Rose (2002, p. 78): "children who are allowed to play freely will demonstrate a genius for lateral thinking and problem solving of which we adults should be envious."

The OECD report on *Starting Strong Curricula and Pedagogies in Early Childhood Education and Care* (2004) argues that a point of controversy in ECEC curriculum making has been the opposition proposed between associative (narrative) thinking and logical analytical thinking. Although both aspects exist constantly in everyday life with children, one or the other will often become more visible in different programmes. In High/Scope, for example, logical analytical thinking is central; whereas in Te Whariki and Reggio Emilia, free associative thinking is more in evidence. The Swedish curriculum, following Bruner (1996), takes the position that children benefit most from curricula and activities that stimulate both narrative and logico-analytic ways of thinking. In order to become skilful learners in creative subjects and natural sciences, the child needs both ways of thinking (Pramling Samuelsson, & Sheridan, 2004). Teachers and pedagogues should encourage both types of thinking in the different topics and tasks that children undertake.

The CTCF (2003) emphasizes the expression of children's thoughts, their communication, and memorial skills as well as their classification and reasoning abilities and the development of critical thinking. The following quotes are indicative:

> Provide opportunities for children to use their knowledge to practice their skills and continue to learn constantly promoting exploration, reasoning, critical thinking, decision making, problem solving. (p. 587)

> [Children should] express their thoughts, preferences, interest through the arts in many ways. [They are] encouraged to improvise, to express thoughts and feelings and to experiment with movement, voice, sound, light and music. (p. 610)

> Emphasis is given on acquiring knowledge processes in creative work conditions and emerging communication skills of children, getting accountability through collaborative work, research and critical thinking. (p. 592)

The Capability of Affiliation

The notion of affiliation is perceived as bringing, receiving, associating into close connection as a member within a community. Dewey argued that

> human beings are generated only by union of individuals; the human infant is so feeble in his powers as to be dependent upon the care and protection of others; he cannot grow up without the help given by others; his mind is nourished by contact with others and by intercommunication; as soon as the individual graduates from family life he finds himself taken into other associations, neighbourhood, school, village, professional or business associates. Apart from the ties which bind him to others, he is nothing (as cited in Winn, 1959).

In line with this, the Te Wariki curriculum states that children learn through responsive and reciprocal relationships with people, places, and things. Interaction provides a rich social world for children to make sense of and gives opportunities for them to learn by trying out their ideas with adults and other children. Cooperative aspirations, ventures, and achievements should be valued (Te Whàriki, 1996).

Social and emotional competence is the ability to understand, manage, and express the social and emotional aspects on one's life in ways that enable the successful management of life tasks such as learning, forming relationships, solving everyday problems, and adapting to the complex demands of growth and development (Elias et al., 2007). The Reggio Emilia approach places a strong emphasis on children's social construction of knowledge through their relationships within the context of collaboration, dialogue, conflict, negotiation, and cooperation with peers and adults (Mercilliott Hewett, 2001). Fabes, Eisenberg, Jones, Smith, Guthrie, Poulin, Shepard, and Friedman (1999) argue that socially competent children display emotions that are responsive to group norms and strike a balance between their own desires and interests and those of other children. They claim that children's social competence is related to their ability to identify and express emotions and emotional intentions, and that evidence supports the importance of regulation and emotion to children's social competence and adjustment.

Wolf and De-Shalit (2007) argue that the lack of social affiliation and relationships, which can in turn result from racism, stigmatization, hostility, and unemployment, may lead to lower life expectancy. Jensen (2009) refers to Sweden's national curriculum Lpfö 98 (2011) that aims to promote children's "social readiness to act in order to establish solidarity and tolerance." The preschool should be a living social and cultural environment that stimulates children into taking initiative and developing their social and communicative competence. The CTCF (2003) focuses on the socialization of the children, the enrichment of their communication skills, and the reinforcement of interaction among children.

> The pre-primary school as a socializing institution of the child (after family) should ensure the conditions for children to grow and socialize smoothly and versatile. (p. 586)

Furthermore, Norway's national curriculum (Ministry of Education and Research, Norway, 2006a) in which, according to the framework, the educational strategy has to contribute to children's development of social interaction skills, language and communication skills in the broadest sense, the learning process includes play as having content in itself and as an independent educational method (Jensen, 2009).

The Capability of Emotions

Emotion and emotional development are further ambivalent terms used widely in early childhood education. More often than not, early childhood curricula stress the significant role of children's emotional development. Sheffield Morris, Silk, Steinberg, Myers, and Rachel Robnson (2007) argue that in the last two decades, there has been a substantial increase in psychology and popular culture's interest in human emotionality and the ways in which individuals express and manage emotions. According to them, this interest is due in part to an increase in developmental research and theory suggesting that an essential component of children's successful development is learning how to regulate emotional responses and related behaviours in socially appropriate and adaptive ways. However, the definition of emotions is challenging. Frijda (2000) notes:

> That there is no generally accepted definition of emotions is in part because emotions involve so many different component phenomena. More precisely, the concept of emotion is used to denote a large variety of phenomena, both in daily interaction and in scientific discourse. These include feelings, evaluations of and cognitions about objects and events…. Emotions are multi-componential phenomena. Each of the component phenomena can form the core of a definition of emotions, and actually have done so …. he various components do not always occur together. (p. 207)

Eisenberg (2006) argues that emotions are viewed as motivational forces that play a role in much of our social behaviour. As noted by Parke (1994), contemporary psychology views emotions as "both products and processes of social interactions, relationships, and contexts" (Eisenberg, 2006, p. 1). Sroufe (1997) defines emotion as an organized reaction to an event that is relevant to the needs, goals, and interests of the individual and is characterized by physiological, experiential, and overt behavioural change. Oatley and Johnson-Laird (1987) postulate that there is a small number of basic emotion modes that occur universally in the human species. They argued:

> Each has a characteristic phenomenological tone, though no meaning as such, as each is based on a non-propositional signal. On the basis of a variety of classificatory studies reviewed by Ekman, Friesen and Ellsworth (1982) one may infer that there are at least five basic emotion modes: they correspond to happiness, sadness, anxiety (or fear), anger, and disgust. One important criterion for a basic emotion is that the facial expression associated with it should be recognised panculturally. (p. 33)

Froebel used to encourage children to express their emotion (Doliopoulou, 2003). In general it is believed that emotions influence behaviour significantly together with social relationships and communication. Goleman and Gardner place great emphasis on this. Goleman argues that cognitive capabilities alone are insufficient. In the seven different types of intelligence within his theory of multiple intelligences, Gardner proposes including interpersonal intelligence that is used to understand and interact with other people.

According to Goelman et al. (2003), Freud hypothesized that play fulfils a special function in children's emotional development. Since it enables children to relieve themselves of negative emotions and replace them with more positive ones, play achieves a cathartic effect. The catharsis facilitates children's ability to deal with the consequences of negative feelings and traumas. Consequently, children play to disengage themselves from any negative feelings brought on by traumatic experiences or personal confrontations, and this allows them to develop a better emotional equilibrium.

Mayer, Salovey, and Caruso (2008) clarify the concept of emotional intelligence as the capacity to carry out sophisticated information processing about emotions and emotion-relevant stimuli and to use this information as a guide to thinking and behaviour. They argue that "individuals high in emotional intelligence pay attention to, use, understand, and manage emotions, and these skills serve adaptive functions that potentially benefit themselves and others" (p. 503).

Emotional competence is crucial to children's ability to interact and form relationships with others (Parke, 1994; Saarni, 1990) Ashiabi (2000) argues that relationships with caregivers and peers are necessary for emotional development to take place, because they provide differing experiences and serve disparate functions. Ashiabi concludes that in essence, the caregiver–child relationship is a training ground for emotional skills, because the skills acquired in it are transferred into relationships with peers.

The Te Wāriki curriculum (1996), under the goal "children experience an environment where their emotional well-being is nurtured," stresses the need to nurture the ability to identify children's own emotional responses and those of others, the confidence and ability to express emotional needs, and the trust that their emotional needs will be responded to.´

Raver (2003) claims that research indicates that young children's emotional adjustment matters because children who are emotionally well-adjusted have a significantly greater chance of early school success, whereas children who experience serious emotional difficulty face grave risks of early school difficulty.

Finally, the CTCF (2003) offers the following suggestion to the pedagogues on emotion:

provide opportunities to children to develop and express ideas and emotions in many ways, such as play, drama, writing, painting, among others. (p. 587).

With movement, voice, speech and materials chosen by the child, it expresses, alone or in cooperation with others, experiences, emotions and ideas (p. 589).

Children should develop positive emotions about themselves ....evelop feelings of love and brotherhood for all creatures of the earth. (pp. 600–601)

The abovementioned capabilities of play, senses – imagination – thought, affiliation, and emotions are the cornerstones of this empirical study and will be further discussed.

Chapter 3: Research Model

None of the talents, which are hidden like buried treasure in every person, must be left untapped.
These are, to name but a few, memory, reasoning power, imagination, physical ability, aesthetic
sense, the aptitude to communicate with others, and the natural charisma of the group leader.
All of this goes to prove the need for greater self-knowledge.

Fryer

The purpose of this chapter is to present the research problems identified in the literature review, to unfold the research questions in the current work, and to construct the research model investigated and analyzed in the following chapters with the use of the research data.

3.1 Research Problems

Three research problems were identified from the literature review of studies on teachers' beliefs and practices in the field of early childhood education:

Society in general, and educational researchers in particular, have long been interested in children's academic achievement. A plethora of empirical studies in educational psychology has stressed the importance of children's academic achievement and investigated how intuitively appealing factors for researchers such as the socioeconomic status of the child (Brooks-Gunn & Duncan, 1997; Caldas & Bankston, 1997; Coleman, 1988) and parental involvement (Christenson, Rounds, & Gorney, 1992; Epstein, 1991) impact on children's academic achievement/success. It seems that in the current climate, the emphasis given to the outcome achievement of education is gradually corroding early childhood education.

The "academic" nature of the curriculum in many pre-primary classrooms stands out as one of the major issues in early childhood education. The pre-primary school is conceived as a preparation stage for children's school success, and primary school academic activities are therefore pushed down into pre-primary programs. The aforementioned phenomenon is named schoolification and can be contrasted with the social pedagogical approach that provides broad orientations for children rather than prescribed outcomes, and in which the acquisition of developmental skills is perceived as a by-product rather than the driver of the curriculum (Bertrand, 2007). Debates on the schoolification phenomenon have arisen over the Greek Cross-Thematic Curriculum Framework (CTCF) that outlines the direction for planning and developing activities in the context of the subjects of language, mathematics, environmental studies, creation and expression, and computer science. Although the CTCF has been criticized intensively for demanding the systematic application of specialized content of the aforementioned subjects to structure pre-school curriculum activities and for attempting to schoolify pre-primary school (Bikos, 2005; Chrysafidis 2004, 2006; Doliopoulou, 2002; Fragkos, 2002, 2005; Kiprianos, 2007; Kitsaras, 2004; Koutsouvanou 2006), there is a lack of empirical evidence on either its effectivity or its implementation in pre-primary school. Up to now, no research has been conducted on this issue, indicative of the scarcity of research in the early childhood education field in Greece. In addition, although school improvement and accountability have become an international issue, the Greek state has failed to deliver a meaningful assessment/evaluation of pre-primary (and not only pre-primary) practice that would clear the foggy landscape of pedagogical activities. The lack of evaluation of the Greek educational system has led not only to the outlay of significant amounts of money without a specific direction and without addressing an actual problem to be faced but also to teachers spending their time on inessential training in frequent curriculum training courses.

Teachers are considered to be the front-line implementers of educational reform and the most influential actors in educational practice, because they are the ones who formulate the setting for children's development. They bear an even heavier burden than parents, because they are expected to exhibit a high degree of professionalism when handling the parents' most precious asset entrusted to them. Pre-primary teachers in Greece live at the maelstrom of rhetoric over ameliorating the early childhood education and care system. However, although they are expected to shape and implement the educational reforms, they are not respected partners in the process because they are the last to be consulted and are kept marginalized from planning and design. Kitsaras (2004) stresses the need to take into account teachers' views and arguments when drawing up the curriculum – and not in an ostensibly democratic process, but in an honest dialogue that discards compliments and political party positions. The absence of teachers in the dialogue and decision-making on educational reform constitutes a serious omission, because it predisposes to implementation failure. If reform is to be successful, any attempt to improve and alter teachers' work should take their beliefs and views into consideration. As Vartuli (1999) notes, it is important to study teachers' pedagogical beliefs because they are a major determinant of behaviour when teachers make classroom decisions. In his paper on *Implementing Educational Change*, Michael Fullan (1989) clarifies the undisputed necessity of taking into consideration teachers' beliefs and practices if effective use of a reform implementation is to be delivered. Several researchers have examined the relationship between beliefs and practices and found modest to strong intercorrelations (Charlesworth et al., 1991, 1993; Vartuli, 1999). Despite the widespread acknowledgement of the significance of teachers' beliefs by scholars in the field and their impact on teachers' practices (Charlesworth et al., 1990; Fang, 1996; Kagan, 1992; Pajares, 1992; Vartuli, 1999), hardly any research on teachers' beliefs has been conducted in the Greek pre-primary context (Doliopoulou, 1996; Tsafos & Sofou, 2010). Doliopoulou (1996) conducted a quantitative study on the beliefs and practices about developmentally appropriate and inappropriate practices in a sample of 67 pre-primary teachers. More recently, Tsafos and Sofou (2010) conducted a qualitative study on teachers' understandings of the curriculum. However, there is a gap when it comes to teachers' beliefs and practices regarding the two pedagogical approaches, namely, the social pedagogical and the pre-primary (schoolification) approach. The present study attempts to fill the current gap in research on Greek teachers' beliefs and practices regarding the aforementioned curricula approaches.

Furthermore, there is only a small body of research in the field of teachers' beliefs and practices addressing the antecedent factors influencing teachers' thinking and perceptions. Fang (1996) argues that a teacher's beliefs are shaped by many factors such as the influence of discipline subculture, the quality of pre-service experience in the classroom, and the opportunity for reflection on the pre-service experience. He also notes that contextual factors can have powerful influences on teachers' beliefs and, in effect, influence their classroom practice. Emphasis has been given to examining the teachers' educational level, training, years of experience, teaching efficacy, and internal locus of control (Cassidy Buell, Pugh-Hoese, & Russell, 1995; Hardy Snider & Fu, 1990; McMullen, 1997, 1999; McMullen & Alat, 2002; Stipek, Daniels, Galluzzo, & Milburn, 1992). Despite the efforts that have been made to identify the antecedent factors, more research is needed in order to grasp the complex and interrelated processes of beliefs and practices.

3.2 Research Questions and Hypotheses

In response to the research problems highlighted above, three research questions were conceptualised for the current work, and specific hypotheses informed by previous literature were formulated.

Research Question 1: Do teachers' beliefs predict their practices?

1.1 Do capabilities- and performance-based beliefs predict their respective practices?

The associations between capabilities- and performance-based beliefs and their respective practices will be investigated in order to gain a deeper insight into the relations between teachers' beliefs and their practices. Teachers' beliefs and practices have been associated with being developmentally appropriate or inappropriate (Charlesworth et al., 1991, 1993; Doliopoulou, 1996). However, other studies have also found inconsistencies between beliefs and practices (Vartulli, 1999). Moreover, a study by Stipek and Byler (1997) revealed significant associations between beliefs and practices on child-centred versus more didactic, basic-skills approaches. Based on the reviewed literature, the present study hypothesizes that teachers' self-reported beliefs will be congruent with their self-reported practices. More specifically, it hypothesizes that capabilities-based beliefs will predict teachers' capabilities-based practices, whereas performance-based beliefs will predict performance-based practices. It is assumed that teachers will have a coherent set of beliefs that map on to the theoretical frameworks seen in each approach. Based on this hypothesis, the study will examine which of the capabilities (imagination, senses, thought, emotions, affiliation and play) is most influential in the formation of the respective beliefs – namely, capabilities- and performance-based.

1.2 Do capabilities-based beliefs influence performance-based practices?

The current work also seeks to investigate whether capabilities-based beliefs influence performance-based practices. It hypothesizes that capabilities-based beliefs will have a negative effect on performance-based practices. This hypothesis is based on the assumption that due to the strong differences between the two sorts of pedagogy, it will be highly unlikely that capabilities-based beliefs will go hand in hand with performance-based beliefs. If teachers' beliefs are in accordance with their practices, as suggested in the literature (Fang, 1996; Kagan, 1992; Stipek et al., 2001), then there should be a disharmony in the relationship between contradictory sorts of beliefs and practices.

1.3 Do performance-based beliefs influence capabilities-based practices?
In the same line, this study aims to investigate performance-based beliefs in relation to capabilities-based practices. It examines the hypothesis that performance-based beliefs will relate negatively to capabilities-based practices. As explained above, a contrast between teachers' beliefs and their practices is not anticipated.

Research Question 2: Do pre-primary teachers favour performance- or capabilities based beliefs?

This study aims to uncover the prevailing sort of belief in teachers' perceptions. Are teachers trying to implement the academic orientation emphasized in the Greek pre-primary curriculum, or do they believe in a capabilities-mode upbringing of children in which knowledge acquisition is a side effect of the process? It is hypothesized that teachers' perceptions will tend to cohere around one of these two pedagogical dimensions. Answering this question will indicate whether or not the fears regarding the schoolification of Greek pre-primary schools are justified. This should end speculations on this topic and introduce much-needed empirical evidence to this debate.

Research Question 3: Are teachers' beliefs predicted by the antecedent factors of years of experience, administrative control, self-efficacy, and decision latitude?

Do factors such as years of experience, self-efficacy, (administrative) control, and decision latitude facilitate or hinder teachers' beliefs and practices regarding the two approaches? It is hypothesized that positive associations will be found between teachers' capabilities-based beliefs and their years of experience, self-efficacy, and decision latitude, whereas a negative association is expected between this sort of belief and administrative control. In contrast, it is hypothesized that negative associations will be found between teachers' performance-based beliefs and their years of experience, self-efficacy, and decision latitude, whereas a positive association is envisaged with administrative control. The following section performs a detailed analysis of all the model constructs and discusses the interrelations between the variables.

3.3 Research Model Constructs

This section presents the main constructs of the research model. The major constructs in this study are teachers' educational level, years of experience, self-efficacy, administrative control, and decision latitude along with teachers' capabilities-based and performance-based beliefs as well as their capabilities-based and performance-based practices.

It is assumed that **teachers' educational level** influences their beliefs and contributes to the outcome of their practices. Benson, McMullen, and Alat (2002) found that teachers' educational level significantly influenced their self-reported developmentally appropriate beliefs scores. In addition, Buchanan, Burts, Bidner, White, and Charlesworth (1998) identified teachers' certification as a predictor of their beliefs and practices.

Historically, personnel in the early childhood education arena in Greece have received training and support from a wide range of systems, primarily because of the development of different curricula with diverse curricular goals and pedagogy but also because of the different study programmes in each Department of Early Childhood Education. The core of the study programmes in Departments of Early Childhood Education emphasizes the didactics of natural sciences, biology, math, ICT, language, and early literacy. One much undervalued fact is that the majority of the academic staff members in these Departments have been trained in various disciplines that have little to do with pedagogy and early childhood education.

Teachers' **year of experience** is among the factors that have been scrutinized in the field. Rich (1993) argues that many studies document supremacy of experienced teachers over non-experienced teachers on a variety of issues, including teacher understanding of classroom events. Palaiologou and Tsapakidou (2009) stress that novice teachers make up a special group of in-service teachers facing enhanced difficulties at the beginning of their teaching career, expressing fears concerning their teaching efficacy, and lacking adequate support when practicing their profession. Doliopoulou (1996) found that well-experienced Greek teachers tended to adopt more developmentally inappropriate beliefs. Also, Rust (1994) in his study stresses the newness and rawness of a teacher's first year of experience. Schempp, Tan, Manross, and Fincher (1998) found differences between novice and competent teachers in assessing student learning difficulties, conceptions of knowledge, and reflective practice. Moreover, some studies have established a relationship between years of experience and teachers' practices (Vartuli, 1999) while others did not find such a relationship (Buchanan et al., 1998). Based on the literature review and earlier empirical evidence, it seemed important to investigate the effect of teachers' years of experience on teachers' beliefs.

Administrative control was one additional factor considered to influence teachers' beliefs. The Greek education system is highly centralized and governed by the Ministry of Education, Lifelong Learning and Religious Affairs. Ifanti (1995) stated that there is a strict centralized, bureaucratic, and authoritarian control over education in Greece. Pre-primary teachers, like all educators working in public education, have a civil-servant status and are dependent on the state, its legislation, and its administration. The Ministry of Education issues and controls which curricula and textbooks should be implemented in schools. Ifanti (1995) recognizes that centralization helps to make overall reform more efficient; however, she stresses the potentially negative effects of a strict central control over all educational concerns. Terhart (1998) argues that

> the teachers' relation to school administration is somewhat ambiguous: they depend on it, yet often come to see it as a barrier which prevents them from doing the positive things pedagogy expects of them.

Ma and MacMillan (1999) argue that the context provided by the administration influences interactions among staff, teachers' feelings of being valued for their work, and the sense of substantive involvement in the operation of school. In their study, they found that school administration is important not only to promote teachers' satisfaction with their work, but also to reduce the negative impact of different levels of teaching experience. Apple and Jungck (1990) state:

> Despite all of the rhetoric about teaching and professionalism, about enhancing teachers' power, and about raising pay and respect, the reality of many teachers' lives bears little resemblance to the rhetoric. Rather than moving in the direction of increased autonomy, the daily lives of teachers in classrooms in many nations are becoming ever more controlled, ever more subject to administrative logic that seeks to tighten the reins on the processes of teaching and curriculum. Teacher development, cooperation, and "empowerment" may be the talk, but centralization, standardization, and rationalization are the tendencies.

But despite the design of the curriculum, it is significant to reveal what the front-line implementers, namely pre-primary teachers, preach and practice. It is necessary to discover how free the educators are to apply their own ideas within educational practice or whether the administration fetters their pedagogical liberty and ambitions.

The term *self-efficacy* encompasses a person's specific belief about her or his ability to carry to completion a prescribed course of action or bring about an intended outcome. The term epitomizes a core concept of Bandura's (1977) social-cognitive theory. According to Bandura (1977, 1986), motivation is determined by judgements of the capability to execute particular courses of action ("efficacy expectations") and beliefs about the likely consequences of those actions ("outcome expectations"). Efficacy expectation is the conviction that one

93

can successfully execute the behaviour required to produce the outcomes. Kagan (1992) argues that self-efficacy refers to a teacher's generalized expectancy concerning the ability of teachers to influence students, as well as the teacher's beliefs concerning his or her own ability to perform certain professional tasks (Ashton & Webb, 1986; Bandura, 1977; Gibson & Dembo, 1984).

Teachers may believe either that they are effective in teaching or that they lack the ability to make a difference with their students. It has been found that a strong sense of personal efficacy is related to better health, higher achievement, and better social integration (Schwartzer, R. et al., 2002). It has also been confirmed empirically that a healthy school climate is conducive to the development of teachers' beliefs that they can influence student learning (personal teaching efficacy) (Hoy & Woolfolk, 1993). Self-efficacy beliefs determine how people feel, think, motivate themselves, and behave. Within the pre-primary school context, teachers are the decision-makers and determine the evolution of the educational process. Therefore, it is a paramount issue to bring to the forefront their self-efficacy beliefs, because these could deliver in-depth insights for policy planners as well as those responsible for training teachers. Bandura (1993) argues that teachers' beliefs in their personal efficacy to motivate and promote learning **influence the types of learning environments they create** and the level of academic progress their students achieve. Ashton (1985) points out that self-efficacy is expected to influence the teachers' choice of instructional activities, the amount of effort they expend in teaching, and the degree of persistence they maintain when confronted with difficulties. Moreover, teachers' beliefs in their efficacy "affect their general orientation toward the educational process as well as their specific instructional activities" (Bandura, 1997, p. 241) Ma and MacMillan (1999) refer to the three ways that teachers' professional competence can be expressed; these being teachers' beliefs that they have the prerequisite subject-content knowledge and skills in sufficient detail to be able to teach the particular course effectively and with confidence, that they have access to effective and current instructional strategies and skills for their use, as well as that they are able to use the subject-content knowledge in conjunction with instructional techniques to enable students to meet the standards for the course they are being taught. Researchers assess self-efficacy beliefs by asking individuals to report the level, generality, and strength of their confidence in being able to accomplish a task or succeed in a certain situation (Pajares, 1996). In this study, teachers' self-efficacy is perceived as influencing teachers' beliefs in the way they nurture, cultivate, and educate children (See Appendix for the table with the item indicators of teachers' self-efficacy).

Decision latitude (decision authority or skill level): Job "decision latitude" is defined as the working individual's potential control over job-related decision making (Karasek et al., 1981). This most commonly used definition of job decision latitude indicates the degree of actual influence over the actual decision made and describes *features of jobs*, primarily the ability of the worker to use his or her skills on the job, to have the authority to make decisions regarding how the work is done, and to set the schedule for completing work activities. This level of decision latitude focuses on the worker's abilities to control his or her own activities and skill use, not to control others. According to Gulielmi and Tatrow (1998), lack of decision latitude is considered to be a stressor in the working environment as well as one of the determinants of job strain. They suggest that the lowest amount of strain should be expected in jobs characterized by low demands and high decision latitude, whereas the greatest strain will result from a combination of high demands and low decision latitude.

Teachers' capabilities-based beliefs and practices represent the social-pedagogic approach according to which the focus is on developmental goals, interactivity between pedagogues and children, and a high quality of life in the early childhood setting within a broad developmental framework and a local curriculum development. This approach offers broad orientations for children rather than prescribed outcomes, and the acquisition of developmental skills is perceived as a by-product rather than as the driver of the curriculum. The aim is to enhance children's capabilities in the emotional, social, aesthetic, and cognitive sector.

Teachers' performance-based beliefs and practices represent the pre-primary or schoolification approach in which the curriculum, as a product of a centralized development, often contains detailed goals and outcomes stated as learning expectations, and these are related to school readiness tasks and skills. According to this approach, pedagogues tend to interact with children around activities related to these learning expectations and rely more on direct instruction strategies. The current Greek pre-primary curriculum espouses the pre-primary approach.

The following figure illustrates the main research model in the current study and indicates the assumed interrelations among the variables and factors.

Figure 3.1. Main Research Model

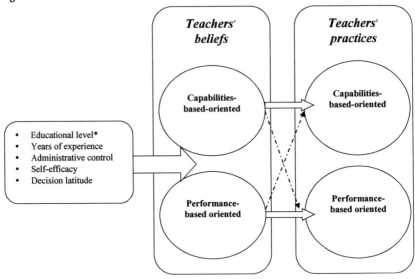

* Had to be withdrawn (see Chapter IV)

3.4 Research Aims

In conclusion, this study pursues three research aims:

- To formulate a theoretical model informed by the current literature to depict the interrelation among teachers' capabilities-based and performance-based beliefs and practices
- To develop an appropriate instrument for the investigation of teachers' capabilities-based and performance-based beliefs and practices
- To test the model empirically using SEM and quantitative data analysis

Chapter 4: Methodology

To err is human, to forgive divine;
but to include errors into your design is statistical.
- Leslie Kish

The purpose of this chapter is to delineate the research methodology and the related concepts, procedures, and tools used in the empirical investigation. This chapter examines the psychometric properties of the instrument designed to operationalize teachers' beliefs regarding performance-based and capabilities-based learning. The study examined the reliability and validity of the instrument. The research design, population sample, procedures, instrument development and statistical methods that were used are reported below.

4.1 The Study

The aim of this study is to discover whether Greek pre-primary teachers' beliefs predict their practices. Moreover, it seeks to detect which concept they favour, namely either (a) the expansion (enhancement) of children's capabilities or (b) the acquisition of the academic learning considered useful for their further school career. Furthermore, it investigates whether teachers' personal characteristics (which served as independent variables) such as teachers' years of experience, their self-efficacy, the experienced administrative control, as well as their decision latitude, predict teachers' beliefs.

The research methodology design used in this study is categorized as a cross sectional quantitative research with purposeful selection of subjects organized into two groups: novice and experienced. According to Field (2009), cross-sectional designs are a form of research in which researchers observe what naturally goes on in the world without directly interfering with it. This term specifically implies that data come from people at different age points with different people representing each age point. The design was structured so to provide self-reported data with respect to the current status of the issues surrounding the variables of the study. In that way, it was possible to gather a broad range of information from a large number of respondents. The literature highlights the problems occurring in studies from the use of self-report instruments. Fang (1996) argues that teachers' written responses in these studies may reflect what should be done rather than what is actually done in class. However, as Pajares (1992) states, self-report instruments help to detect inconsistencies and areas that merit attention.

Studies designed to investigate teachers' beliefs and practices were reviewed to determine the method used in this study. This revealed a great variety of approaches. By recognizing the paucity of research with large numbers of participants within the field with a considerable number of participants (above 150 subjects), it was perceived necessary to proceed to a quantitative empirical study with a respectable sample size.

The researcher developed a questionnaire consisting of the measureable concepts used to operationalize the research hypotheses. The instrument was divided into three major categories: (a) background sociocultural information about teachers, (b) beliefs and practices rating scales, and (c) a professionalization scale from which self-efficacy and decision-latitude scales were derived.

4.2 Population and Sample

The population of this study was Greek pre-primary school teachers working in kindergartens (*nipiagogeia*) run under the supervision of the Ministry of Education who were enrolled in a training programme. A purposive sampling method was used to select the training and retraining programmes in which the respondents were enrolled. Although this method may not be representative of the whole population and may lack generalizability, it does however provide an in-depth understanding of curriculum praxis in the field of Greek pre-primary education.

The selection was made purposively between novice and well-trained pre-primary teachers in diverse regions of Greece. The selection of regions depended on the operation of the training and retraining programmes, namely PEKs (Perifereiaka Epimorfotika Kentra) and Didaskaleia, and access into these institutions. These institutions offer government-subsidized training courses for in-service teachers.

The distinction between novice and well-trained teachers was based on applying the developmental stages suggested by Katz (1972) to preschool teachers (see Figure 4.1). Although Katz supports the fact that individual teachers may vary greatly in the length of time spent in each of the four stages, a rough estimation of the length of each stage is made. During these four developmental stages teachers pass from anxiety to knowledge and skill acquisition, to improvement of techniques and repertoire of activities before reaching the stage of maturity in which they can become reflective on their profession. Maturity may be reached by some teachers within 3 years, by others in 5 or more. The teacher at this – last – stage has come to terms with herself as a teacher (Katz, 1972).

Figure 4.1. **Stages of development and training needs of preschool teachers** *(adapted from L.G. Katz (1972, p. 3, Figure. 1): Developmental Stages of Preschool Teachers. Clearinghouse on Early Childhood Education, Urbana, IL. Retrieved from http://eric. ed.gov/PDFS/ED057922.pdf*

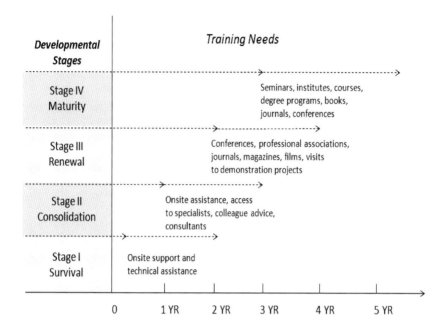

Based on these developmental stages, a novice pre-primary school teacher was defined for the present study as a public pre-primary school teacher with between 0 and 5 years of experience. An *experienced teacher* was defined as a public pre-primary school teacher who had more than 5 years of experience. An additional factor contributing to the aforementioned distinction between novice and well-experienced teachers was the fact that a precondition for joining the retraining programme offered in the universities (Didaskaleio) was to have a minimum of 5 years teaching experience.

The approximate sample size was defined by following Taro Yamane's table (cited in: Israel, 1992) with the size of the target population determined to be a minimum of 201. The level of accuracy (confidence level) was established at 95 percent to indicate the margin of error (associated *p* level .05). However, because the population was distinguished by the teacher experience variable, a more purposeful and larger sample size of approximately 350 was estimated to be needed to obtain reasonable distributions for the experience variable and to ensure representativeness.

Table 4.1 shows the distribution of the sample with respect to experience grouping and gender. The final sample comprised 341 pre-primary school teachers 124 (37 percent) of them were novices and 217 (63 percent) were well-experienced. A total of 98 percent of the teachers were women (333) and only 2 percent were men (8).

Table 4.1. Teachers' analysis experience grouping

Group	Gender		Overview
	Female	Male	
Novice teachers	121(35.50%)	3(0.90%)	124 (36.40%)
Well-experienced teachers	212(62.20%)	5(1.50%)	217 (63.60%)
Total	333(97.70%)	8(2.30%)	341(100.00%)

The low number of male participants also reflects the fact that a low number of males attend of the training and retraining programmes. In Greece, as in many Western countries, pre-primary education is in principle a gender-skewed profession saturated by women. According to Kitsaras (2001), the teaching staff of pre-primary schools consists of pre-primary teachers, who, until today, are almost all female. Since 1984, when the first male pre-primary teachers graduated in Greece, the percentage of men who have studied at pedagogical departments of pre-primary education has never exceeded 3–4 percent (Kitsaras, 2001). Doliopoulou (2006) provides a table showing the number of teaching personnel in public pre-primary schools between 1999 and 2005 and she argues that very few males seem to be entering this arena every year. She states that the figure was 0.44 percent in 1999–2000 and rose to 0.60 percent in 2004–2005. According to the to statistical data from the Greek National Statistical Service, for the year 2010–2011, out of a total of 13,496 preschool teachers, only 162 were men, that is., about 1.2 percent.

The field of pre-primary education worldwide is challenged by gender bias and in the literature it is claimed that there is a dire need for the elevation of the profession (Jalongo et al., 2004). It is considered that the equalization of salaries between pre-primary teachers and primary and secondary teachers as well as an equal accreditation would contribute to improving of preschool teachers' status and professionalization (Jalongo et al., 2004; Lindsay & Lindsay, 1987). However, despite what Arreman and Weiner (2007) call the "universification" resemblances of the Greek educators within the educational system with regard to standards of training as well as their salaries, it is clear that preschool teachers still face a low prestige not only in the society but also within the educational system in comparison to primary and secondary school teachers.

Although the age of teachers varies within qualification groups, the majority of novice teachers belong to the 21–30 age group whereas the majority of the well-experienced teachers belong to the 31–40 age group. Table 4.2. presents the cross-tabulation analysis on the consistency of the groups depending on age.

Table 4.2. Cross-Tabs on teachers' categories and age

Group	Age			Overview
	21–30	31–40	Above 41	
Novice teachers	64(18.60%)	48(14.20%)	12(3.60%)	124 (36.40%)
Well-experienced teachers	3(0.90%)	120(35.50%)	94(27.20%)	217 (63.60%)
Total	67(19.50%)	168(49.70%)	106(30.80%)	341(100.00%)
Cramér's V score with teachers' age	.62		p	.00

Note Cramér's V correlation coefficient

As a backdrop to the analysis that follows in the next chapter, it was considered important to investigate teachers' background characteristics such as their educational level, their marital status as well as their parents' education. Descriptive and inferential techniques were employed for the analysis of the data. The respondents' background analysis results are reported in Table 4.3.

With regards to teachers' educational level, it can be observed that the vast majority of respondents in every age group hold a bachelor degree, followed by pedagogical academy graduates and master graduates, whereas doctoral graduates were few and far between. After discovering that the sample of the study is rather homogeneous with respect to educational level, it was considered wise to not include this factor as a predictor variable in the main research model because it would not provide any useful information.

With regard to the marital status of the respondents, the majority of the teachers were married (63.05 percent), and 31.67 percent were single. It is worth noting the percentage of divorced teachers (5.28 percent), because this does not match the general trend in Greek divorce rates. According to Eurostat (2011), the Greek divorce rate for 2010 was 1.2 per thousand inhabitants. An interpretation of this inconsistency may be that the following: teachers, being public servants, are financially independent and have guaranteed a state of employment for the rest of their professional lives. They are also well-educated. Therefore, the prevalent traditional family model dominated by marriage and child-rearing values may depend highly on the professional, financial and educational status of Greeks. Finally, the low levels of teachers' parents' education could be explained by the fact that the majority of the respondents were older than 31 years when the study was conducted and consequently their parents should be the first generation after World War II, who grew up in a crushed country in which education was not considered a priority.

Table 4.3. Teachers' background characteristics

Background characteristic	N	%
Teachers' educational level		
Pedagogical academy	32	9.40
Bachelor's degree	277	81.20
Master's degree	30	8.80
PhD	2	0.60
Total	341	100
Marital status		
Single	108	31.67
Married	215	63.05
Divorced	18	5.28
Total	341	100
Teachers' maternal education		
Illiterate	20	5.87
Elementary graduate	170	49.85
Lower secondary school grad.	35	10.27
Upper secondary school grad.	77	22.58
Bachelor's degree	37	10.85
Master's degree	1	0.29
PhD	1	0.29
Total	341	100

Background characteristic	N	%
Teachers' paternal education		
Illiterate	11	3.23
Elementary graduate	140	41.06
Lower secondary school grad.	56	16.42
Upper secondary school grad.	75	21.99
Bachelor's degree	54	15.84
Master's degree	2	0.59
PhD	3	0.87
Total	341	100

4.3 Questionnaire Development

Because one of the major aims of this study was to investigate the teachers' beliefs and practices, it was necessary to develop an instrument that operationalizes the theoretical framework and measures teachers' capabilities-based and performance-based beliefs and practices in a way that is adjusted to the Greek pre-primary education context. The development of the instrument derived from the need to gauge which antecedents influence teachers' beliefs concerning an instruction method to achieve academic goals (performance-based beliefs) or to develop or enhance capabilities for children, by valuing the process and not the outcome (capabilities-based beliefs) as well as to discover a potential relationship between teachers' beliefs and practices with regard to this dichotomy (performance-based vs./& capabilities-based).

The construct of "teachers' capabilities-based and performance-based beliefs and practices" was developed by synthesizing theory, the Greek Cross-Thematic Curriculum Framework and relevant published instrumentations in the pre-primary field It contains four main factors/scales; capabilities-based beliefs, performance-based beliefs, capabilities-based practices and performance-based practices. The capabilities-based beliefs and practices factors contain items categorized as CA-Thought, CA-Play, CA-Affiliation, CA-Senses, CA-Imagination and CA-Emotions whereas the performance-based beliefs and practices contain items categorized as AG-Thought, AG-Play, AG-Affiliation, AG-Senses, AG-Imagination and AG-Emotions (see Table 4.4.).

Table 4.4. – Questionnaire Items – Beliefs in Enhancing Children's Capabilities

Item No.	Questionnaire statement: How important is it for the children to...	Factor Loading	M	SD
Thought CA				
2	interact with the possible alternative solutions in a problem-solving activity.	.46	3.74	.45
5	have freedom to determine the progress of an activity	.35	3.60	.53
25	be encouraged to write in any way they can	.28	3.53	.57
43	express their thoughts when listening to a narrative	.49	3.57	.54
Play CA				
6	have the freedom to plan and organize their dramatic play	.43	3.55	.59
9	have time for free play	.31	3.86	.37
10	take part in recreational activities	.39	3.61	.51
11	engage in playful activities based on their interests	.37	3.83	.41
Affiliation CA				
19	enrich their knowledge through peer interaction	.37	3.59	.53
21	become friends with their peers	.35	3.71	.51
22	develop their communicative skills	.50	3.81	.39
23	learn to cooperate	.40	3.91	.30
35	accept people from different linguistic, cultural, or religious backgrounds	.47	3.80	.44
Senses CA				
39	use their senses to explore their surroundings	.61	3.66	.47
40	choose and use different materials creatively	.55	3.67	.47
Imagination CA				
15	have the freedom to use their imagination to define the course of an activity	.48	3.65	.49
29	be involved in role-playing games	.50	3.66	.49
30	use their imagination and narrate a fairy tale of their own	.47	3.71	.48
31	imagine the outcome of a narrative	.49	3.33	.56
33	have their imagination and resourcefulness stimulated	.59	3.82	.39
38	experiment with the objects to be found in the pre-primary school	.60	3.54	.52
Emotions CA				
18	discuss the emotional effect of an argument, fight, etc. with their pre-primary school teacher	.32	3.72	.53
32	share their fears and anxieties	.45	3.78	.42
34	negotiate possible conflicts or tensions that may arise when they cooperate	.43	3.74	.48

Table 4.5. – Questionnaire Items – Beliefs in Academic Learning Orientation

Item No.	Questionnaire statement: How important it is for the children to…	Factor Loading	M	SD
Thought AG				
1	improve their mathematical skills through problem-solving activities	.47	3.23	.56
3	develop the capacity to recognize familiar words in the environment and within texts	.51	3.29	.63
4	memorize very short texts in order to grasp elements of the language progressively (e.g. syllables)	.52	2.73	.77
26	get used to memorizing, reciting poems, learning similes, using word puns etc	.56	2.65	.78
27	recognize and compare different forms of written speech, e.g. a manuscript and a printed text in the Greek language as well as others.	.54	3.03	.67
Play AG				
7	enrich their knowledge through play	.30	3.90	.30
12	have organized activities included in their outdoors play	.49	2.65	.75
41	involve themselves in writing activities through games	.38	3.45	.57
Affiliation AG				
8	participate in activities organized by the teacher	.37	3.10	.58
24	learn the social rules that they have to follow when taking part in a circle discussion	.51	3.59	.52
28	participate in team games, so as to broaden their knowledge through peer interaction	.21	3.80	.40
Senses AG				
14	learn through a lesson plan (even if they may not use all their senses)	.42	2.97	.70
Imagination AG				
16	engage in activities organized in advance so as to avoid unexpected consequences	.50	2.13	.85
17	have their imagination reinforced as part of their learning abilities	.27	3.48	.57
36	learn not to interrupt the course of an activity and wait until it is completed	.51	2.87	.81
37	engage themselves as much as possible with computers	.42	2.30	.71
Emotions AG				
20	develop positive feelings towards learning	.27	3.78	.42
42	learn to control their feelings in the pre-primary school	.42	3.38	.71
44	Accept any rules and restrictions that apply in the pre-primary school	.50	3.49	.52

With respect to the beliefs and practices rating scales, a self-reported format was used with a 4-point rating scale. The Beliefs Scale asked teachers to indicate the relative degree of importance for each statement on a rating scale ranging from 1 *(not important at all)* to 4 *(extremely important)*, and the Practices Scale asked teachers to indicate the frequency for each statement on a scale ranging from 1 *(almost never)* to 4 *(very often)*.

The purpose of a rating scale is to allow respondents to express both the direction and the strength of their opinion about a topic (Garland, 1991). For the original draft version of this part of the questionnaire, the author generated a pool of 49 and 19 items containing statements on aspects of children's learning for beliefs and practices respectively. It was anticipated that teachers who favoured a child-centred approach might respond quite differently to each of these statements in comparison with teachers who favoured a more skills-based approach. The items chosen for the Teachers' Beliefs Scale were influenced by the professional literature and were adjusted to the requirements of the Greek Cross-Thematic Curriculum Framework (CTCF).

Table 4.6. – Questionnaire Items – Practices in Enhancing Children's Capabilities

Item No.	Questionnaire statement: Please indicate the extent to which you usually involve children in the following activities	Factor Loading	M	SD
1	Dramatic play	.55	3.18	.64
5	Narrating stories	.56	3.34	.59
8	Singing	.35	3.75	.48
11	Defining the evolution of an activity	.62	3.15	.58
12	Playing freely	.36	3.75	.45
16	Being involved in playful activities that the children themselves have chosen	.67	3.56	.55
17	Discussing social dilemmas and issues (e.g. people with special needs)	.65	3.15	.66

Table 4.7. – Questionnaire Items – Practices in Academic Learning Orientation

Item No.	Questionnaire statement: Please indicate the extent to which you usually involve children in the following activities	Factor Loading	M	SD
3	Activities emphasizing the acquisition of mathematical skills	.57	3.28	.51
6	Writing their names	.35	3.77	.44
9	Counting	.72	3.27	.72

Item No.	Questionnaire statement: Please indicate the extent to which you usually involve children in the following activities	Factor Loading	M	SD
10	Memorizing texts	.71	2.38	.79
15	Being asked to recognize familiar writing in their environment	.54	3.27	.60
18	Cutting out and painting outlines	.32	2.28	.90

The content of the instrument was also influenced in a moderate way by the Teachers Belief Scale (TBS) and Instructional Activities Scale, two well-known and frequently used quantitative measures of kindergarten teachers' beliefs and practices in the USA developed by Charlesworth et al. (1991, 1993). These measures were developed on the basis of the guidelines for developmentally appropriate practice issued by the National Association for the Education of Young Children (NAEYC). The items that were included in Charlesworth et al.'s instruments cover many important aspects of the early childhood curriculum based on broad curriculum concepts that could be related to an extensive range of principles or theories of young children's development and learning. The original draft of the present questionnaire was administered to experienced teachers and to professors in order to examine item clarification and provide the author with feedback.

After this process, the wording of certain items had to be revised to increase their clarity, and some items were eliminated because they did not discriminate between the child-centred and skill-centred approach. The final corpus of the Beliefs Scales contained 44 items (See Appendix).

The questionnaire constructed for this study consists of three major categories: sociocultural background information about teachers, beliefs rating scales, practices rating scales, and the professionalization scale.

With regard to the sociocultural background information on the teachers, the study focused on teachers' background from a demographic, educational, and socio-economic perspective. Teachers reported their gender, age, years of experience, education level attained, marital status, number of children, spouse's occupational status, as well as the educational level of their mother and father. Several scholars have related the level of teachers' education and years of experience to their behaviours, beliefs, and practices. (Cassidy et al., 1995; Benson McMullen, 1999; Benson McMullen & Alat, 2002; Hardy Snider & Fu, 1990, Vartuli, 1999). The research literature on early childhood settings has reported an association between high levels of education and positive teachers' behaviour. Snider and Fu (1990) found a relationship between level of education and knowledge of developmentally appropriate practices (DAP). Moreover, Huberman (1992, 1993) suggested that, as teachers gain more teaching experience, they often follow one of two tracks: either one defined as proactive and professionally content or one defined by self-doubts and conservatism.

With respect to the third category, items were included from the Professionalization scale (see Ziegler et al. (manuscript, in press 2012) Professionsfragebogen from the "Evaluation sozialer Frühwarnsysteme in NRW und Schutzengel Schleswig-Holstein"). Two subscales were derived from this scale, namely, Self-Efficacy, and Decision Latitude. Sample items from each scale can be found below (Tables 4.8. & 4.9.).

Table 4.8. – Self-Efficacy Scale Items

Self-Efficacy Items	Factor Loading	M	SD
1) I am convinced that my educational practice in the pre-primary school is appropriate.	.74	3.06	.47
2) The children's parents accept me as a teacher.	.62	3.35	.51
3) I am convinced that my educational practice contributes to the child's development and socialization.	.78	3.22	.53
4) I can easily handle any problems occurring in the pre-primary school.	.73	3.03	.52
5) My job contributes significantly to prompt provision of help and support to children who need it.	.51	3.31	.56

Table 4.9. – Decision-Latitude Scale Items

Decision-Latitude Items	Factor Loading	M	SD
1) I decide alone what methods to use in my educational practice.	.88	2.82	.78
2) I decide and define alone the aims of my educational practice.	.89	2.78	.81
3) I decide and define alone the context of my educational practice.	.88	2.62	.83
4) I decide alone on the way to solve educational problems.	.76	2.61	.76

4.4 Pilot Study

A pilot study was conducted in order to investigate the internal consistency (reliability) and content validity of the constructed scales. The aim was to reduce measurement error by examining the characteristics of validity and reliability of the measure. The researcher has established reliability and validity for this instrument by conducting a pilot study in May 2010. The respondents were 31 pre-primary school teachers, (93.50 percent female and 6.50 percent male) attending a retraining program held by the University of Ioannina. Sixteen (51.60 percent) respondents were aged between 30 and 39 years; the other 15 (48.40 percent) were aged above 40. Most of the teachers had either a Bachelor's degree ($n = 18$, 58.10 percent) or a degree from a pedagogical academy ($n = 11$, 35.50 percent), and the rest were Master's graduates ($n = 2$, 6.50 percent). Their experience varied from 5 years ($n = 13$, 41.90 percent), to between 6 and 10 years ($n = 15$, 48.40 percent) and to between 11 and 20 years ($n = 3$, 9.70 percent).

Testing the reliability delivers information about the extent to which an instrument used is consistent with itself. According to Fishbein and Ajzek (1975), reliability refers to the degree to which a measure is free of variable error. Therefore, the lower the reliability of an instrument the less useful it is.

Cronbach's alpha is one of the most frequent and pervasive statistical measures in research involving test construction and use. Basically, Cronbach's Alpha shows how well each individual item in the scale correlates with the sum of the remaining items. An acceptable value of Cronbach's alpha is considered to be .7 to .8 (Field, 2009; Kline, 1999). However, several scholars recommend being cautious when formulating general guidelines on alpha (Cortina, 1993; Schmitt, 1996). Schmitt (1996) perceives the use of any cut-off value as short-sighted because satisfactory levels of alpha depend on test use and interpretation. In addition he notes that alpha increases as a function of test length. "When a measure has other desirable properties, such as meaningful content coverage of some domain and reasonable unidimensionality, this low reliability may be not a major impediment to its use" (Schmitt, 1996).

The scales were found to be reliable at the indicator and item level as well as the overall scale level. The internal consistencies across all items for the 43 items assessing Teachers' Beliefs and the 18 Instructional Activities items were reasonably satisfactory with values of α= .84 and α= .70, respectively. The 24-item capabilities-based beliefs (BCA) subscale (α=.77) and the 19-item performance-based beliefs (BAG) subscale had acceptable Cronbach's alphas of .77 and .70, respectively. Finally, the 7-item capabilities-based practices (PCA) subscale and the 5-item performance-based practices (PAG)subscale had questionable alphas of

.60 and .63. Therefore 2 and 3 items respectively were eliminated from the initial scales in order to achieve better internal consistency (See Appendix).

4.5 Administration of the Questionnaire and Main Data Collection Process

The investigator e-mailed a brief summary of the project, explaining the purpose of the survey and asking for permission and help along with a short CV to the professors who were directing the training and retraining programmes in each region (see Appendix 1 for a copy of the material). Follow-up calls were made to the heads and the secretaries of each programme by both the researcher and Prof. Dr. Spyros Pantazis to encourage participation and answer any questions that might have emerged. During these phone calls, information was gathered about the exact number of participants in each programme as well as about the schedule of study programme they were attending. This process offered an estimation of the number of possible participants. Data collection did not occur until permission was granted.

The administration of the questionnaire as well as the collection of data was done directly by the researcher herself in four Greek universities: University of Ioannina, Kapodistrian University of Athens, Aristotelian University of Thessaloniki and University of Crete. However, in the case of Didaskaleio of Rhodes (Aegean University), both the administration and the collection of data were carried out by the secretary of the institution at that time. Table 4.10 presents the targeted and actual sample distribution within institutions and Figure 4.2 illustrates the survey instrument distribution. As can be observed, the number of participants from Rhodos University was lower than the others because of the small number of attendees in the specific retraining programme. The phenomenon of having a small number of participants in institutions located in the periphery and a higher number of attendees in big cities such as Athens and Thessaloniki is not unexpected.

Table 4.10. Sample distribution within recruitment institutions

		% of Distribution	Target Number	Actual Number
Didaskaleia	Kapodistrian University of Athens	21.11	*100*	72
	University of Crete	8.80	*30*	30
	University of Ioannina	7.63	*30*	26
	Aegean University (Rhodos)	3.52	*15*	12
	Aristotelian University of Thessaloniki	22.29	*100*	76

		% of Distribution	Target Number	Actual Number
PEKs	PEK Ioannina	17.60	*90*	60
	1st PEK Thessaloniki	9.38	*60*	32
	2st PEK Thessaloniki	9.67	*60*	33

It should be noted that none of the participants received any incentive or remuneration for their participation. The sampling frame began with 485 participants. Of the 485 questionnaires distributed, 341 were completed and returned. The overall participation rate was 70.3 percent.

Figure 4.2. Survey instrument distribution

Source: Google, Note: The green dots represent the locations of retraining programmes for well-experienced teachers (Didaskaleia); the red dots, the training programmes for novice teachers (PEKs).

For better and accurate results for this survey, it is necessary to put some basic requirements. Firstly, to be able to make correlations that correspond to reality between years of service, beliefs and practices should be assumed that all answers given by teachers are true and not influenced by any external factor. Also the fact that they were surveyed by anonymous questionnaires permits to conceive that teachers were objective in their responses.

4.6 Psychometric Properties

An instrument must fulfil two broad categories of psychometric properties in order to be considered as a good measure of a construct: reliability and validity. Reliability represents the measure's ability to measure the construct of interest consistently, whereas validity indicates how well it accurately measures the construct of interest. The concepts of reliability and validity, which are further analysed, concern the degree to which the measuring instrument is free of measurement error. Hence, they were explored in order to ensure the appropriateness of the instrument used.

4.6.1 Reliability

The scales used were expected to display acceptable levels of internal and temporal consistency. The reliability coefficients of each scale met the criterion. Construct reliability ranged from 0.63 to 0.88. Cronbach's alpha for each scale and subscale is shown in Table 4.4. (see Appendix for intercorrelations of the items of each scale). The Beliefs Scale demonstrated sound reliability, whereas the Practices Scale was at the limits of what is permissible. The Self-Efficacy and Decision Latitude scales had adequate reliability. Although the PCA and PAG scales were at the cut-off point (also rather low), conceptually, it makes sense to retain them.

Table 4.11. Scales reliabilities

Scales	Sample item	Number of items	Cronbach's α
			$(N = 431)$
1. Teachers' Beliefs Scale			
1.1. Capabilities-based beliefs (BCA)	It is _____ for the children to interact with possible alternative solutions during problem-solving activities.	24	.83

Scales	Sample item	Number of items	Cronbach's α
			(N = 431)
1.2. Performance-based beliefs (BAG)	It is ____ for the children to improve their mathematical skills.	19	.75
	Total	43	.84
2. Teachers' practices scale			
2.1. Capabilities-based practices	How often do children play freely?	7	.63
2.2. Performance-based practices	How often do you involve/engage children in activities focusing on the acquisition of mathematical skills?	6	.60
	Total	13	.67
3. Self-Efficacy Scale	I can handle problems occurring in the pre-primary school well.	5	.71
4. Decision –Latitude Scale	I can decide on my own about the methods I use in educational practice. I decide and set the content of my educational practice on my own.	4	.88

4.6.2 Validity

Although a test may be reliable, it may not measure what it sets out to measure. For that reason, it is important to test the validity of the instrument. The concept of validity involves the examination of the extent to which a measure or a set of measures correctly represents the concept of study (Hair, Black, Babin, & Anderson, 2010). The scales and subscales of the questionnaire were examined for content and construct validity. In terms of validity, the literature distinguishes two kinds of validity: content validity and internal consistency.

4.6.2.1 Content Validity

The validity of the measure was checked with field experts. The scale items were sent to independent experts in the field who were asked for their feedback. According to the experts, most of the items achieved the intended goal of measuring teachers' capabilities-based-oriented and performance-based (academic knowledge and goals-oriented) beliefs and practices.

"the developed material can achieve the aims in measuring teachers' capabilities-based & performance-based beliefs & practices. However, some of these items need to be amended or replaced."

"The items are totally understandable for me. All statements are linked with the Cross-Thematic Curriculum."

The initial version of the questionnaire had a 5-point Likert scale. One of the experts recommended using another scale.

"I suggest you to use a 4-type rating scale and not a 5-type Likert scale, as a substantial number of the respondents in a questionnaire tend to select the mid-point category without indicating an opinion on the topic asked."

A review of the literature revealed that there is empirical evidence that the presence or absence of a mid-point in a scale influences the results obtained. Garland (2001) argues that social desirability bias, arising from respondents' desires to please the interviewer or appear helpful or not be seen to give what they perceive to be a socially unacceptable answer, can be minimized by eliminating the mid-point category from Likert scales. Based on this, it was decided to exclude the mid-point category in the scales.

It was also indicated that certain components of the scales were not important and should be eliminated whereas some other items were ambiguous and needed to be modified. It was recommended that the wording of 8 of the 45 items should be changed.

A concern was raised by the experts about the sincerity of the teachers' self-reported practices. The teachers may present an ideal self, or fill in what they think that the researcher should or wants to hear. Social desirability is a phenomenon in which respondents seek to boost their esteem in the eyes of the researcher by providing the response that is considered to be desired or expected.

The solution for this concern was obtained from the expert discussion: randomization of the scale items and amendment of the response scale. Some corrections were made as a result of comments emerging from the discussions.

4.6.2.2 Construct Validity

The construct validity of each subscale was assessed by the correlations between and within the scales. These were found to be moderately strong. Construct validity was also examined by applying confirmatory factor analysis (CFA) to all measurement models. CFA (Albright & Park, 2009) is a special case of structural equation modelling (SEM), that is theory- or hypothesis-driven. Factor analysis refers to a "wide array of statistical techniques used to examine relationships between items and latent factors with which items associate" (Hinson, DiStefano & Daniel, 2003). CFA outcomes provide information on each indicator's significance. The relationship between indicators should be strong. If they do not interrelate among each other, it is a disadvantage for any further analysis (Yotyodying, 2006). CFA is shown as a path diagram in which squares represent observed variables and circles represent latent variables. Single-headed arrows are used to imply a direction of assumed effect influence, and double-headed arrows represent covariance between two latent variables.

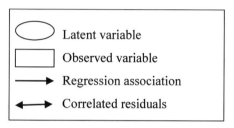

Many tests exist to assess how well a model matches the observed data (Albright & Park, 2009). CFA offers a variety of goodness-of-fit measures to evaluate a model. Schreiber, Nora, Stage, Barlow and King (2006) provide a chart of several fit index evaluations as well as with the cut-off levels for determining model fit. To evaluate model fit, I considered the χ^2 test, the ratio of χ^2 to df, and four other fit indices: goodness of fit index (GFI), comparative fit index (CFI), the root mean square residual (RMR), and the root-mean-square-error of approximation (RMSEA).

The CFA was employed for teachers' beliefs predictors (self-efficacy & decision-latitude), capabilities-based beliefs, and performance-based beliefs as well as capabilities-based practices and performance-based practices. Without introducing some constraints, a confirmatory factor model is not identified. The problem lies in the fact that the latent variables are unobserved and hence their scales are unknown. To identify the model, it is necessary to set the metric of the latent variables in some manner. The two most common constraints are to set either the variance of the latent variable or one of its factor loadings to one (Rindskopf & Rose, 1988). To construct the measurement models, scale items were used as indicators (manifest variables) for each measurement model.

After testing correlation among indicators, it was found that all measurement models were statistically significant ($p < .01$ level). This indicated that the correlation matrix of each measurement model differed from the identity matrix (no indicators had a relationship). Kaiser-Meyer-Olkin measures of sampling

(KMO) of all measurement models varied from .761 to .803. The details are shown in Table 4.5.

Table 4.12. Pearson's correlation coefficient Bartlett's test of sphericity and the Kaiser-Meyer-Olkin measures of Sampling (KMO) of measurement models

	Pearson's correlation coefficient	Bartlett's test of sphericity	KMO
Predictors of beliefs			
Self-Efficacy	.315–.534	283.303**	.761
Decision-Latitude	.531–.752	716.165**	.803
Teachers' Beliefs			
Teachers' capabilities-based beliefs	.224–.580	450.931**	.792
Teachers' performance-based beliefs	.156–.351	716.165**	.803
Teachers' Practices			
CA practice	.112–.360	206.458**	.703
Performance practice	.128–.314	149.576**	.732

*Note: ** p < .01*

4.6.2.3 Factorial Validity of Subscales

CFA was used to test the factorial validity of each subscale included in the model. The factor in each model is the subscale, whereas the indicators are items preserved after the content validity analysis. To evaluate the model fit of the models, the following fit indices were selected and used: Chi-square (χ^2), the goodness of fit index (GFI), the comparative fit index (CFI), the root mean-square residual (RMR), and the root mean-square error of approximation (RMSEA).

The results showed that the models fit the data well. These models are Self-Efficacy and Decision Latitude, Capabilities-Based Beliefs and Performance-Based Beliefs, as well as Capabilities-Based Practices and Performance-Based Practices. Apart from this, teachers' years of experience and administrative control were measured by single items (See Appendix).

The measurement model of self-efficacy was measured by five indicator items predicting the latent construct of self-efficacy (See Table 4.8.). The coefficient of Item C 1.1 was constrained to one in order to ensure identification. The findings revealed that the measurement model of Self-Efficacy was valid.

*Figure 4.3. Validated Measurement Model of Teachers' Self-Efficacy (**p<.01)*

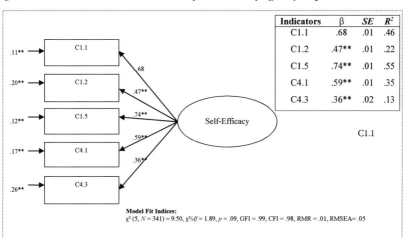

Indicators	β	SE	R²
C1.1	.68	.01	.46
C1.2	.47**	.01	.22
C1.5	.74**	.01	.55
C4.1	.59**	.01	.35
C4.3	.36**	.02	.13

Model Fit Indices:
χ² (5, N = 341) = 9.50, χ²/df = 1.89, p = .09, GFI = .99, CFI = .98, RMR = .01, RMSEA= .05

Model structure as well as standardized parameter estimates and model fit indices are presented in Figure 4.3. The findings revealed that the measurement model yielded reasonably good fit indices [χ² (5, N = 341) = 9.50, χ²/df = 1.89, p = .09, GFI = .99, CFI = .98, RMR = .01, RMSEA = .05]. All indicators were significant, and the factor loadings of indicators ranged from 0.36 to 0.74. Among them, Item C 1.5., "I am convinced that my educational practice contributes to the child's (all-round) development and socialization", proved to be was found as the most important indicator whereas Item C 4.3., "My job contributes significantly to prompt provision of help and support to children who need it", the least important.

The validity of the decision-latitude measurement model was also assessed by specifying four indicator items predicting the latent construct of decision latitude (see Table 4.9.). The coefficient of Item C 2.1 was constrained to one in order to ensure identification. Model structure as well as standardized parameter estimates and model fit indices are presented in Figure 4.4. Reasonably good fit indices for the measurement model were found [χ² (1, N = 341) = .09, χ²/df = .09, p = .86, GFI = 1.00, CFI = 1.00, RMR = .00, RMSEA = .00]. All indicators were significant and the factor loadings of indicators ranged from 0.68 to 0.91. Among them, Item C 2.2., "I define the aims of the educational practice on my own", was found to be the most important indicator whereas Item C 2.4., "I decide the way of solving educational problems on my own", was the least important.

Figure 4.4. Validated Measurement Model of Teachers' Decision Latitude

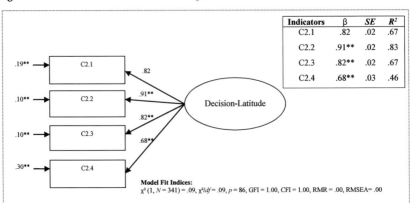

Indicators	β	SE	R²
C2.1	.82	.02	.67
C2.2	.91**	.02	.83
C2.3	.82**	.02	.67
C2.4	.68**	.03	.46

Model Fit Indices:
χ² (1, N = 341) = .09, χ²/df = .09, p = 86, GFI = 1.00, CFI = 1.00, RMR = .00, RMSEA= .00

In the same vein, the measurement model of teachers' beliefs in CA was tested by specifying six indicators, CA-thought, CA-play, CA-affiliation, CA-senses, CA-imagination, and CA-emotions, predicting the latent construct of teachers' beliefs in CA. To reduce the number of estimated parameters in the structural model, factor scores of all measurement models were computed and used as manifest variables. The coefficient of CA-Thought was constrained to one in order to ensure identification. Model structure as well as standardized parameter estimates and model fit indices are presented in Figure 4.5. Once again, good fit indices were found [χ^2 (N = 341) = 8.87, χ^2/df = 1.48, p = .18, GFI = .99, CFI = .99, RMR = .00, RMSEA = .04]. All indicators were significant and the factor loadings of indicators ranged from 0.45 to 0.79. Among them, CA-Imagination was found to be the most important indicator whereas CA-Emotions was the least important.

Figure 4.5. Validated Measurement Model of Capabilities-Based Beliefs (*p < .05. ** p < .01.)

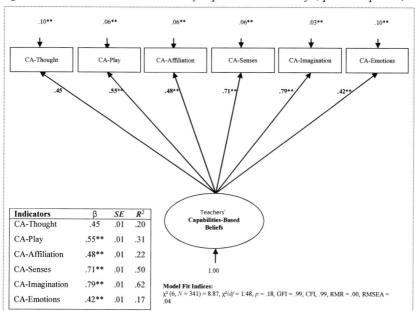

Indicators	β	SE	R²
CA-Thought	.45	.01	.20
CA-Play	.55**	.01	.31
CA-Affiliation	.48**	.01	.22
CA-Senses	.71**	.01	.50
CA-Imagination	.79**	.01	.62
CA-Emotions	.42**	.01	.17

Model Fit Indices:
χ² (6, N = 341) = 8.87, χ²/df = 1.48, p = .18, GFI = .99, CFI, .99, RMR = .00, RMSEA = .04

The measurement model of teachers' beliefs in AG was measured by six indica-tors, AG-thought, AG-play, AG-affiliation, AG-senses, AG-imagination, and AG-emotions, predicting the latent construct of teachers' beliefs in AG. To reduce the number of estimated parameters in the structural model, factor scores of all measurement models were computed and used as manifest variables. The coef-ficient of AG-Thought was constrained to one in order to ensure identification. Model structure as well as standardized parameter estimates and model fit in-dices are presented in Figure 4.6. The findings revealed that the measurement model yielded reasonably good fit indices [χ² (N = 341) = 7.53, χ²/df = .84, p = .58, GFI = .99, CFI = 1.00, RMR = .01, RMSEA = .00]. All indicators were significant and the factor loadings of indicators ranged from 0.39 to 0.69. Among them, AG-Imagination was the most important indicator whereas AG-Senses was the least important.

Figure 4.6. Validated Measurement Model of Performance-Based Beliefs (*p < .05. ** p < .01.)

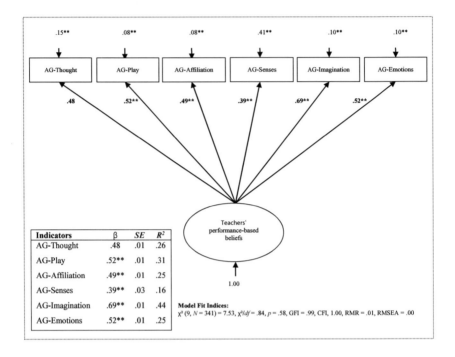

Indicators	β	SE	R²
AG-Thought	.48	.01	.26
AG-Play	.52**	.01	.31
AG-Affiliation	.49**	.01	.25
AG-Senses	.39**	.03	.16
AG-Imagination	.69**	.01	.44
AG-Emotions	.52**	.01	.25

Model Fit Indices:
χ² (9, N = 341) = 7.53, χ²/df = .84, p = .58, GFI = .99, CFI, 1.00, RMR = .01, RMSEA = .00

The measurement model of CA-Practice was measured by specifying seven indicator items predicting the latent construct of capabilities-based practices. The coefficient of Item b1 was constrained to one in order to ensure identification. Model structure as well as standardized parameter estimates and model fit indices are presented in Figure 4.7. The results of CFA showed that fit indices were achieved [χ^2 (11, N = 341) = 21.18, χ^2/df = 1.93, p = .03, GFI = .98, CFI = .95, RMR = .01, RMSEA = .04]. All indicators were significant and the factor loadings of indicators ranged from 0.27 to 0.62. Among them, Item b16,"Being involved in playful activities that have been chosen by the children", was found to be the most important indicator whereas Item b8, "Singing", was the least important.

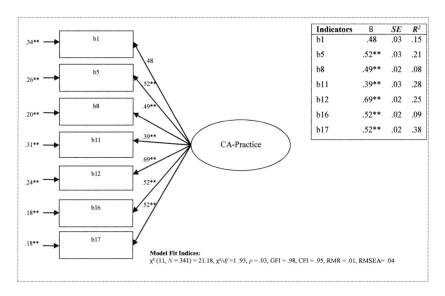

Figure 4.7. Validated Measurement Model of Capabilities-Based Practices (*p < .05. ** p < .01.)

A CFA was conducted to examine the validity of the measurement model of AG-Practice, which includes seven items as indicators of the latent construct of performance-based practices. The coefficient of Item b1 was constrained to one in order to ensure identification. Model structure as well as standardized parameter estimates and model fit indices are shown in Figure 4.8. The fit indices demonstrated a good model fit [χ^2 (8, N = 341) = 15.02, χ^2/df = 1.88, p = .06, GFI = .98, CFI = .95, RMR = .01, RMSEA = .05]. All indicators were significant and the factor loadings of indicators ranged from 0.20 to 0.61. Among them, Item b10, "memorize texts", was found to be the most important indicator whereas Item b6, "write their name", was the least important.

Figure 4.8. Validated Measurement Model of Performance-Based Practices (*p < .05. ** p < .01.)

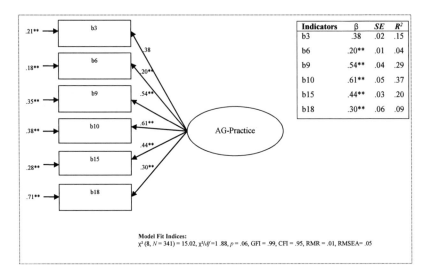

Indicators	β	SE	R^2
b3	.38	.02	.15
b6	.20**	.01	.04
b9	.54**	.04	.29
b10	.61**	.05	.37
b15	.44**	.03	.20
b18	.30**	.06	.09

Model Fit Indices:
χ^2 (8, *N* = 341) = 15.02, χ^2/df =1 .88, *p* = .06, GFI = .99, CFI = .95, RMR = .01, RMSEA= .05

4.7 Statistical Analysis

The researcher utilized IBM SPSS Statistics 20 and IBM SPSS Amos 20 to assist in the data analysis of the survey. Both the data entry and the coding process were conducted by the researcher. One of the most widely used methods of imputation is the mean substitution that replaces the missing values of a variable with the mean value of that variable calculated from all valid responses (Hair, Black, Babin, & Anderson, 2010). However, this imputation method is suggested only in studies with relatively low levels of missing data. In this study, missing data were less than 5 percent for each item, and were therefore replaced with the mean of each case. Based on the collected data, the following types of analyses were employed to explore the research questions. It worth noting that the statistical methods used are mentioned without in depth elaboration, but cross-reference is given to facilitate further reading or description of the methods.

Primary descriptive analysis was performed to obtain a general distribution of the social and educational background of the pre-primary school teachers. Cronbach's alpha was used to determine the reliability of the scales and subscales of the questionnaire.

Correlation analysis was used to determine the statistical significance of the items used in the scales and subscales. The correlation is a measure of association between two variables. If two variables are highly correlated, the Pearson's correlation will be close to either to -1.0 or +1.0. A correlation of zero shows no relationship. When there is a negative correlation between two variables, as the value of one increases, the value of the other variable decreases and vice versa. If something has been identified as highly correlated, that does not mean that there is a one-to-one relationship between the two variables.

Analysis of variance (ANOVA) was employed to investigate whether there was a significant effect of teachers' beliefs on group level. Field (2009) defines the analysis of variance as a statistical procedure that uses the F ratio to test the overall fit of a linear model.

Cross-tabulation analysis was used to explore teachers' group membership. Cross-tabs are frequency tables in which two categorical variables can be assessed (Coolican, 2004).

Finally, structural equation modelling was employed to test the model of this study empirically. The term structural equation modelling (SEM) does not designate a single statistical technique but instead refers to a family of related procedures (Kline, 2010). Structural equation modelling is a cutting-edge technique in multivariate analysis which enables the researcher to simultaneously estimate multiple dependence relationships. Structural equation models (SEMs) are a flexible class of models that allow complex modelling of multivariate data. This method merges the logic of CFA, multiple regression, and path analysis within a single data-analytic framework. In essence, SEM makes it possible to test whether a hypothesized causal structure is consistent or inconsistent with the data.

To understand SEM it is necessary to grasp two fundamental concepts: the measurement model and the structural model. The measurement model establishes relationships between latent (unobserved) variables and multiple observable items. This makes up the CFA portion of the model. The structural model tests a set of hypothesized associations among two or more variables. All structural equation models must be over-identified, which means that there are more equations in the model than unknown parameters.

Path diagrams use various symbols to represent model assumptions graphically. Variable names are drawn inside boxes when the variables are observed, or inside ovals, when the variables are latent. The relationships among the variables can be described with the use of either directed (single-directed) or double-headed arrows. Directed arrows represent causal relationships among variables, whereas double-headed arrows between variables imply a nonzero correlation. A lack of arrows indicates that the variables are conditionally independent.

Chapter 5: The Empirical Findings

However beautiful the strategy,
you should occasionally look at the result.
Winston Churchill

This study was undertaken to gain a better understanding of not only the relationship between teachers' capabilities- and performance-based beliefs and practices but also the antecedent factors of teachers' beliefs. The present chapter reports the empirical findings in the following sequence. Section 5.1. presents a comparison of the mean scores among the main variables of the study. Section 5.2. reports the correlational analysis of these variables is presented. Section 5.3. shows the relationship between the two measurement models of beliefs. The two following sections (5.4. and 5.5.) report the results of the structural equation model analysis with the last section reporting the results of the second-order model. Throughout the chapter, statistical analyses are followed by a substantive discussion on the findings.

5.1 Descriptive Analysis of the Main Research Variables

The descriptive analysis of the key variables used in the main model is presented in Tables 5.1 and 5.2 as a first step towards gaining a deeper understanding of each variable. These key variables were derived from the calculation of factor scores of (sub)scales on the basis of the data from 341 questionnaires. In order to interpret the mean scores it is necessary to define the range of the 4-type rating scale. This was as follows:

1= Not important at all/Almost never/I entirely disagree   1.00–1.74
2= Not that important/Rarely/I rather disagree   1.75–2.50
3= Fairly important/Regularly/I rather agree   2.51–3.25
4= Extremely important/Very Often/I entirely agree   3.26–4.00

Table 5.1. Descriptive Statistics for the 17 Key Variables (N = 341)

Research Variable	Min	Max	Mean	SD
Thought CA	2.33	4.00	3.62	.35
Thought AG	1.40	4.00	2.98	.45
Play CA	2.75	4.00	3.71	.29
Play AG	2.33	4.00	3.33	.33
Affiliation CA	2.80	4.00	3.76	.27
Affiliation AG	2.67	4.00	3.49	.32
Senses CA	2.67	4.00	3.64	.36
Senses AG	1.00	4.00	2.97	.70
Imagination CA	2.83	4.00	3.62	.29
Imagination AG	1.50	4.00	2.69	.44
Emotions CA	2.33	4.00	3.74	.34
Emotions AG	2.33	4.00	3.54	.38
Practices CA	2.22	4.00	3.42	.27
Practices AG	2.33	3.89	3.12	.29
Administrative Control	1.00	4.00	1.87	.63
Self-Efficacy	1.75	4.00	3.16	.37
Decision Latitude	1.00	4.00	2.54	.57

It can be observed that teachers score higher on CA variables (Thought CA, Play CA, Affiliation CA, Senses CA, Imagination CA and Emotions CA). It should also be noted that the dispersion of AG variables is higher than that of CA variables. As shown in Table 5.1., the mean scores of Thought CA and AG indicate that both variables are perceived as fairly important for the teachers, and their standard deviations (*SD*) do not suggest any great diversifications in their answers. Play CA and Play AG mean scores are 3.71 and 3.33, indicating that teachers conceive play to be extremely important for the children. In the same vein, Affiliation CA and Affiliation AG with mean scores of 3.76 and 3.49 respectively seem to go hand in hand with each other, but the former is ranked as more important than the latter. However, Senses CA and Senses AG represent a different case because the *SD* of Senses AG is so high that it slips away from the range of fairly important cases and includes ones that are not important at all. Similarly, Imagination AG's *SD* indicates that teachers' responses are loosely clustered around the mean. Emotions CA also has a higher score than Emotions AG. With respect to practices, it can be observed that teachers perform more practices that emphasize children's capability expansion followed by practices that focus on the acquisition of academic learning. With regards to Administrative Control, it seems that teachers tend to disagree on the inflexibility and strictness of the educational system's structure, whereas the Self-Efficacy mean score of 3.16 suggests that they have a high sense of efficacy. Lastly, the Decision Latitude score is at the edge of the "rather agree" range and its *SD* indicates that the answers given are not closely clustered around the mean.

In addition, it was considered significant to provide the frequencies of the variable "Years of Experience" because this is also a key variable (see Table 5.2.) As the table shows, a large proportion of the respondents have up to 4 years of experience, whereas the majority have from 5 to 9 years of experience in the field of early childhood education. A significant number of the respondents belong to the 10–19 years of experience group, whereas a minor number has above 20 years of experience in the field.

Table 5.2. Frequency Table of "Years of Experience" (YoE)

	Frequency	Per cent%	Cummulative per cent
0–4 YoE	124	36.36	36.36
5–9 YoE	126	36.95	73.31
10–19 YoE	76	22.29	95.60
20+ YoE	15	4.40	100
Total	341	100	100

5.2 Correlation Analysis of the Key Variables

This part of the analysis examined the correlations among the key variables in the study in order to gain preliminary insights into their interrelationships. Table 5.3 displays the correlation matrix. It can be seen that the significant correlations for the main research variables ranged from .11 ($p < .05$) to .58 ($p < .01$). Moreover, correlations among teachers' beliefs variables ranged from .12 ($p < .05$) to .58 ($p < .01$). Specifically, all teachers' capabilities-based beliefs variables (CA) had significant positive intercorrelations ranging from .22 ($p < .01$) to .58 ($p < .01$). Imagination CA and Senses CA yielded the highest significant correlation coefficient, .58 ($p < .01$), followed by Imagination CA and Play CA, .40 ($p < .01$); Imagination CA and Affiliation CA, .37 ($p < .01$); and Imagination CA and Thought CA, .36 ($p < .01$). The lowest correlation among teachers' capabilities-based beliefs' variables was Emotions CA and Thought CA, .22 ($p < .01$), followed by Emotions CA and Senses CA, .27 ($p < .01$); Emotions CA and Play CA, 28 ($p < .01$); and Senses CA and Thought CA, .22 ($p < .01$).

In the same vein, all teachers' performance-based beliefs variables (AG) yielded significant positive intercorrelations ranging from .16 ($p < .01$) to .35 ($p < .01$). Imagination AG and Thought AG, .35 ($p < .01$), yielded the highest significant correlation, followed by Imagination AG and Play AG, Imagination AG and Affiliation AG as well as Imagination AG and Emotions AG, all with .34 ($p < .01$). The lowest correlation was between Emotions AG and Senses AG, .16 ($p < .01$); followed by Senses AG and Thought AG, .18 ($p < .01$); and Affiliation AG and Thought AG, .20 ($p < .01$).

Practices CA correlated with all teachers' capabilities-based beliefs variables (CA), yielding the highest correlation with Imagination CA, .40 ($p < .01$), and the lowest with Thought CA, .21 ($p < .01$). Practices AG correlated with nearly all teachers' performance-based beliefs variables (AG). It showed the highest correlation with Thought AG, .39 ($p < .01$) and the lowest with Affiliation AG, .12 ($p < .05$). It is worth noting that Practices AG did not correlate with Senses AG, .07 ($p > .05$), which needs to be discussed in the following chapter. There was also a significant correlation.

Table 5.3. *Correlation Matrix for the Main Research Variables (N = 341)*

Research Variable	1	2	3	4	5	6	7	8	9	10	11	12	13	14	15	16	17	18
1. THOUGHT CA	—																	
2. THOUGHT AG	.19**	—																
3. PLAY CA	.29**	-.02	—															
4. PLAY AG	.24**	.32**	.23**	—														
5. AFFILIATION CA	.33**	.07	.33**	.19**	—													
6. AFFILIATION AG	.14*	.20**	.27**	.27**	.33**	—												
7. SENSES CA	.28**	.19**	.30**	.28**	.29**	.20**	—											
8. SENSES AG	.17**	.18**	.13*	.26**	.19**	.23**	.16**	—										
9. IMAGINATION CA	.36**	.20**	.40**	.31**	.37**	.31**	.58**	.12*	—									
10. IMAGINATION AG	.08	.35**	.07	.34**	.10	.34**	.23**	.26**	.22**	—								
11. EMOTIONS CA	.22**	.05	.28**	.16**	.35**	.15**	.27**	.08	.32**	.05	—							
12. EMOTIONS AG	.15**	.26**	.09	.26**	.26**	.29**	.10	.16**	.14**	.34**	.18**	—						
13. PRACTICES CA	.21**	.06	.29**	.09	.28**	.17**	.25**	.05	.40**	.13*	.25**	.03	—					
14. PRACTICES AG	-.03	.39**	-.07	.22**	.00	.12*	.02	.07	.05	.33**	-.05	.24**	.17**	—				
15. YEARS OF EXPERIENCE	-.10	.01	.09	-.07	.04	-.01	-.03	-.06	.03	-.09	.04	-.06	.12*	.00	—			
16. ADMINISTRATIVE CONTROL	-.08	.08	-.09	.07	-.01	.01	-.06	.02	-.03	.15**	-.05	-.03	-.05	.11*	-.07	—		
17. SELF-EFFICACY	.03	.11*	.03	.01	-.05	.14*	.11*	.19**	.16**	.12*	.02	.02	.25**	.09	.00	-.19**	—	
18. DECISION LATITUDE	.01	.01	-.02	.05	-.04	.11*	.06	.09	-.05	.15**	.06	.13*	.00	.08	-.05	-.07	.18**	—

Note. Teachers' beliefs variables (1–12). Teachers' practices variables (13–14). Antecedent factors (15–18). *p < .05. **p < .01.

between Practice CA and Practice AG with a value .17 ($p < .01$). Moreover, the table shows that there is a number of significant correlations among specific teachers' capabilities-based and performance-based beliefs variables. This indicated the need to further investigate the relationship between these two constructs in a subsequent part of analysis.

With respect to factors, Years of experience did not relate to any capabilities-based or performance-based beliefs variables except for one significant correlation with Practices CA, .12 ($p < .05$). Administrative control correlated significantly with Imagination AG, .15 ($p < .01$) and also with Practices AG, .11 ($p < .05$). Self-Efficacy correlated significantly with Thought AG, .11 ($p < .05$), Affiliation AG, .14 ($p < .05$), Senses AG, .19 ($p < .01$), and Imagination AG, .12 ($p < .05$). It also correlated negatively with Administrative Control with a correlation coefficient of -.19 ($p < .01$). Finally, Decision Latitude correlated positively with Affiliation AG, .11 ($p < .05$), Imagination AG, .15 ($p < .01$), and Emotions AG, .12 ($p < .05$). It also correlated significantly with Self-Efficacy, .18 ($p < .01$). The findings from the correlation analysis are encouraging. However, because a correlation does not imply causation it is necessary to continue the analysis with structural equation modelling.

5.3 Beliefs: Second-order two-factor model

After empirically verifying the interrelation between teachers' beliefs and practices, it was necessary to investigate whether either capabilities-based beliefs or performance-based beliefs prevail in teachers' thinking. An answer to this question based on the empirical findings of the preceding models would make it easy to derive the sort of practices that predominates in preschools.

The preceding models were first-order factor models. According to Hair et al. (2010), a first-order factor model is the one in which the covariances between measurement items are explained with a single latent factor layer (think of a layer as one level of latent constructs). In order to examine the factorial validity of teachers' capabilities-based and performance-based beliefs, it was necessary to conduct a confirmatory factor analysis by testing a second-order measurement model containing two layers of latent constructs (Figure 5.3). Hair et al. (2010) argue that a second-order factor model should be used only in relationships with other constructs of the same general level of abstraction. In the respective case, the introduction of a second-order factor changes the designation of the constructs. The latent construct of teachers' beliefs becomes an exogenous construct, having no measurement variables, whereas capabilities-based and performance-based beliefs become endogenous constructs.

Normally, if there is only one second-order factor in a model, there must be at least three first-order factors for the model to be identified. However, additional degrees of freedom may sometimes be gained in second-order models by making equality restrictions on factor loadings when sets of tests are thought to be equivalent, and by making further equality restrictions on error variances when sets of tests are thought to be parallel. In some special cases, models with such restrictions will be identified when they would not be identified without the restrictions (Rindskopf & Rose, 1988).

According to Rindskopf and Rose (1988), a second-order factor model contains at least one second-order factor, and the first-order factors are linear combinations of the first-order factors, plus a unique variable for each first-order factor. The observed variables are linear combinations of the first-order factors plus a residual variable for each observed variable. In the model (Figure 5.3), the capabilities-based beliefs and performance-based beliefs as well as CA-Thought and AG-Thought were set at one by default using AMOS. The model fitted the data well ($\chi^2 = 57.90$, $df = 46$, $p = 0.11$ $\chi^2/df = 1.26$, CFI = 0.98, RMSEA = 0.03). The regression coefficients for both capabilities-based beliefs' and performance-based beliefs were positively significant with coefficients of .80 and .65 respectively. These findings indicate that capabilities-based beliefs gain mastery over teachers' beliefs and consequently over their practices. However, it is clear that teachers' do not disregard performance-based beliefs. Instead it can be concluded that their relation is not opposing but more complementary and supplementary.

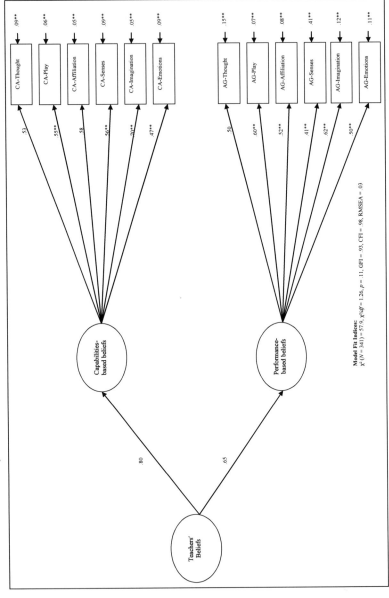

Figure 5.1. Second-order model of teachers' beliefs (* p < .05 **p < .01.)

Model Fit Indices:
χ^2 (N = 341) = 57.9, χ^2/df = 1.26, p = .11, GFI = .93, CFI = .98, RMSEA = .03

5.4 Interrelation of the Measurement Models

The confirmatory analysis of the measurement models demonstrated that the variables fitted the empirical data well. However, before proceeding to the full model analysis explaining the structural relationship among the exogenous and endogenous variables, it was necessary to test the interrelation of the two measurement models in order to exclude the case of perfect collinearity. According to Field (2009), perfect collinearity exists when at least one predictor is a perfect linear combination of the others (the simplest example being two predictors that are perfectly correlated and have a correlation coefficient of 1.0). If there is a perfect collinearity between predictors, it becomes impossible to obtain unique estimates of the regression coefficients because there are an infinite number of combinations of coefficients that would work equally well.

Therefore, a model with a double-headed arrow representing the covariance of the two latent variables/constructs was tested. The fit indices of this model indicated that the model had a good fit [χ^2 ($N = 341$) = 93.90, χ^2/df = 2.29, p = .00, GFI = .96, CFI = .93, RMR = .01, RMSEA = .06]. All indicators were significant with factor loadings ranging from 0.39 to 0.78. The covariance between the two latent variables was significantly high with a correlation coefficient of .54 ($p<$ .01), indicating a strong relationship between the two sorts of beliefs. Nevertheless, no perfect linear relationship could be observed between the two latent variables, permitting a continuation to the analysis of the full model. The results of this data analysis indicate that the two sorts of beliefs, capabilities-based and performance-based, are characterized by an interrelation rather than a dichotomy. This positive path coefficient cannot be characterized as spurious but rather as expected on the basis of the study's theoretical framework.

The structural regression model explaining the relationships among the main research variables was tested using structural equation modelling (SEM) with IBM SPSS Amos Versions 19 and 20. The exogenous variables in the proposed model (see Figure 5.2) were four manifest variables: the antecedent factors of teachers' beliefs (i.e. years of experience, administrative control, self-efficacy, and decision latitude). The endogenous variables in the model were two latent and two manifest variables:

Figure 5.2. Empirically validated measurement model of capabilities-based beliefs.

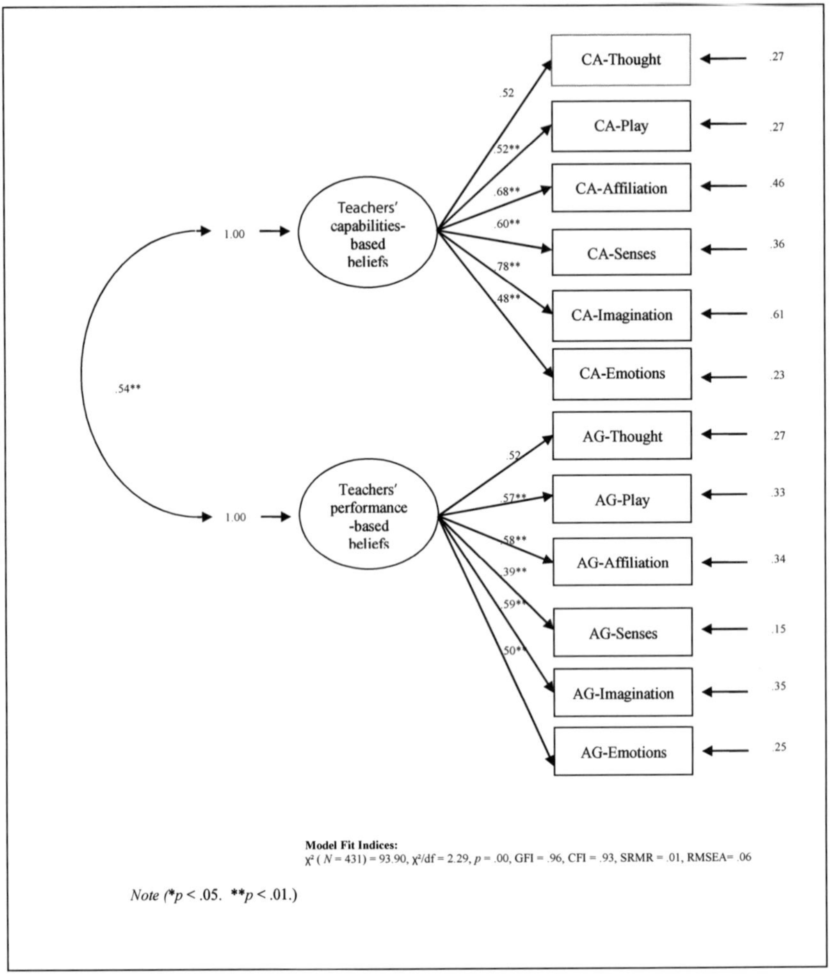

teachers' capabilities-based beliefs and teachers' performance-based beliefs as well as Practices CA and Practices AG respectively. It is worth noting that the sample size (N= 341) was satisfactory for a latent variables structural equation model.

According to Hair et al. (2010), when the sample size for maximum likelihood estimation is relatively small, the precision of estimating complex models becomes lost as the number of parameters increases. Therefore, it was preferable to compute the factor scores of the variables indicated as manifest in the model in order to reduce the number of estimated parameters in the structural model.

5.5 Structural Regression Model

The first part examined the structural model of relations between the latent constructs of teacher's beliefs and teachers' practices manifest variables.

Afterwards, the structural model of antecedent factors and the latent constructs of teachers' beliefs was tested with a path analysis computed with IBM SPSS Amos (Versions 19 and 20).

The results of the data analysis indicate that the structural regression model describing the relationship between teacher's beliefs and practices was valid. The fit indices indicated that the model had an adequate (marginally good) fit with the empirical data (χ^2 (100, N = 341) = 225.30, χ^2/df = 2.25, p = .00, CFI = .90, GFI =.94, AGFI = .89, RMR = .02, RMSEA = .06). The estimated parameter coefficients between the latent variables in the model demonstrated the structural relationship between these variables. It can be seen that teachers' capabilities-based beliefs were a significant predictor of teachers' practices in both CA and AG. Capabilities-based beliefs had a positive association with practices in CA, β = .60 ($p < .01$) but a negative association with practices in AG, β = -.37 ($p < .01$). This implies that the more a teacher believes in a capabilities-based pedagogical approach, the more likely it is that the teacher will practice capabilities-based activities and the less likely it is that she or he will practice performance-based activities. Teachers' performance-based beliefs predicted teachers' practices in AG, β = .66 ($p < .01$), which is in line with the theoretical claims and empirical findings reported in prior studies such as Charlesworth et al. (2001). Moreover, it can be seen that this was not the case for the reverse pair, namely, teachers' performance-based beliefs and practices on CA because these revealed a non significant negative coefficient.

Therefore, it became clear that teachers' beliefs are inextricably interwoven with their practices. It is also important to pay attention to parameter estimates because relationships among variables may well be weak even when there is a good model fit. Looking at the standardized parameters, significant relationships can be seen in several specified paths. All belief indicators were significant with factor loadings ranging from .38 ($p < .01$) to .87 ($p < .01$). Among these, CA-Imagination, β = .87 ($p < .01$), and AG-Imagination, β = .68 ($p < .01$), were found to be the most important indicators, whereas CA-Emotions, β = .44, and AG-Senses, β = .38 ($p < .01$), were the less important.

With regard to the relations between the antecedent variables and the latent constructs of teacher's beliefs, the regression coefficients of Years of Experience, Administrative Control, and Decision Latitude on teachers' capabilities-based beliefs were not significant, with path coefficients of β = .04, -.06 and -.03 respectively. Self-Efficacy was a significant indicator (β = .14, p < .05) of teachers' capabilities-based beliefs. As expected due to the non-significant effect of the antecedent variables, teachers' capabilities-based beliefs explained only 3 percent of the variance in the data (R^2 = .03). This result indicates that the higher the teachers' self-efficacy, the greater the teachers' capability-based beliefs.

However, teachers' Self-Efficacy (β= .10, p < .05) and Decision Latitude (β= .05, p < .05) as well as Administrative Control (β = .06, p < .05) had significantly positive effects on teachers' performance-based beliefs (academic goals oriented), whereas Years of Experience (β = -.01, p < .05) revealed negative effects. Teachers' performance-based beliefs explained 6 percent of the data's variance in the data (R^2 = .06). These results indicate that:

- the higher the teachers' self-efficacy, the more their performance-based beliefs rise;
- the higher teachers' decision latitude, the more teachers are likely to espouse performance-based beliefs;

Figure 5.3. Empirically validated structural model of teachers' beliefs and practices (*p < .05. **p < .01.)

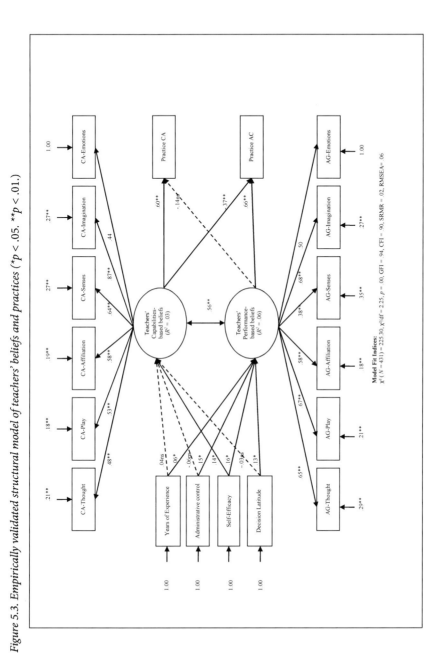

- the more administrative control teachers are experiencing, the more they are likely to adopt performance-based beliefs;
- the less years of experience teachers have the more they osculate performance-based beliefs,

With regard to the role self-efficacy in the two sorts of teachers' beliefs, it seems to have self-efficacy has a significant effect on teachers' beliefs but it did not contribute significantly to the sort of belief that prevails in the teachers perceptions.

Although the antecedent factors did not explain a high percentage of the variance in the data, it was decided to retain these predictors in the model without disregarding the prospected need for more explanatory variables.

The results of the data analysis indicate that the structural model describing the relationship among antecedent factors, teachers' beliefs and teachers' practices was a valid model with an adequate fit that provides a plausible explanation of the relationship among these variables, even though this does not imply that it is the only possible model. The results of the data analysis of the current study have been presented in this chapter and the previous chapter. The following chapter will discuss the results found in the study.

Chapter 6: Discussion

All truth passes through three stages:
First, it is ridiculed.
Second, it is violently opposed.
Third, it is accepted as being self-evident.
Arthur Schopenhauer

Following the presentation of the data analysis, this chapter discusses the main research findings in the context of the theoretical background. Interpreting the results first required a thorough understanding of the Greek context in relation to related studies in the field conducted in Europe and the United States. This is summarized before reviewing the main objectives of the study and its methodology. The findings are then summarized and discussed. After that, the limitations and implications of these findings for policy in the field of early childhood education are outlined. Finally, potential directions for future research are suggested.

6.1 Summary

The general purpose of the current study was to develop and empirically validate the conceptual model describing the linkages between teachers' beliefs and practices. More specifically, "linkages" here refers to relationships among the antecedent factors and teachers' capabilities- and performance-based beliefs, between teachers' capabilities- and performance-based beliefs, and between teachers' beliefs and practices. Additionally, the study investigates which sort of belief, namely, capabilities- or performance-based beliefs, is stronger and more predominant in teachers' perceptions. To review, the study investigated the following research questions:

- Do teachers' beliefs predict teachers' practices?
- Do Greek pre-primary teachers favour performance-based or capabilities-based beliefs?
- Are teachers' beliefs predicted by antecedent factors (i.e. years of experience, administrative control, self-efficacy, and decision latitude)?

The participants in this study were pre-primary teachers attending training or retraining programmes at the time of data collection. The total sample consisted of 341 teachers, the majority of whom were women. The research instrument was a questionnaire outlining specific descriptions of teachers' views about children, the curriculum, instruction, and learning in Greek pre-primary classrooms. It comprised three parts:

a. Background socio-cultural information about teachers.
b. Beliefs and practices rating scales.
c. A professionalization scale from which self-efficacy and decision-latitude scales were derived.

Items were rated on a 4-point scale. The instrument's internal consistency and validity were tested through a pilot study and discussions with experts in the field. The results of pilot testing indicated that the factors in this study were statistically significant and conceptually logical.

Data collection was carried out during three training programmes in PEKs located in Thessaloniki and Ioannina, as well as in retraining programs (*Didaskaleia*) at the Universities of Athens (Kapodistrian), Thessaloniki (Aristotle), Ioannina, Crete (Rethymno), and the Aegean (Rhodes). The paper-and-pencil questionnaire was administered during the teachers' courses.

The conceptual model of the current study was sketched on the basis of a literature review describing a system of linkeages among a number of variables. A cutting-edge technique in multivariate analysis – structural equation modelling (SEM) – was used to validate the conceptual model.

The present study investigated the relationship between teachers' beliefs and practices. Furthermore, it examined the emphasis placed by the teachers on either the children's capabilities enhancement or on academic learning acquisition, based on the assumption that teachers' suggestions and self-reported practices reflect their underlying beliefs and values regarding their students' needs and their implicit theories of teaching and learning. Two broad categories of teachers' beliefs delineated teachers' perceptions of over-focusing on academic goals and a preference for enhancing students' capabilities. These two schools of thought could be seen, namely, by expressing a preference for performance-based beliefs representing the pre-primary curriculum, or favoring the capabilities-based beliefs representing the social pedagogic curriculum. The beliefs of the latter group were tested within the spectrum of four basic human capabilities as described in Martha's Nussbaum's (2011) list, including *Senses, Imagination, and Thought; Play; Affiliation;* and *Emotions.* In the performance-based beliefs, the respective capabilities served as an instrument for the fulfilment of academic success, and the achievement of academic objectives was the primary aim. In the capabilities-based beliefs, on the other hand, these acts had an intrinsic value for children's capabilities enhancement. It was assumed that each type of belief would lead to the respective practice, and that it would have a reverse linkage with the contradictory belief–practice dyad. The conceptual model contained four predictor variables as antecedents influencing teachers' beliefs, including teachers' years of experience, administrative control over teachers' pedagogical work, teachers' self-efficacy, and decision latitude.

The conceptual model was tested empirically with structural equation modelling (SEM). The step-by-step investigation of each causal path was considered to be a logical approach that would lead to gaining deeper insight into the interrelations between the variables in the main model. First, the interrelations among the capabilities- and performance-based beliefs and practices were investigated, followed by an examination of the predictor constructs of teachers' capabilities- and performance-based beliefs. In addition, a second-order, two-factor model was employed in order to detect which offset of beliefs the teachers would favour.

6.2 Discussion of the Main Findings

This is the first investigation ever conducted on Greek pre-primary teachers' beliefs and practices within the framework of capabilities- and performance-based pedagogy, and the findings from the SEM analysis indicated that the models indeed fitted the data well. The results of this study suggest several interesting relationships that shed light on curriculum implementation and planning. In addition to this, the findings also point out directions for future research in the field and confirm most of the assumptions expressed in the proposed model. The following sections present and discuss the primary findings of this study in line with the research questions as posed by the researcher.

Research Question 1:
Do teachers' beliefs predict teachers' practices?
Data analysis indicated that teachers' beliefs were largely in accordance with their self-reported actions. More specifically, teachers' capabilities-based beliefs predicted capabilities-based practices, whereas teachers' performance-based beliefs predicted performance-based practices. This finding is consistent with the widely recognized principle that teachers' beliefs directly influence their teaching practices (Fang, 1996; Kagan, 1992; Stipek et al., 2001). Empirically, Charlesworth et al. (1991, 1992) found a moderate but statistically significant correlation between teachers' beliefs and practices regarding developmentally appropriate teaching. Moreover, several other empirical studies have indicated that teachers' practices are associated with their beliefs (Hollon, Anderson, & Roth, 1991; Janesick, 1982; Morine-Dershimer, 1983; Smith & Shepart, 1988; Stipek, Daniels, Galluzzo, & Milburn, 1992). The findings in this current study serve as further confirmation

of previous findings because the SEM method of data analysis used here enables the researcher not only to assess the strength of a dependence relationship between two variables more accurately than a correlation, but also to designate the causal direction. Therefore, it can be deduced that teachers' beliefs have a direct positive effect on their respective practices.

The study also revealed that there is a direct negative relationship between teachers' capabilities-based beliefs and performance-based practices, suggesting that when capabilities-based perceptions are embraced, teachers are likely to reject performance-based activities. This finding implies that teachers who value capabilities-based pedagogy tend not to practice activities solely for the sake of academic achievement. It is likely that teachers who tend towards capabilities-based beliefs will be interested in and eager to offer students alternative activities that foster capability enhancement.

However, a reverse effect of teachers' performance-based beliefs on capabilities-based practices could not be confirmed, suggesting that the more teachers tend to believe in performance-based pedagogy, the less likely they are to reject capabilities-based activities. It should be noted here that this result contradicts the hypothesis made at the beginning of this research process, which predicted that teachers' performance-based beliefs would negatively influence capabilities-based practices. Yet, the lack of a direct negative effect could be inferred as an encouraging result, suggesting that teachers who favour performance-based pedagogy may not necessarily disregard capabilities-based activities. It may indeed be the case that the teacher as a decision-maker determines whether, how, and when to use a certain method. If teachers are performance-based driven but do not disregard the enhancement of children's capabilities, then this may be a balance that serves both of the pedagogical approaches presented in the OECD thematic review of early childhood education and care policy (Bennett, 2005; OECD, 2006). The OECD review describes two broad curricula approaches: the social pedagogical and the pre-primary. For Bertrand (2007), the social pedagogic curriculum is marked by a broad orientation towards teaching children, rather than on prescribed outcomes, and the acquisition of developmental skills is perceived as a by-product rather than as the driver of the curriculum. In contrast, the pre-primary approach, which is sometimes referred to as the so-called schoolification of the early years, has specific goals and outcomes often stated as learning standards or expectations related to acquiring skills and practicing tasks for school readiness. Of these two curricular approaches, the Greek curriculum embodies the pre-primary approach, as it is characterized by centralised development and contains detailed goals and outcomes that influence or determine curriculum decisions regarding what and how children learn. In the Greek curriculum, the emphasis has moved away from childhood development and socialisation towards teaching specific academic skills. However, the findings of this study indicate that it may well be the case that teachers do not disregard children's capabilities while applying the pre-primary (performance-based) approach. Nevertheless, further analysis of teachers' prevailing sort of belief was required, as will be discussed below.

From the indicators of the two types of beliefs, *Imagination* seems to play the most significant role in pre-primary teachers' pedagogy, regardless of whether the role of *Imagination* in an activity is instrumental to acquiring an academic skill or is a meaningful process for encouraging children's creative capacity. Studies investigating the impact of imaginative activity on children's emotional and social behaviour, as well as on their cognition, highlight their benefits in these areas (see Richards & Sanderson, 1999; Udwin, 1983). This finding indicates that teachers find it important to nourish and spark children's imaginations. In the literature to date, however, few attempts have been made to further explore this issue. There is thus a need for more research in order to gain a deeper understanding of pre-primary teachers' beliefs about the role of *Imagination*.

To briefly summarize the results of this study, teachers' beliefs were found to be in alignment with their practices and translate into their behaviour in the classroom. Teachers' beliefs predict teachers' practices; and more concretely, capabilities- and performance-based beliefs predict their respective practices, whereas capabilities-based beliefs have a direct negative effect on performance-based practices.

Research Question 2:
Do pre-primary teachers favour performance- or capabilities-based beliefs?
The research findings suggested that the prevailing type of belief iheld by teachers was the capabilities-based one. It seems that teachers tend to favour a more pedagogical approach, in which the enhancement of children's capabilities is prioritized over teaching formal facts and skills. This finding provides solid evidence offers an optimistic response to scholars' concerns regarding the schoolification of Greek pre-primary school. As previously discussed in the theoretical part of this study, a number of scholars (Chrysafidis, 2006; Doliopoulou, 2002, 2003; Fragkos, 2002; Koutsouvanou, 2006; Tsafos & Sofou, 2010) have stressed their concerns over the academic goal-driven curriculum. They are concerned that pre-primary school is being converted into *"a misprint of primary school"* (Chrysafidis, 2006). Chrysafidis (2006) argues that by pursuing scientific knowledge, pre-primary school may be sacrificing creative activities and adopting

strategies very similar to those that will be later used on students by their primary school teachers. Furthermore, Tsafos and Sofou (2010) report empirical evidence from a qualitative study indicating that teachers themselves are sceptical about the areas of the curriculum that closely resemble primary school, fearing that these aspects are contributing to schoolification. However, the present study empirically demonstrates that teachers demand to make systematic use of specialised content from science, mathematics, and other subjects to structure pre-primary activities, regardless of the curriculum in place. As such, they are still capabilities-driven and prioritize a social-pedagogic approach that emphasizes the expansion of children's capabilities. Teachers seem to acknowledge the importance of offering children experiences that are valuable in their own right. As Diehm (2011) stresses, this phase of education so dominated by play should not be misunderstood as a purely preliminary stage of schooling, although nobody would deny that it is an important phase for cognitive and social development – and Greek pre-primary teachers seem to be aware of this. Although this finding is encouraging, it does raise concerns about the money spent on teachers' seminars and training, because it would appear that the curricula have not had a particularly strong impact on shaping teachers' beliefs.

This result does not imply that the performance-based sort of beliefs were disregarded and/or overlooked by teachers. Indeed, teachers expressed appreciation for performance-based beliefs, but on a slightly lower level. The CFA analysis revealed that pre-primary teachers' perceptions of these two constructs did not cluster into a dichotomy. Their association would be better characterized as an interrelation or better, as a *dialogic* relation, because it seems that teachers value an approach that combines aspects from both schools of thought. This is in line with Bertand's (2007) argument that, in practice, most education systems use approaches that blend elements of both, but lean towards either a pre-primary or a social pedagogic approach. Based on her argument, it can be inferred from the data of the present study that Greek pre-primary teachers tend towards the social pedagogic approach, as the findings revealed that capabilities-based beliefs prevail in teachers' thinking. This was expected because it was assumed that these two constructs, representing as they do two widely discussed trends in the field of early childhood education, would both have an influence teachers' thinking and perceptions. As such, teachers do appreciate both capabilities- and performance-based beliefs, a point that should be taken into account in future research. In conclusion, teachers are likely to choose a middle or interactive position, one which allows them to recognize and perceive practices that are both appropriate for the instructional circumstances and for the needs of the children.

Research Question 3:
Are teachers' beliefs predicted by antecedent factors (e.g. years of experience, administrative control, self-efficacy, and decision latitude)?
Overall, it was found that the predictor constructs significantly influenced teachers' beliefs. While all the antecedent factors significantly predicted teachers' performance-based beliefs, this was actually not the case for capabilities-based beliefs. The effect of each antecedent factor on teachers' beliefs is discussed in the following sections.

Years of Experience
Teachers' years of experience have a significantly negative and direct effect on their performance-based beliefs, which indicates that less experienced teachers are likely to embrace pedagogy designed to achieve academic goals. These findings support the hypothesis of this study because it had been assumed that teachers with less experience would bow to parents' pressure regarding their children's academic advancement, making them thus more likely to adhere to curricular guidelines. Chrysafidis (2006) argues that pre-primary teachers, by following parents' prompts and their personal priorities, invest their efforts in the pursuit of augmenting children's academic knowledge. In their study, Kelly and Berthelsen (1995) found that disputes with children's parents proved to be one of the main stressors for teachers in the preschool environment. Doliopoulou (1996) found that dealing with government regulations and parents were the factors that had most influence on Greek pre-kindergarten teachers. Although Doliopoulou's study showed that Greek parents tend to influence teachers towards making their kindergarten-aged children engage in more developmentally appropriate practices, Hopf and Hatzichristou (1999) stressed that Greek parents do place a lot of emphasis on the education of their children, exert a good deal of pressure on scholastic achievement, and associate academic success with the upward social aspirations of their family.

Here is it important to note that novice teachers are at a stage in which they are still learning how to teach, and they certainly need time to overcome their anxieties and reach a higher level. During this phase of refining their craft, they expand and elaborate their professional knowledge and develop critical stances towards the pedagogical methods they use in practice. Many studies document the superiority of experienced teachers over non-experienced teachers on a variety of issues. Rich (1993) refers to the empirical studies that confirm the superiority of expert over to novice teachers when it comes to important instructional phenomena such as understandings classroom events and using routines for classroom management and instruction. In the Greek context, employment conditions in Greece mean that the vast majority of novice teachers have must take teaching assignments far from their homes and families. The personal challenges that arise with relocating place additional pressures on the new pre-primary teachers above and beyond the professional demands of the classroom.

Nevertheless, this study found that teachers' years of experience did not influence their capabilities-based beliefs. This result runs counter to theoretical expectations, and leads to the conclusion that experience cannot be considered a predictor of capability-based pedagogy. It may be the case that the formation of capabilities-based beliefs is not influenced by years of experience, but rather by the degree to which teachers' reflect on the pedagogical activity itself. Perhaps a capabilities-based approach cannot be learned through the years, but is rather a value that teachers' form for themselves through their own critical thinking on the subject.

Administrative Control
Administrative control yielded a significantly positive direct effect on teachers' performance-based beliefs, indicating that teachers who experience intense administrative control are prompted to adopt performance-based pedagogy. This was expected, as it was assumed that the burden teachers may feel from such "a strict centralized, bureaucratic, and authoritarian control as the Greek educational system" (Ifanti, 1995) would lead them to follow the curriculum quite closely, particularly its academic dimension of speeding up cognitive processes, in order to gain approval from superiors. As Flouris and Pasias (2003) note, schools are governed primarily by a central authority – the Ministry of Education – and the local school personnel rarely make important decisions regarding what is to be taught, by whom, and for what purposes. Woolfolk and Hoy (1990) refer to this as a 'bureaucratic orientation' in which the individual is committed to the set of attitudes, values, and behaviours characteristically encouraged by bureaucracies. According to them, a bureaucratic orientation emphasizes self-subordination, impersonality, conformity to rules, traditionalism, and loyalty to the organization. In a top-down system, where plans, rules, regulations, and decision-making are implemented by the head administrators, as is the case in the Greek educational system, it would be hard for a teacher not to give in to the pressure from colleagues and superiors who champion academic skills.

However, administrative control did not have a significant effect on capabilities-based beliefs, a finding that indicates that administrative control does not influence the formation of teachers' capabilities-based beliefs. It was hypothesized that administrative control would have a negative effect on this set of beliefs. As mentioned previously, one explanation for this would be that the formation

146

of capabilities-based beliefs may demand a high level of reflective and critical thinking from teachers, and the level of administrative control does not influence this process. The apparent lack of influence of administrative control on capabilities-based beliefs highlights the need to search for other qualities that may better predict teachers' capabilities-based beliefs.

Self-Efficacy

This study's findings revealed that teachers' self-efficacy had significantly positive and direct effects on both capabilities-based and performance-based beliefs. Teachers' belief in their own ability to have a positive effect on children's development and learning is a significant factor for both pedagogical stances. Indeed, the degree to which teachers believe in their own efficacy to motivate and promote learning influences the types of learning environments they create and the level of academic progress their students achieve (Bandura, 1993). The hypothesis set forth in this study was that having a high level of self-efficacy would positively influence teachers' capabilities-based beliefs. Kagan (1992) refers to Smylie's (1988) study in which greater self-efficacy was related to a change in practices. Low levels of self-efficacy were expected to lead teachers to follow the approach prescribed in the curriculum. Kagan (1992) also refers to Poole, Okeafor, and Sloan's (1989) study with elementary teachers, which found that self-efficacy was positively associated with the tendency to use new curricula. Tsigilis, Grammatikopoulos, and Koustelios (2007) argue that teachers' strong self-efficacy beliefs are frequently been related to a variety of positive teaching behaviours and student performance outcomes, such as being more open to new ideas and innovations, exhibiting greater commitment to teaching, investing greater effort in teaching, being less critical of students who make mistakes, and providing assistance to low-achieving students. This finding may indicate that self-efficacy is crucial to a teacher's belief system, but it cannot define the type of beliefs that teachers ultimately endorse. Bearing in mind that teachers' beliefs about their own competencies have significant implications for the pedagogical process, further research on self-efficacy in this field is warranted.

Decision Latitude

Decision latitude had a significantly positive and direct effect on performance-based beliefs: as the results of this study indicate, the higher a teachers' decision latitude, the more they will tend to endorse performance-based beliefs. In contrast, there was no significant effect of decision latitude on capabilities-based beliefs. This finding is not in line with the theoretical expectations outlined earlier in this study because it was assumed that the stronger the teachers' decision latitude, the less they would adopt performance-based beliefs and the more they would champion capabilities-based beliefs. This result is also rather confusing in relation to the findings on the second research question regarding teachers' beliefs preference, in which capabilities-based beliefs were dominant. Previous literature on the subject would suggests thatlack of decision latitude would be a stressor and one of the determinants of job strain (Gulielmi & Tatrow, 1998). Indeed, previous research has shown that the lowest amount of strain is experienced in jobs characterized by low demands and high decision latitude, and the greatest strain results from a combination of high demands and low decision latitude in the workplace. Accordingly, it may be that high decision latitude predicts performance-based beliefs and resultant practices, because a low task demand may result in a low amount of strain on teachers. In contrast, capabilities-based beliefs and practices may call for high-demand tasks, thus resulting in a high amount of strain on teachers. For instance, preparing a dramatic play activity to enhance children's capabilities may be more demanding than preparing mathematical problem-solving activities. As Chrysafidis (2006) points out, most pre-primary teachers turn to ideas and techniques used in elementary school to teach reading and writing, due to the effort, knowledge, and high degree of sensitivity required to implement a proper activity that attends to young children's capacities.

In contrast to the theoretical expectations, findings showed that antecedent factors did not contribute as strongly to the capabilities-based beliefs as anticipated. It was a matter of great concern that the predictor indicators of the model, apart from self-efficacy, did not influence teachers' capabilities-based beliefs. This emphasizes the need for further investigation in order to find out which (other) factors may influence this type of belief. However, all antecedent factors were predictors of performance-based beliefs, providing a favourable basis for further research in the field.

Although the relationships were moderate and the antecedent factors did not explain a notably high percentage of the variance in the data, this study does deliver significant associations between antecedent factors and teachers' beliefs. Despite the fact that key predictor variables were identified through the literature, it should be noted that other factors which could potentially influence teachers' beliefs (e.g. age, gender, personality, specialized courses, and training) were not included in the study. Given that this is a preliminary study of beliefs and practices, the significant prediction based on these variables is encouraging, particularly since most of the associations among variables took the expected directions. However, these results invite further exploration into the antecedent factors influencing teachers' beliefs.

6.3 Limitations of the Study

The main limitation in this study stems from the self-reported, survey data collection method. One advantage of using self-reports is the possibility of re-cruiting a significant number of participants. Input from a large number of par-ticipants, in turn, affords a more accurate glimpse into the issued addressed. But as Chng (2012) argues, although self-reports deliver a substantially larger and more homogeneous data set sample, this may be due to common source and method variance. It would thus be preferable to combine quantitative and quali-tative methods in an empirical study, as this would also offer an in-depth look at the issue being investigated. Future studies, both quantitative and qualitative, are needed to determine more effectively the actual curriculum being implemented in a classroom. The field would also benefit from research on the factors that hin-der or promote the pedagogical praxis aimed at enhancing children's capabilities, regardless of their socio-economic background. Understanding teachers' beliefs is important in understanding classroom practices. Teachers, as professionals and front-line implementers, should be the ones who bear the responsibility for creating a pre-primary school environment in which children can flourish. The challenge of improving one's ways of exercising pedagogy to better serve the in-terests of children – and by extension, the community – is accomplished only by studying teachers' beliefs and how they put knowledge into practice in the classrooms. More specifically, this study's findings can be used as background information to perform focused intervention studies on teachers' beliefs and practices, especially with respect to socially disadvantaged children. The current research was designed as a cross-sectional study, and it does not permit inference of causal relations among the different variables. Longitudinal designs, which could be used to draw causal conclusions, would be of great value and are thus highly recommended for future research.

One source of threat to internal data validity is selection. Participants were not randomly assigned. As described above, study participants were drawn in a convenience sampling, because the subjects for the study were from a specif-ic geographical region and state. In contrast to random sampling, this directly limits making generalisations about the research findings from the respondents to apply to the entire target population, namely, pre-primary teachers currently working for the Ministry of Education and Religious Affairs in Greece. Due to the convenience sampling method, this sample may well be biased.

The researcher created the questionnaire for the purposes of this specific study. Therefore, there is no known validity or reliability information beyond the specific data collected here. Although the tool was pilot tested by the researcher, the questionnaire should be retested using other data samples to confirm validity and reliability.

A further limitation of this study is the absence of both male and minority voices. Because male pre-primary teachers are a single digit percentage of all pre-primary teachers, and due to the fact the vast majority of educators have Greek ethnicity and citizenship, it was not possible to investigate differences between male and female pre-primary teachers within this study, or to examine possible discrepancies among teachers from diverse ethnic backgrounds.

Despite these methodological limitations, this research still provides certain reliable inferences and especially critical indications of how to understand and explain pre-primary teachers' beliefs and practices. In addition, it provides a springboard for the use of the capability approach as a normative framework and as a counter narrative to a narraw and impoverished conception of early childhood education curriculum and it sets priorities for further research in similar fields. Given the fact that this is one of the first studies to ever investigate this particular subject, there are opportunities to refine and improve the methodologies developed here.

6.4 Future Implications

Despite the limitations of the current study, it still contributes to the theoretical and empirical understanding of teachers' perceptions and teaching in response to children's capabilities enhancement and academic learning acquisition. It also sheds light on teachers' professional development and support in Greece.

This study has served to initiate the process of gathering information on Greek pre-primary teachers' beliefs and practices, and it has opened a path towards unveiling the actual curriculum used in Greek pre-primary school. Its importance is both theoretical and practical, because it contributes to our understanding of teachers' thinking, particularly since the importance of pre-primary experiences is well acknowledged. If pre-primary school can help to ameliorate the effects of social disadvantage, then the role of the teachers in this process is undoubtedly critical. Certainly, teachers' beliefs and practices have an impact on the quality of children's pre-primary experience and on the benefits that it brings to children. Pre-primary teachers have a strong influence on children by their role in nurturing and teaching them, particularly in the present societal context in which the family is becoming de-/re-institutionalized and parents face highly demanding pressures from their workplaces. Pre-primary teachers are entrusted with the responsibility of shaping an optimal environment where children can flourish irrespective of their SES status; now more than ever, teachers are required to nurture their students. As a result, there is a need to address the over-emphasis on learning for the sake of obtaining purely academic knowledge at the exclusion of other kinds of knowledge or skills.

A comparison from an international perspective is helpful in expanding understanding of the cultural and international diversity in this field. In this Greek case, the findings have shown that teachers' beliefs predict classroom practices, and that antecedent factors do influence teachers' beliefs. However, the research was designed as a cross-sectional study and does not permit inferences on causality among the variables investigated. Therefore, causal attributions will require further longitudinal research.

This study was an initial step in the investigation of Greek pre-primary teachers' beliefs and practices. How teachers' ways of thinking recognise capabilities expansion and academic knowledge achievement offers insight into the actual curriculum being applied in Greek pre-primary education. In turn, these findingds could also be used as a tool in further teacher training. The model itself serves as a conceptual tool to understand how efficiently training should be designed, and where emphasis should be placed, namely to the pedagogues' beliefs which shape the information they receive from formal preparatory training and direct their subsequent decision-making in the classroom. Although the results must be viewed as tentative, a model for future research has been established here by the development of useful procedures for identifying the associations among teachers' beliefs and their practices, as well as the effect of certain antecedent factors on teachers' beliefs. It is worth noting that this study has provided data in an area where there had been previously much speculation, but little empirical evidence. More specifically, it constitutes an enlightening piece of work on the Greek case because the limited and sporadic research on the field in Greece up until this point did not provide a clear view of teachers' beliefs and practices. This study also serves as an alternative look at the vast body of literature that has accumulated on maximizing children's academic gains in pre-primary school.

The data gleaned from this study also provides information about how teachers are likely to respond to policy initiatives and curriculum innovations. The findings highlight the complexity of teaching, which should be of interest to policymakers, school administrators, and those responsible for teacher training in Greece.

Furthermore, this study contributes to further research on the Capability Approach by offering a new spectrum of thinking about capabilities at the earliest stage of the educational system. Although empirical and theoretical efforts have been made to shed light on the relationship between the Capability Approach and education, little attention has been given to early childhood education. Schooling may be extremely important in securing and expanding children's capabilities. The present study is unique in the field of early childhood education, as, there has been little (if any) research investigating an official curriculum from the perspective of the Capability Approach up until this point.

Not only could the findings of this study be used by policy implementers to understand current teachers' beliefs and practices, but the empirical model could also be used as a guide to plan better policy implementation and application in the educational context. In addition, these results could be beneficial to school administrators and teachers themselves who are looking to improve their school environments or professional practices, respectively. The questionnaire appears to be a promising instrument for the study of teachers' beliefs and practices. While the results indicate preliminary supportive evidence for this instrument; further work is needed to establish the potential value of the tool.

6.5 Recommendations

Based on the findings of this present study, the following directions for future research are suggested:

Further training based upon the needs of the teachers. Competent and well-trained early educators are the key to ensuring positive emotional, social, and cognitive outcomes in children. Professional preparation does not end by obtaining a university degree. On the contrary, educators have a constant need for continuing re-education, whether formal or informal, and should be engaging in continuous reflection of their own practices. Teachers constitute the most important factor in helping young children to adjust to the social sphere and flourish both socially and academically. It is therefore necessary to provide teachers with situations for self-examination and self-improvement, which in turn will help to enhance educational outcomes. Now more than any time in the past, there is greater awareness of the types of support professionals can provide to create productive learning environments for children. Political will, local leadership, engaged parents, and committed teachers are the ingredients needed to create a beneficial pre-primary setting for children. As Ryan & Grieshaber (2005) argue, enhancing children's language, cognitive, and early reading skills are important for early childhood teachers to know how to do, but if they are to be able to respond effectively to diverse student populations, then it is also necessary that they have an understanding of the politics of their work and the role of education in creating productive and socially competent members of society.

Researchers, policymakers, and teachers in the field, as along with parents, should be cautious about placing too much focus on academic achievement. The aim of the educational setting should be the all-round development of children and enhancing their capabilities, not predominantly on preparing them academically for entry into school. Human beings in general and children in particular acquire much more knowledge in informal settings than in a formal context. The debate on formal and informal learning in the literature draws on the image of an iceberg: the tip of an iceberg symbolizes formal learning while the bulk of learning takes place informally, below the surface. As Livingstone (2002) notes, informal learning is mostly invisible and massive. Katz (1999) suggested that the younger the children are, the more informal the learning environment should be. Although the aim of the formal context is to improve the current educational conditions, the result is often the opposite. Instead of providing enrichment to the children, it may result in intellectual burnout or social and emotional damage. It is important here to reflect more on what kind of a future a society wants to have. The current era is characterized by abundant information and advanced technology in a rapidly changing society. It seems unlikely that it will be possible to predict what knowledge will need to be acquired today to meet the requirements of the future. However, educators can certainly provide the nurturement to support the development of physically, emotionally, socially, and intellectually healthy children.

Children need to be seen as persons with a voice and as socially competent agents. Early childhood should not be perceived as a merely preparatory stage, a rehearsal for adulthood; children should not be regarded as passive receivers of an implemented policy and/or an applied pedagogy, but as actors who are able and deserve to be part of the process. Sünker and Bühler-Niederberger (2012) refer to the problem raised in Bernfeld's study *Sisiphos oder die Grenzen den Erziehung* [*Sisyphus, or the Limits of Education*], namely, that pedagogic work often fails to correspond to the reality of children's lives. They go on to argue that:

> it is now much more common to find acknowledgement that childhood should be regarded as a part of society and culture rather than a precursor of it; and that the children should be seen as already social actors not beings in the process of becoming such.

Empirical work in the field of early childhood (Dandy & Baker, 1998) has shown that children are competent social agents and have an active social world that is located beyond the audible and visual scrutiny of the teacher. The United

Nations Convention on the Rights of the Child (UNCRC) has advanced the debate and altered the view of children from being merely recipients of freedoms and services or beneficiaries of protective measures, to being subjects with rights and active participants in the actions impacting on them. The fundamental difference between present discussions about children's rights and those of previous years lies partly in this different conception of the child as deserving personal rights rather than simply protectionist rights (Sünker & Swiderek, 2007). Sünker and Moran-Ellis (International Encyclopaedia of Political Science) categorize those rights as: (a) relating to participation; and (b) seeking to enable children's voices to be heard in the process of decision making and democratic participation.

The concept of "minor politics" presented in Dahlberg and Moss (2005) reflects a wide political arena in which children as social agents address everyday issues that occur in pre-primary schools. Minor politics refer to "minor engagements which are cautious, modest, pragmatic, experimental, stuttering, tentative and concerned with the here and now, not with some fantasized future, with small concerns, petty details, the everyday and not the transcendental" (Dahlberg & Moss, 2005, p. 14). By transferring minor politics to the pre-primary school, children can have some control over the selection, pacing, and sequencing of the curriculum and act as agents throughout the pedagogical process.

References

Albright, J., & Myoung Park, H. (2009). Confirmatory *factor analysis using Amos, LISREL, Mplus, SAS/STAT CALIS*. Working paper. The University Information Technology Services (UTIS) Centre for Statistical and Mathematical Computing, Indiana University. Retrieved from http://www.indiana.edu/~statmath/stat/all/cfa/index.html

Alkire, S. (2003). *The capability approach as a development paradigm?* Material for the training session preceding the 3rd international conference on the capability approach, Pavia, pp. 1–18. Retrieved from http://www.capabilityapproach.com/pubs/461CAtraining_Alkire.pdf

Alkire, S. (2005). Why the capability approach? *Journal of Human Development*, 6(1), pp. 115–133. Retrieved from: http://websie.eclac.cl/mmp/doc/Alkire%20(2005)%20Why%20the%20capability%20approach.pdf

Alkire, S. (2007). *Choosing dimensions: The capability approach and multidimensional poverty* (Chronic Poverty Research Centre, Working Paper No. 88). Retrieved from: http://dx.doi.org/10.2139/ssrn.1646411

Andersen, P. L., & Hansen, M. N. (2012). Class and cultural capital – the case of class inequality in educational performance. *European Sociological Review*. 28(5), 607–621.

Andresen, S., Otto, H.- U., & Ziegler, H. (2006). Education and welfare: A pedagogical perspective on the capability approach. In *Freedom and social justice. Documentation of the 2006 International Conference of the Human Development and Capability Association* (pp. 1–34). Retrieved from http://www.capabilityapproach.com/pubs/3_3_Andresen.pdf

Andresen, S., Otto, H.- U., & Ziegler, H. (2008). Bildung as human development: An educational view on the capabilities approach. In H. – U. Otto, & H. Ziegler (Eds), *Capabilities – Handlugsbefähigung und Verwirklichungschancen in der Erziehungswissenschaft* (pp. 165–197). Wiesbaden, Germany: Verlag für Sozialwissenschaften.

Apple, M. (1982). Common curriculum and state control. *Discourse: Studies in the Cultural Politics of Education, 2*(2), 1–10

Apple, M. (1988). Social crisis and curriculum accords. *Educational Theory*, 38(2), 191–201.

Apple, M., & Jungck, S. (1990). You don't have to be a teacher to teach this unit: Teaching, technology and gender in the classroom. *American Educational Research Journal, 27*(2), 227–251.

Apple, M., & Teitelbaum, K. (1986). Are teachers losing control of their skills and curriculum? *Journal of Curriculum Studies, 18*(2), 177–184. Retrieved from http://dx.doi.org/10.1080/0022027860180207

Arreman, I., & Weiner, G. (2007). Gender, research and change in teacher education: A Swedish dimension. *Gender and Education, 19*(3), 317–337.

Ashiabi, G. (2000). Promoting the emotional development of preschoolers. *Early Childhood Education Journal, 28*(2), 79–84.

Atkinson, A. (1999). The contributions of Amartya Sen to welfare economics. *Scandinavian Journal of Economics, 101*(2), 173–190.

Ball, C. (1994). *Start right: The importance of early learning.* London, England: RSA.

Bandura, A. (1993). Perceived self-efficacy in cognitive development and functioning. *Educational Psychologist, 28*(2), 117–148.

Barnett, S. (1992). Benefits of compensatory preschool education. *The Journal of Human Resources, 27*(2), 279–312.

Bennett, J., & Kaga, Y. (2010). The integration of early childhood systems within education. *International Journal of Child Care and Education Policy, 4*(1), 35–43.

Benson McMullen, M. (1997). The effects of early childhood academic and professional experience on self perceptions and beliefs about developmentally appropriate practices. *Journal of Early Childhood Teacher Education, 18*(3), 55–68.

Benson McMullen, M. (1999). Characteristics of teachers who talk the DAP talk and walk the DAP walk. *Journal of Research in Childhood Education, 13*(2), 216–230.

Benson McMullen, & Alat, K. (2002). Education matters in the nurturing of the beliefs of preschool caregivers and teachers. *Early Childhood Research & Practice, 4*(2), 1–25.

Bernstein, B. (1975). Class and pedagogies: Visible and invisible, *Educational Studies, 1*(1), 23–41.

Bernstein, B. (1996). *Pedagogy, symbolic control and identity: theory, research, critique.* London: Taylor & Francis.

Bertrand, J. (2007). Preschool programs: Effective curriculum. Comments on Kagan and Kauerz and on Schweinhart. In E. Tremblay, G. Barr, & V. Peters (Eds.), *Encyclopedia on early childhood development [online]* (pp. 1–7). Montreal, Quebec: Centre of Excellence for Early Childhood Development. Downloaded from http://www.child-encyclopedia.com/documents/Bertran dANGxp.pdf

Bevanot, A., & Resh, N. (2003). Education governance, school autonomy and curriculum implementation: A comparative study of Arab and Jewish schools in Israel. *Journal of Curriculum Studies, 35*(2), 171–196.

Biggeri, M., Libanora, R., Mariani, S., & Menchini, L. (2004, September). Children establishing their capabilities: Preliminary results of the survey during the first children's world congress on child labour. Paper presented at the 4th International Conference on the Capability Approach, "Enhancing Human Security, University of Pavia, Italy. Retrieved from http://cfs.unipv.it/ca2004/papers/biggeri.pdf

Bredekamp, S. (1993). Myths about developmentally appropriate practice: A response to Fowell and Lawton. *Early Childhood Research Quarterly, 8*(1), 117–119.

Bredekamp, S, & Copple, C. (1997). *Developmentally appropriate practice in early childhood programs.* Washington, DC: National Association for the Education of Young Children (NAYEC).

Brooks-Gunn, J., & Duncan, G. J. (1997). The effects of poverty on children. *The Future of Children, 7*(2), 55–71.

Broström, S. (2009, September). Early childhood education – actual positions and future possibilities. *Paper presented at the conference "Konturen frühpädagogischer Hochschulbildung – Forschung, Lehre und Praxis verzahen," Berlin, Germany: Robert Bosch Foundation.*

Brown, F. (2012): The play behaviours of Roma children in Transylvania. *International Journal of Play, 1*(1), 64–74.

Buchanan, T., Burts, D., Bidner, J., White, F., & Charlesworth, R. (1998). Predictors of the developmental appropriateness of the beliefs and practices of first, second, and third grade teachers. *Early Childhood Research Quarterly, 13*(3), 459–483.

Burts, D., Hart, C., Charlesworth, R., & Kirk, L. (1990). A comparison of frequencies of stress behaviours observed in kindergarten children in classrooms with developmentally appropriate versus developmentally inappropriate instructional practices. *Early Childhood Research Quarterly, 5*(1), 407–423.

Burts, D., Hart, C., Charlesworth, R., Fleege, P., Mosley, J., & Thomasson, R. (1992). Observed activities and stress behaviours of children in developmentally appropriate and inappropriate kindergarten classrooms. *Early Childhood Research Quarterly, 7*(1), 297–318.

Caldas, S. J., & Bankston, C. (1997). Effect of school population socioeconomic status on individual academic achievement. *Journal of Educational Research, 90*(5), 269–277.

Campbell, F., Ramey, C., Pungello, E., Sparling, J., & Miller-Johnson, S. (2002). Early childhood education: Young adult outcomes from the Abecedarian project. *Applied Developmental Science, 6*(1), 42–57.

Cassidy, D., Buell, M., Pugh-Hoese, & S., Russell, S. (1995). The effect of education on child care teachers' beliefs and classroom quality: Year one evaluation of the TEACH early childhood associate degree scholarship program. *Early Childhood Research Quarterly, 10*(1), 171–183.

Charlesworth, R., Hart, C., Burts, D., & Hernandez, S. (1991). Kindergarten teachers' beliefs and practices. *Early Child Development and Care, 70*(1), 17–35. Retrieved from http://dx.doi.org/10.1080/0300443910700103

Charlesworth, R., Hart, C., Burts, D., Thomasson, R., Mosley, J., & Fleege, P. (1993). Measuring the developmentally appropriateness of kindergarten teachers' beliefs and practices. *Early Childhood Research Quarterly, 8*(1), 255–276.

Child, D. (1973). *Psychology and the teacher.* London, England: Hold, Rinehart and Winston.

Chng, G. (2012). Children's informal reasoning skills and epistemological beliefs within the family: The role of parenting practices, parental epistemological beliefs and family communication patterns (Dissertation. Bielefeld University, Germany). Retrieved from http://pub.uni-bielefeld.de/publication/2519185

Christenson, S. L., Rounds, T., & Gorney, D. (1992). Family factors and student achievement: An avenue to increase students' success. *School Psychology Quarterly, 7*(1), 178–206.

Chrysafidis, K. (2004). *Epistemological principles of preschool education: The preschool in the space of ideology and science,* Athens: tupothito – Giorgos Dardanos.

Chrysafidis, K. (2006). The new curriculum of the Greek kindergarten: Innovations in service of DEPPS. *Modern Kindergarten, 53*(1), 108–115.

Clark, D. (2005). Sen's capability approach and the many spaces of human wellbeing. *The Journal of Development Studies, 41*(8), 1339–1368.

Clark, D. (2006). The capability approach: Its development, critiques, and recent advances. GPRG-WPS-032. Retrieved from http://economics.ouls.ox.ac.uk/14051/1/gprg-wps-032.pdf

Clarke, K. (2006). Childhood, parenting and early intervention: A critical examination of the Sure Start national programme. *Critical Social Policy, 26*(4), 699–721.

Cohn, M., & Kottkamp, R. (1993). *Teachers: The missing voice in education.* Albany, NY: State University of New York Press.

Coolican, H. (2004). *Research methods and statistics in psychology.* London, England: Hodder & Stoughton.

Cortina, J. (1993). What is coefficient alpha? An examination of theory and applications. *Journal of Applied Psychology, 78*(1), 98–104.

Dahlberg, G., & Moss, P. (2005). *Ethics and politics in early childhood education. Contesting early childhood.* New York, NY: Routledge Falmer.

Danby, S., & Baker, C. (1998). "What is the problem?" Restoring social order in the preschool classroom. In I. Hutchby & J. Moran-Ellis (Eds.), *Children and social competence: Arenas of action* (pp. 157–186). London, England: Falmer Press.

Dean, H. (2009). Critiquing capabilities:the distractions of a beguiling concept. *Critical Social Policy, 29*(1), pp. 261–278.

Deci, E., Schwartz, A., Sheinman, L., & Ryan, R. (1981). An instrument to assess adult's orientation toward control versus autonomy with children: Reflections on intrinsic motivation and perceived competence. *Journal of Educational Psychology, 75*(5), 642–650.

Diehm, I., & Magyar-Haas, V. (2010). Language education – for the "good life"? In S. Andresen, I. Diehm, U. Sander, & H. Ziegler (Eds.), *Children and the good life: New challenges for research on children* (pp. 103–114). Dordrecht, Netherlands: Springer.

Diehm, I. (2011). Children as competent agents of their social realty, *BI.research, 38*(1), 22–25.

DiTommaso, M. (2006). *Measuring the well being of children using a capability approach: An application to Indian data.* Centre for household, income, labour & demographic economics, Working papers ChilD n. 05/2006.

Doliopoulou, E. (2000). The new curriculum for the kindergarten: Some first thoughts. *Modern Kindergarten, 26*(1), 72–77.

Doliopoulou, E. (2002). The full-day kindergarten and the Unified Cross-Thematic Curriculum Framework on kindergarten. *Modern Kindergarten, 35*(1), 8–12.

Doliopoulou, E. (2006). *System of early education/care and professionalization in Greece, SEEPRO Report, 1–19.* Retrieved from http://www.ifp.bayern.de/im peria/md/content/stmas/ifp/commissioned_report_greece.pdf

Education, Audiovisual and Culture Executive Agency (2009). *Tackling social and cultural inequalities through early childhood education and care in Europe.* Retrieved from http://www.eurydice.org

Edwards, C. (2002). *Three approaches from Europe: Waldorf, Montessori, and Reggio Emilia.* Paper 2, Faculty Publications, Department of Child, Youth, and Family Studies, Lincoln, NE: University of Nebraska. Retrieved from http://digitalcommons.unl.edu/famconfacpub/2

Einarsdottir, J., & Gardarsdottir, B. (2009). Parental participation: Icelandic play-school teachers' views. In Th. Papatheodorou & J. Moyles (Eds.), *Learning together in the early years: Exploring relational pedagogy* (pp. 196–217). London, England: Routledge.

Eisenberg, N. (2006). Handbook of child psychology. Vol. 3: Social, emotional and personality development. New York, NY: Willey.

Epstein, J. L. (1991). Effects on student achievement of teachers' practices of parent involvement. In S. Silvern (Ed.), *Advances in Reading/Language Research: Literacy through family, community, and school interaction* (Vol. 5, pp. 261–276). Greenwich, CT, JAI Press.

Eurostat (2011). *Marriage and divorce statistics*. Retrieved from: http://epp.euro stat.ec.europa.eu/statistics_explained/index.php/Marriage_and_divorce_sta tistics

Eurydice/Eurybase (2010). *Organisation of the education system in Greece 2009/ 2010*. Retrieved from http://eacea.ec.europa.eu/education/eurydice/docu ments/eurybase/eurybase_full_reports/EL_EN.pdf

Fabes, R., Eisenberg, N., Jones, S., Smith, M., Guthrie, I., Poulin, R., Shepard, S., & Friedman, J. (1999). Regulation, emotionality and preschoolers' socially competent peer interactions. *Child Development, 70*(2), 432–442.

Fang, Z. (1996). A review of research on teacher beliefs and practices. *Educational Research, 38*(1), 47–65.

Fendler, L. (2001). Educating flexible souls: The construction of subjectivity through devellopmentality and interaction. In K. Hultqvist & G. Dahlberg (Eds.), *Governing the child in the new millenium* (pp. 119–142). London, England: Routledge Falmer.

Fenech, M., Sumsion, J.,(2007): Early Childhood Teachers and Regulation: complicating power relations using Foucauldian lens, in: Contemporary Issues in Early Childhood, Vol. 8, No. 2, pp. 109–122.

Field, A. (2009). *Discovering statistics using SPSS* (3rd ed.). London, England: Sage.

Fishbein, M., & Ajzen, I. (1975). *Belief, attitude, intention and behavior: An introduction to theory and research*. Reading, MA: Addison-Wesley.

Fleer, M, Anning, A., & Cullen, J. (2009). A framework for conceptualising early childhood education. In: A. Anning, J. Cullen, M. Fleer (Eds.), Early childhood education. Society and Culture. Los Angeles, pp. 187–204.

Flouris, G., & Pasias, G. (2003). A critical appraisal of curriculum reform in Greece (1980-2002): Trends, challenges, and perspectives. *European Education, 35*(3), 73–90.

Fowell, N., & Lawton, J. (1992). An alternative view of developmentally appropriate practice in early childhood education. *Early Childhood Research Quarterly, 7*(1), 53–73.

Frangos, C. (1993). A Child Development Centre (C.D.C.) based on the world of work and everyday life: A case of quality education provision for 2.5–5 year old children. *European Early Childhood Education Research Journal, 1*(1), 41–52. Downloaded from http://dx.doi.org/10.1080/13502939385207341

Frangos, C. (2002). The curricula and the "new" study programs. *Modern Education, 125*(1), pp. 60 – 68 (in greek: Διάλογος για την παιδεία και την εκπαιδευση: Τα αναλυτικά προγράμματα και τα «νέα» προγράμματα σπουδών, *Σύγχρονη Εκπαίδευση*)

Frijda, N. (2000). Emotions. In K. Pawlik & M. Rosenzweig (Eds), *International handbook of psychology* (pp. 207–222). Thousand Oaks, CA: Sage.

Fullan, M. (1989). *Implementing educational change: What we know*. PHREE Background Paper Series, Document No. PHREE/89/18. Retrieved from http://www-wds.worldbank.org/external/default/WDSContentServer/WDSP/IB/1989/07/01/000009265_3960929042553/Rendered/PDF/multi_page.pdf

Garland, R. (1991). The mid-point on a rating scale: Is it desirable? *Marketing Bulletin, 2*(1), 66–70. Retrieved from http://marketing-bulletin.massey.ac.nz/v2/mb_v2_n3_garland.pdf

Gasper, D. (2004). Human well-being: Concepts and conceptualizations. *UNU – WIDER, Discussion Paper, 2004/06*, 1–34. Retrieved from http://www.wider.unu.edu/publications/working-papers/discussion-papers/2004/en_GB/dp2004-006/_files/78091738193724471/default/dp2004-006.pdf

Gess-Newsome, J. (2002). Pedagogical content knowledge: An introduction and Orientation. *Contemporary Trends and Issues in Science Education, 6*(1), 3–17.

Goelman, H., Andersen, C., Anderson, J., Gouzouasis, P., Kendrick, M., Kindler, A., Porath, M., & Koh, J. (2003). Early childhood education. In W. Reynolds & G. Miller (Eds.), *Handbook of psychology, Vol. 7, Educational psychology* (pp. 285–331). New York, NY: Wiley.

Green, K. (2000). Exploring the everyday "philosophies" of physical education teachers from a sociological perspective. *Sport, Education, and Society, 5*(2), 109–129.

Grieshaber, S. (2009). Equity and quality in the early years of schooling. *Curriculum Perspectives, 29*(1), 91–97.

Grinsburg, K. (2007). The importance of play in promoting healthy child development and maintaining strong parent-child bonds. *Pediatrics, 119*(1), 182–191.

Guimaraes, A., & Youngman, M. (1995). Portuguese preschool teachers' beliefs about early literacy development. *Journal of Research in Reading, 18*(1), 39–52.

Gulielmi, S., & Tatrow,K. (1998). Occupational stress, burnout and health in teachers: A methodological and theoretical analysis. *Review of Educational Research, 68*(1), 61–99. Retrieved from http://rer.sagepub.com/content/68/1/61. full.pdf

Guskey, T. (2002). Professional development and teacher change. *Teachers and Training: Theory and Practice, 8*(3), 381–391.

Hair, J., Black, W., Babin, B., & Anderson, R. (2010). *Multivariate data analysis. A global perspective.* Upper Saddle River, NJ: Prentice-Hall.

Hardy Snyder, M., & Fu, V. (1990). The effects of specialized education and job experience on early childhood teachers' knowledge of developmentally appropriate practice. *Early Childhood Research Quarterly, 5*(1), 69–78.

Hertzog, N. (2001). Reflections and impressions from Reggio Emilia: "it's not about art". *Early Childhood Research and Practice, 3*(1), 1–10.

Hinson, J., DiStefano, Ch., & Daniel, C. (2003). The Internet Self-Perception Scale: Measuring elementary students' levels of self-efficacy regarding Internet use. *Journal of Educational Computing Research, 29*(2), 209–22.

Hirsh-Pasek, K., Hyson, M., & Rescorla, L. (1990). Academic environments in preschool: Do they pressure or challenge young children. *Early Education & Development, 1*(6), 401–403.

Hirsh-Pasek, K. (1991). Pressure or challenge in preschool? How academic environments affect children. *New Directions for Child Development, 53*(1), 39–46.

Hopf, D., Hatzichristou, C. (1999): Teacher gender-related influences in Greek schools, in: British Journal of Educational Psychology, Vol. 68, No. 1, pp. 1–18

House, R. (2002). The central place of play in early learning and development. *The Mother* Magazine, *2*(1), 44–46. Reprinted in V. and P. Robinson (eds*), Stretch Marks: Selected Articles from* The Mother *Magazine*, Penrith, Cumbria: Starflower Press, 2009, 378–384. Retrieved from: http://openeyecampaign. wordpress.com/research-and-supporting-literature/the-central-place-of-play-in-early-learning-and-development/

Howes, C., Burchinal, M., Pianta, R., Bryant, D., Early, D., Clifford, R., & Barbarin, O. (2008). Ready to learn? Children's pre-academic achievement in pre-kindergarten programs. *Early Childhood Research Quarterly, 23*(3), 27–50.

Hughes, B.(2003). *Evolutionary playwork and reflective analytic practice.* New York: Routledge.

Israel, G. (1992). Determining sample size. *Fact Sheet PEOD-6,* 1–5. Retrieved from http://edis.ifas.ufl.edu/pdffiles/PD/PD00600.pdf

Jalongo, M., Fennimore, B., Pattnaik, J., Laverick, D., Brewster, J., & Mutuku, M. (2004). Blended perspectives: A global vision for high-quality early childhood education. *Early Childhood Education Journal, 32*(3), 143–155.

Jensen, B. (2009). A Nordic approach to early childhood education (ECE) and socially endangered children. *European Early Childhood Education Research Journal, 17*(1), 7–21.

Jones, L., Burts, D., Buchanan, T., & Jambunathan, S. (2000). Beginning pre-kindergarten and kindergarten teachers' beliefs and practices: Supports and barriers to developmentally appropriate practices. *Journal of Early Childhood Teacher Education, 21*(3), 397–410. Retrieved from http://dx.doi.org/10.1080/0163638000210310

Kagan, D. (1992). Implications of research on teacher belief. *Educational Psychologist, 27*(1), 65–90.

Kamerman, S. (2006). *A global history of early childhood education and care.* Background paper prepared for the Education for All Global Monitoring Report 2007, Strong foundations: early childhood care and education. Retrieved from http://unesdoc.unesco.org/images/0014/001474/147470e.pdf

Karras, K. (2010). Teacher education in Greece: Training, issues and challenges for teacher profession,. In K. G. Karras & C.C. Wolhuter (Eds.), *International Handbook on Teacher Education Worldwide* (Vol. 1, pp. 291–304). Athens, Greece: Atrapos.

Katz, L. (1972). *Developmental stages of preschool teachers.* Clearinghouse on Early Childhood Education, Urbana, Illinois. Retrieved from http://eric.ed.gov/PDFS/ED057922.pdf

Katz, L. (1999). *Another look at what young children should be learning.* ERIC Digest. Champaign, IL: ERIC Clearinghouse on Elementary and Early Childhood Education.

Kauppinen, K., Haavio-Mannila, E., Kandolin, I. (1989): Who benefits from working in non-traditional workroles? Interaction patterns and quality of work, Acta Sociologica, Vol. 32, No. 4, pp. 389–403

Kelly, A., & Berthelsen, D. (1995). Preschool teachers' experience of stress. *Teaching and Teacher Education, 11*(4), 345–357.

Kessler, S. (1991). Alternative perspectives on early childhood education. *Early Childhood Research Quarterly, 6*(1), 183–197.

Kitsaras, G. (2001). *Preschool pedagogy.* Self-published.

Kitsaras, G. (2004). *Programs and methodology of preschool didactics.* Self-published.

Kline, R. (2011). *Principles and practice of structural equation modelling.* New York, NY: Guilford Press.

Koutsouvanou, E. (2006). Some views on the Unified Cross-Thematic Curriculum Framework (DEPPS). *Modern Kindergarten, 53*(1), 96–106.

Kuklys, W., & Robeyns, I. (2004). Sen's capability approach to welfare economics, CWPE 0415. Retrieved from https://papers.econ.mpg.de/esi/discussionpapers/2004-03.pdf

Lascarides, C., & Hinitz, B. (2000). *History of early childhood education*. New York. NY: Falmer Press.

Lee Stevenson, D., & Baker, D. (1991). State control of the curriculum and classroom instruction. *Sociology of Education, 64*(1), 1–10.

Lindsay, P., & Lindsay, C. (1987). Teachers in preschools and child care centres: Overlooked and undervalued. *Child & Youth Care Quarterly, 16*(2), 91–105.

Livingstone, D. (2002). Mapping the iceberg. *NALL Working Paper, 54*. Retrieved from http://www.nall.ca/res/54DavidLivingstone.pdf

Mahon, R. (2010). After Neo-Liberalism? The OECD, the World Bank and the child. *Global Social Policy, 10*(2), 172–192.

Mayer, J., Salovey, P., & Caruso, D. (2008). Emotional intelligence: New ability or eclectic traits? *American Psychologist, 63*(6), 503–517.

McLachlan, C., Fleer, M., & Edwards, S. (2010). *Early childhood curriculum: Planning, assessment and implementation*. Cambridge, England: Cambridge University Press.

Mercilliott Hewett, V. (2001). Examining the Reggio Emilia approach to early childhood education. *Early Childhood Education Journal, 29*(2), 95–100.

Ministry of Education (1996). *Te Wariki, Early Childhood Curriculum*. Wellington, New Zealand: Learning Media.

Morris, S., Silk, S., Steinberg, L., Myers, S., & Robnson, R. (2007). The role of the family context in the development of emotion regulation. *Social Development,16*(2), 361–368.

Moss, P., & Bennett, J. (2006). *Toward a new pedagogical meeting place? Bringing early childhood into the education system*. Briefing paper for a Nuffield Educational Seminar, 26 September 2006. Retrieved from http://89.28.209.149/fileLibrary/pdf/briefingpaper_Moss_Bennett.pdf

National curriculum guidelines on early childhood education and care in Finnland (2003). *STAKES*. Retrieved from http://www.thl.fi/thl-client/pdfs/267671cb-0ec0-4039-b97b-7ac6ce6b9c10

Norberg, K., & Johansson, O. (2010). The ethical dimensions of curriculum leadership in Scandinavian countries. *Journal of Educational Administration, 48*(3), 327–336.

Nores, M., Belfield, C., Barnett, S., & Schweinhart, L. (2005). Updating the economic impacts of the High/Scope Perry preschool program. *Educational Evaluation and Policy Analysis, 27*(3), 245–261.

Nutbrown, C., & Abbot, L. (2001). *Experiencing Reggio Emilia – Implications for preschool provision*. Buckingham, England: Open University Press.

Nussbaum, M. (2006). Education and democratic citizenship: Capabilities and quality education. *Journal of Human Development, 7*(3), 385–395.

Nussbaum, M. (2007). *Frontiers of justice: Disability, nationality, species membership social contracts and three unsolved problems of justice*. Cambridge, MA: Harvard University Press.

Nussbaum, M. (2010). *Not for profit – why democracy needs humanities*. Princeton, NJ: Princeton University Press.

Nussbaum, M. (2011). *Creating capabilities – the human development approach*. Cambridge, MA: Belknap/Harvard University Press.

Oatley, K., & Johnson-Laird, P. (1987). Towards a cognitive theory of emotions. *Cognition & Emotion, 1*(1), 29–50.

Oberhuemer, P., Schreyer, I., & Neuman, M. (2010). *Professionals in early childhood education and care systems: European profiles and perspectives*. Opladen, Germany: Barbara Budrich Publishers.

Opper, S. (1993). Kindergarten Education: Cinderella of the Hong Kong education system. In A. B. M. Tsui & I. Johnson (Eds.), *Teacher education and development* (pp. 80–89). Hong Kong: The University of Hong Kong, Faculty of Education (Education Papers No. 18).

Osmani, S. (2000). Human rights to food, health, and education. *Journal of Human Development, 1*(2), 273–298.

Pajares, F. (1992). Teachers' beliefs and educational research: Cleaning up a messy construct. *Review of Educational Research, 62*(3), 307–332.

Papadopoulos, F., & Tsakloglou, P. (2005). *Social exclusion in the EU: A capability-based approach*. EI Working Paper. Retrieved from http://www2.lse.ac.uk/europeanInstitute/LEQS/EIWP2005-01.pdf

Penn, H. (2002). The World Bank's view of early childhood, *Childhood, 9*(1), 118–132.

Piaget, J. (1951). *Psychology of intelligence*. London, England: Routledge.

Phillips, D., & Stipek, D. (1993). Early formal schooling: are we promoting achievement or anxiety? *Applied & Preventive Psychology, 2*(1), pp. 141–150.

RAND (2005). Proven benefits of early childhood interventions. RB–9145–PNC, 1–5. Retrieved from: http://www.rand.org/pubs/research_briefs/RB9145/index1.html

Raver, C. (2003). Young children's emotional development and school readiness. *Clearinghouse on Elementary and Early Childhood Education*, EDO-PS-03-8.

Reynolds, A. (1997). *The Chicago child-parent centers: A longitudinal study of extended early childhood intervention*. Institute for Research on Poverty, Discussion Paper no. 1126–97. Retrieved from http://www.irp.wisc.edu/publica tions/dps/pdfs/dp. 12697.pdf

Rich, Y. (1993). Stability and change in teacher expertise. *Teacher & Teacher Education, 9*(2), 137–146.

Richards, C., & Sanderson, J. (1999). The role of imagination in facilitating deductive reasoning in 2-, 3- and 4- year-olds. *Cognition, 72*(1), B1–B9.

Richardson, V. (2003). Preservice teachers' beliefs. In J.Raths & A. McAninch, *Teacher beliefs and classroom performance: the impact of teacher education,* (pp. 1–22), Advances in teacher education (Vol. 6). United States of America: Information Age Publishing Inc.

Rindskopf, D., & Rose, T. (1988). Some theory applications of confirmatory second-order factor analysis. *Multivariate Behavioural Research, 23*(1), 51–67.

Robeyns, I. (2000). *An unworkable idea or a promising alternative? Sen's capability approach re-examined*. Retrieved from http://www.econ.kuleuven.ac.be/ eng/ew/discussionpapers/Dp. 00/DPS0030.pdf

Robeyns, I. (2003, September). *The Capability Approach: An interdisciplinary introduction*. Paper presented to the Training Course preceding the 3rd International Conference on the Capability Approach, Pavia, Italy. Retrieved from http://www.soc.spbu.ru/img/up/files/File/1.8%20Robeyns%20The%20Capa bility%20Approach.%20An%20Interdisciplinary%20Introduction.pdf

Robeyns, I. (2005). The capability approach: A theoretical survey. *Journal of Human Development, 6*(1), 93–114.

Robeyns, I. (2006). Three models of education: Rights, capabilities and human capital. *Theory and Research in Education, 4*(1), 69–84.

Ryan, S., & Grieshaber, S. (2005). Shifting from developmental to postmodern practices in early childhood teacher education. *Journal of Teacher Education, 56,* 34–45.

Saito, M. (2003). Amartya Sen's capability approach to education: A critical exploration. *Journal of Philosophy of Education, 37*(1), 17–33.

Salais, R. (2011). The capability approach and deliberative democracy. Contribution to the international conference *"Human Development Perspectives"*, Center for Education and Capability Research, Bielefeld University, 26th/27th June, 1–16.

Saracho, O. (2002). Young children's creativity and pretend play. *Early Child Development and Care, 172*(5), 431–438.

Schlotter, M., Schwerdt, G., & Woessmann, L. (2009). Econometric methods for causal evaluation of education policies and practices: A non-technical guide. *Education Economics, 19*(2), 109–137.

Schmitt, N. (1996). Uses and abuses of coefficient alpha. *Psychological Assessment, 8*(4), 350–353.

Schreiber, J., Nora, A., Stage, F., Barlow, E., & King, J. (2006). Reporting structural equation modelling and confirmatory factor analysis results: A review. *Journal of Educational Research, 99*(6), 323–337.

Schweinhart, L., & Weikart, D. (1997). The High/Scope preschool curriculum comparison study through age 23. *Early Childhood Research Quarterly, 12*(1), 117–143.

Sen, A. (1980). Equality of what? In S. McMurrin (Ed.), *The Tanner Lectures on Human Values*, Cambridge University Press. Reprinted in Sen (1982), ch. 16, available from http://tannerlectures.utah.edu/lectures/documents/sen80.pdf

Sen, A. (1993). Capability and well-being. In M. Nussbaum, & A. Sen (Eds.), *The quality of life* (pp. 30–53). Oxford, England: Clarendon Press.

Sen, A. (2010). *The idea of justice*. London, England: Penguin Books.

Sims-Schouten, W. (2000). Child care services and parents' attitudes in England, Finland and Greece. In A. Pfenning & T. Bahle (Eds.), *Families and Family Policies in Europe: Comparative Perspectives* (pp. 270–288). Frankfurt/M, Germany: Peter Lang.

Singer, J., & Singer, D. (2005). Preschooler's imaginative play as precursor of narrative consciousness. *Imagination, Cognition and Personality, 25*(2), 97–117.

Singer, D., & Singer, J. (2007). *Imagination and play in the electronic age*. Cambridge, MA; Harvard University Press.

Smith, M., & Shepard, L. (1988). Kindergarten readiness and retention: A qualitative study of teachers' beliefs and practices. *American Educational Research Journal, 25*(3), 307–333.

Sofou, E., & Tsafos, V. (2010). Preschool teachers' understandings of the national preschool curriculum in Greece. *Early Childhood Education Journal, 37*(1), 411–420. doi:10.1007/s10643-009-0368-2

Sofou, E. (2010). Recent trends in early childhood curriculum: The case of Greek and English national curricula. In D. Mattheou (Ed.), *Changing educational landscapes: Educational policies, schooling systems and higher education – a comparative perspective* (pp. 227–240). Dordrecht, Netherlands: Springer.

Soler, J., & Miller, L. (2003). The struggle for early childhood curricula: A comparison of the English Foundation Stage curriculum, Te Wāriki, and Reggio Emilia. *International Journal of Early Years Education, 11*(1), 57–68.

Sroufe, A. (1997). *Emotional development: The organization of emotional life in the early years.* Cambridge Studies in Social and Emotional Development. New York, NY: Cambridge University Press.

Stipek, D., Daniels, D., Galluzzo, D., & Milburn, S. (1992). Characterizing early childhood education programs for poor and middle-class children. *Early Childhood Research Quarterly, 7*(1), 1–9.

Stipek, D., & Byler, P. (1997). Early childhood education teachers: Do they practice what they preach? *Early Childhood Research Quarterly, 12*(1), 305–325.

Sünker, H., & Swiderek, T. (2007). Politics of childhood, democracy and communal life: Conditions of political socialization and education, *Policy Futures in Education, 5*(3), 303–314.

Sünker, H., & Bühler-Niederberger, D. (2012). From socialization research to the sociology of childhood: Advances and hostages. *Pedagogy – theory & praxis, 5*(1), 7–26.

Terzi, L. (2007). The capability to be educated. In M. Walker & E. Unterhalter (Eds.), *Amartya Sen's capability approach and social justice in education* (pp. 25–43). New York, NY: Palgrave Macmillan.

Tsatsaroni, A., Ravanis, K., & Falagas, A. (2003). Studying the recontextualisation of science in pre-school classrooms: Drawing on Bernstein's insights into teaching and learning practices. *International Journal of Science and Mathematics Education, 1*(1), 385–417.

Tsigilis, N., Grammatikopoulos, V., & Koustelios, A. (2007). Applicability of the teachers' sense of efficacy scale to educators teaching innovative programs. *International Journal of Educational Management, 21*(7), 634–642.

Udwin, O. (1983). Imaginative play training as an intervention method with institutionalized preschool children. *British Journal Educational Psychology, 53*(1), 32–39.

UNESCO Policy Brief on Early Childhood (2004). *The early childhood workforce in "developed" countries: Basic structures and education.* No 27. Paris, France: UNESCO.

Vakil, S., Freeman, R., & Swim, T. J. (2003). The Reggio Emilia approach and inclusive early childhood programs. *Early Childhood Education Journal, 30*(3), 187–192.

Valkenburg, P. (2001). *Television and the child's developing imagination* In J. Singer & D. Singer (Eds.), *Handbook of children and the media* (pp. 121–134). Thousand Oaks, CA: Sage.

Vandell, D. (2004). Early child care: The known and the unknown. *Merrill-Palmer Quarterly, 50*(3), 387–414.

Vartuli, S. (1999). How early childhood teacher beliefs vary across grade level. *Early Childhood Research Quarterly, 14*(4), 489–514.

Vrinioti, K., Kiridis, A., Sivropoulou – Thedosiadou, E., Chrysafides, K., Parents' guide, in Greek: Βρυνιώτη, Κ., Κυρίδης, Α., Σιβροπούλου – Θεοδοσιάδου, Ε., Χρυσαφίδης, Κ., *Οδηγός Γονέα*, ΥΠΕΠΘ, Ειδική Υπηρεσία Επιλογής Προγραμμάτων ΚΠΣ. Retrieved from http://nip-oloimero.sch.gr/appdata/documents/odigos%20gonea(lr).pdf

Vygotsky, L. (2004). Imagination and creativity in childhood. *Journal of Russian and East European Psychology* (English Translation 2004: M. E. Sharpe, Inc., from the Russian text: Voobrazehenie I tvorchestvo v detskom vozraste, Moscow: Prosveshchenie, 1967), *42*(1), 7–97.

Wang, J., Elicker, J., McMullen, M. & Mao, S. (2008). Chinese and American preschool teachers' beliefs about early childhood curriculum. *Early Childhood Development and Care,178*(3), 227–249.

Walker, M., & Unterhalter, E. (2007). The capability approach: Its potential for work in education. In M. Walker & E. Unterhalter (Eds.), *Amartya Sen's Capability Approach and social justice in education* (pp. 1–18). London, England: Palgrave Macmillan.

Weiner, G., Kallos, D. (2000): Positively Women: Professionalism and Practice in Teaching and Teacher Education, paper presented to the symposium "Teacher Education in Europe: Current Tendencies and Prospects in a Comparative Perspective, at AERA, in New Orleans April 24–28

Westwood, P., Knight, B., & Redden, E. (1997). Assessing teachers' beliefs about literacy acquisition – Effects of sophisticated exposure and support for meaning. *Journal of Research Reading, 20*(1), 224–235.

Wien, C. (1996). Time, work, and developmentally appropriate practice. *Early Childhood Research Quarterly, 11*(1), 377–403.

Winn, R. (1959). *John Dewey: Dictionary of Education.* Westport, CT: Greenwood Press.

Williams, L., & Fromberg, D. P. (Eds.). (1992). *Encyclopaedia of early childhood education.* New York, NY: Garland.

Wolff, J., & De-Shalit, A. (2007). *Disadvantage.* Oxford, England: Oxford University Press.

Wood, E., & Attfield, J. (2005). *Play, learning & the early childhood curriculum.* London, England: Sage.

Wood, E. (2010). *New directions in play: Learning, pedagogy and curriculum.* Froebel College Early Childhood Conference, Dublin, May 21st.

Woolfolk, A., & Hoy, W. (1990). Prospective teachers' sense of efficacy and beliefs about control. *Journal of Educational Psychology, 82*(1), 81–91.

Woolley, S., Benjamin, W., & Woolley, A. (2004). Construct validity of a self-report measure of teacher beliefs related to constructivist and traditional approaches to teaching and learning. *Educational & Psychological Measurement,* *64*(2), 319–331.

Yotyodying, S. (2006). Factors affecting decision making on university choice of graduate students in education: A multiple discriminant analysis. *Journal of Research Methodology, 19*(2), 215–248.

Appendix: Questionnaire in Greek and in English

Το παρόν ερωτηματολόγιο απευθύνεται σε νηπιαγωγούς στοχεύοντας να διερευνήσει τις πεποιθήσεις και τις πρακτικές τους, έτσι ώστε να εκμαιεύσει σημαντικές πληροφορίες για την παιδαγωγική εργασία του Νηπιαγωγείου.

Η συμπλήρωσή του είναι εξαιρετικής σημασίας για την ερευνήτρια και σας παρακαλεί να αφιερώσετε 30 λεπτά από τον χρόνο σας. Διαβεβαιώνεται πως θα διασφαλιστεί η ανωνυμία των συμμετεχόντων και οι απαντήσεις που θα δοθούν θα παραμείνουν απόλυτα εμπιστευτικές.

Ευχαριστώ θερμά για την συνεργασία.

A1. Φύλο

Άνδρας ☐
Γυναίκα ☐

A2. Πανεπιστημιακή Εκπαίδευση

ΝΑΙ ☐ ΟΧΙ ☐
Αν ναι, σε ποιό Πανεπιστήμιο:

_____

A3. Εξομοίωση

ΝΑΙ ☐ ΟΧΙ ☐

A4. Σπουδές
Πτυχίο Παιδ. Ακαδημίας ☐ Πτυχίο☐ Μεταπτυχιακό ☐ Διδακτορικό ☐

A5. Ηλικία

20–30 ☐ 31–40 ☐ 41 και άνω ☐

A6. Έτη Προϋπηρεσίας

Πόσα χρόνια εργασιακής εμπειρίας έχετε σαν νηπιαγωγός

Δεν έχω ☐ 1 χρόνο ☐ 2 χρόνια ☐ 3 χρόνια ☐ 4 χρόνια ☐ 5 χρόνια και άνω ☐

Β1. Παρακαλώ συμπληρώστε σταυρώνοντας το κουτάκι που αντικατοπτρίζει σε μεγαλύτερο βαθμό τις προσωπικές σας πεποιθήσεις.

	Καθόλου σημαντικό	Οχι ιδιαίτερα σημαντικό	Αρκετά σημαντικό	Εξαιρετικά σημαντικό
	↓	↓	↓	↓
1) Είναι _____ για τα παιδιά να βελτιώσουν τις μαθηματικές τους δεξιότητες.	☐	☐	☐	☐
2) Είναι _____ για τα παιδιά να αλληλεπιδρούν με τις πιθανές εναλλακτικές λύσεις κατά την διαδικασία επίλυσης προβλημάτων.	☐	☐	☐	☐
3) Είναι _____ για τα παιδιά να αναπτύξουν την ικανότητα να αναγνωρίζουν οικείες λέξεις στο περιβάλλον και μέσα σε κείμενα.	☐	☐	☐	☐
4) Είναι _____ για τα παιδιά να απομνημονεύουν πολύ μικρά κείμενα προκειμένου να συνειδητοποιήσουν, σταδιακά, στοιχεία της γλώσσας (λ.χ. συλλαβές).	☐	☐	☐	☐
5) Είναι _____ για τα παιδιά να έχουν την ελευθερία να καθορίζουν την εξέλιξη μιας δραστηριότητας.	☐	☐	☐	☐
6) Είναι _____ για τα παιδιά να έχουν την ελευθερία να σχεδιάζουν και να οργανώνουν μόνα τους το δραματικό παιχνίδι.	☐	☐	☐	☐

Παρακαλώ επιλέξτε δύο από τις παραπάνω φράσεις που κατά την γνώμη σας είναι οι πιο σημαντικές. Στην ακόλουθη γραμμή σημειώστε τον αριθμό που τις αντιπροσωπεύει (1-6)

α)_____

β)_____

	Καθόλου σημαντικό	Οχι ιδιαίτερα σημαντικό	Αρκετά σημαντικό	Εξαιρετικά σημαντικό
	↓	↓	↓	↓
7) Είναι _____ για τα παιδιά να εμπλουτίζουν τις γνώση τους μέσω του παιχνιδιού.	☐	☐	☐	☐
8) Είναι _____ για τα παιδιά να συμμετέχουν στις δραστηριότητες που οργανώνει η νηπιαγωγός.	☐	☐	☐	☐
9) Είναι _____ για τα παιδιά να έχουν χρόνο για ελεύθερο παιχνίδι.	☐	☐	☐	☐
10) Είναι _____ για τα παιδιά να λαμβάνουν μέρος σε ψυχαγωγικές δραστηριότητες.	☐	☐	☐	☐
11) Είναι _____ οι παιγνιώδεις δραστηριότητες να βασίζονται στα ενδιαφέροντα των παιδιών.	☐	☐	☐	☐
12) Είναι _____ το παιχνίδι των παιδιών σε υπαίθριους χώρους να περιλαμβάνει οργανωμένες δραστηριότητες.	☐	☐	☐	☐

Παρακαλώ επιλέξτε δύο από τις παραπάνω φράσεις που κατά την γνώμη σας είναι οι πιο σημαντικές. Στην ακόλουθη γραμμή σημειώστε τον αριθμό που τις αντιπροσωπεύει (7–12)

α)_____

β)_____

	Καθόλου σημαντικό	Οχι ιδιαίτερα σημαντικό	Αρκετά σημαντικό	Εξαιρετικά σημαντικό
	↓	↓	↓	↓
13) Είναι _____ για τα παιδιά να έχουν την ευκαιρία να συμμετέχουν σε δραστηριότητες όπου οι εμπειρίες τους θα αποκτώνται με την χρήση όλων των αισθήσεων.	☐	☐	☐	☐
14) Είναι _____ για τα παιδιά να μαθαίνουν μέσα από ένα σχέδιο εργασίας (ακόμη κι αν δεν χρησιμοποιούν όλες τους τις αισθήσεις).	☐	☐	☐	☐
15) Είναι _____ για τα παιδιά να έχουν την ελευθερία να χρησιμοποιούν την φαντασία τους προκειμένου να καθορίσουν την πορεία μιας δραστηριότητας.	☐	☐	☐	☐
16) Είναι _____ για τα παιδιά να οργανώνουμε τις δραστηριότητες εκ των προτέρων έτσι ώστε να αποφευχθούν απρόσμενες εξελίξεις.	☐	☐	☐	☐
17) Είναι _____ να ενισχύουμε την φαντασία των παιδιών προς χάρη των μαθησιακών δυνατοτήτων τους.	☐	☐	☐	☐
18) Είναι _____ για τα παιδιά να συζητούν με την νηπιαγωγό για την συναισθηματική επίδραση που έχει σε αυτά ένας διαπλεκτισμός, τσακωμός, κ.τ.λ.	☐	☐	☐	☐

Παρακαλώ επιλέξτε δύο από τις παραπάνω φράσεις που κατά την γνώμη σας είναι οι πιο σημαντικές. Στην ακόλουθη γραμμή σημειώστε τον αριθμό που τις αντιπροσωπεύει (13–18)

α)_____

β)_____

	Καθόλου σημαντικό	Οχι ιδιαίτερα σημαντικό	Αρκετά σημαντικό	Εξαιρετικά σημαντικό
	↓	↓	↓	↓
19) Είναι _____ για τα παιδιά να εμπλουτίζουν τη γνώση τους μέσα από την αλληλεπίδραση με ομιλίκους.	☐	☐	☐	☐
20) Είναι _____ για τα παιδιά να αναπτύξουν θετικά συναισθήματα πρός την μάθηση.	☐	☐	☐	☐
21) Είναι _____ για τα παιδιά να συνάπτουν φιλίες με ομιλίκους.	☐	☐	☐	☐
22) Είναι _____ για τα παιδιά να αναπτύξουν τις επικοινωνιακές τους δεξιότητες.	☐	☐	☐	☐
23) Είναι _____ για τα παιδιά να μάθουν να συνεργάζονται.	☐	☐	☐	☐
24) Είναι _____ για τα παιδιά να μάθουν τους κοινωνικούς κανόνες που οφείλουν να ακολουθούν όταν λαμβάνουν μέρος σε μια συζήτηση στον κύκλο.	☐	☐	☐	☐

Παρακαλώ επιλέξτε δύο από τις παραπάνω φράσεις που κατά την γνώμη σας είναι οι πιο σημαντικές. Στην ακόλουθη γραμμή σημειώστε τον αριθμό που τις αντιπροσωπεύει (19–24)

α)_____

β)_____

	Καθόλου σημαντικό	Οχι ιδιαίτερα σημαντικό	Αρκετά σημαντικό	Εξαιρετικά σημαντικό
	↓	↓	↓	↓
25) Είναι _____ για τα παιδιά να ενθαρρύνονται να γράφουν όπως μπορούν.	☐	☐	☐	☐
26) Είναι _____ για τα παιδιά να εθίζονται να απομνημονεύουν και να απαγγέλουν ποιήματα, να μαθαίνουν λαχνίσματα, αινίγματα, γλωσσοδέτες, κ.α.	☐	☐	☐	☐
27) Είναι _____ για τα παιδιά να αναγνωρίζουν και να συγκρίνουν διαφορετικές μορφές του γραπτού λόγου, όπως π.χ. το χειρόγραφο και το έντυπο κείμενο, αλλά και την ελληνική και άλλες γραφες.	☐	☐	☐	☐
28) Είναι _____ για τα παιδιά να συμμετέχουν σε ομαδικά παιχνίδια, έτσι ώστε να διευρύνουν τη γνώση τους μέσω της αλληλεπίδρασης με τους ομιλίκους.	☐	☐	☐	☐
29) Είναι _____ για τα παιδιά να εμπλέκονται σε παιχνίδια όπου υποδύονται ρόλους.	☐	☐	☐	☐
30) Είναι _____ για τα παιδιά να πλάθουν με την φαντασία τους και να αφηγούνται ένα δικό τους παραμύθι.	☐	☐	☐	☐

Παρακαλώ επιλέξτε δύο από τις παραπάνω φράσεις που κατά την γνώμη σας είναι οι πιο σημαντικές. Στην ακόλουθη γραμμή σημειώστε τον αριθμό που τις αντιπροσωπεύει (25-30)

α)_____

β)_____

	Καθόλου σημαντικό	Οχι ιδιαίτερα σημαντικό	Αρκετά σημαντικό	Εξαιρετικά σημαντικό
	↓	↓	↓	↓
31) Είναι _____ για τα παιδιά να φαντάζονται την εξέλιξη μιας αφήγησης.	☐	☐	☐	☐
32) Είναι _____ για τα παιδιά να μοιράζονται τους φόβους τους και τις ανησυχίες τους.	☐	☐	☐	☐
33) Είναι _____ να ερεθίζεται η φαντασία και η εφευρετικότητα των παιδιών.	☐	☐	☐	☐
34) Είναι _____ για τα παιδιά να δραπραγματεύονται τυχόν συγκρούσεις ή εντάσεις που προκύπτουν σε μια συνεργασία.	☐	☐	☐	☐
35) Είναι _____ για τα παιδιά να αποδέχονται ανθρώπους με διαφορετικές γλωσσικές, πολιτιστικές ή θρησκευτικές καταβολές.	☐	☐	☐	☐
36) Είναι _____ για τα παιδιά να μάθουν να μην διακόπτουν την ροή μιας δραστηριότητας παρά να περιμένουν εως ότου ολοκληρωθεί.	☐	☐	☐	☐
37) Είναι _____ για τα παιδιά να ασχολούνται όσο το δυνατόν περισσότερο με τον υπολογιστή.	☐	☐	☐	☐

Παρακαλώ επιλέξτε δύο από τις παραπάνω φράσεις που κατά την γνώμη σας είναι οι πιο σημαντικές. Στην ακόλουθη γραμμή σημειώστε τον αριθμό που τις αντιπροσωπεύει (31–37)

α)_____

β)_____

	Καθόλου σημαντικό	Οχι ιδιαίτερα σημαντικό	Αρκετά σημαντικό	Εξαιρετικά σημαντικό
	↓	↓	↓	↓
38) Είναι _____ για τα παιδιά να πειραματίζονται με τα αντικείμενα που βρίσκονται στο χώρο του νηπιαγωγείου.	☐	☐	☐	☐
39) Είναι _____ για τα παιδιά να εξερευνούν με τις αισθήσεις τους τον χώρο που τους περιβάλλει.	☐	☐	☐	☐
40) Είναι _____ για τα παιδιά να επιλέγουν και να χρησιμοποιούν δημιουργικά διάφορα υλικά.	☐	☐	☐	☐
41) Είναι _____ για τα παιδιά να εμπλέκονται σε δραστηριότητες γραφής μέσω του παιχνιδιού.	☐	☐	☐	☐
42) Είναι _____ για τα παιδιά να μάθουν να ελεγχουν τα συναισθήματά τους στο νηπιαγωγείο.	☐	☐	☐	☐
43) Είναι _____ για τα παιδιά να έχουν την δυνατότητα να εκφράζουν τις σκέψεις τους όταν ακούν μια διήγηση.	☐	☐	☐	☐
44) Είναι _____ για τα παιδιά να αποδέχονται τυχόν κανόνες και περιορισμούς που ισχύουν στο νηπιαγωγείο.	☐	☐	☐	☐

Παρακαλώ επιλέξτε δύο από τις παραπάνω φράσεις που κατά την γνώμη σας είναι οι πιο σημαντικές. Στην ακόλουθη γραμμή σημειώστε τον αριθμό που τις αντιπροσωπεύει (38–44)

α)_____

β)_____

B2. Παρακαλώ επιλέξτε τον βαθμό που εκφράζει το πόσο συχνά συνηθίζατε να εμπλέκετε τα παιδία στις ακόλουθες δραστηριότητες.

	Σχεδόν ποτέ ↓	Σπάνια ↓	Τακτικά ↓	Πολύ Συχνά ↓
1) Δραματικό παιχνίδι.	☐	☐	☐	☐
2) Παζλ και κατασκευές.	☐	☐	☐	☐
3) Εμπλέκονται σε δραστηριότητες που δίνουν εμφαση στην κατάκτηση των μαθηματικών δεξιοτήτων.	☐	☐	☐	☐
4) Καλούνται να αναγνωρίζουν οικεία γραφή στο περιβάλλον	☐	☐	☐	☐
5) Διηγούνται ιστορίες	☐	☐	☐	☐
6) Γράφουν το όνομά τους	☐	☐	☐	☐
7) Ζωγραφίζουν	☐	☐	☐	☐
8) Τραγουδούν	☐	☐	☐	☐
9) Απαρίθμηση	☐	☐	☐	☐
10) Απομνημονεύουν κείμενα	☐	☐	☐	☐
11) Καθορίζουν την εξέλιξη της δραστηριότητας	☐	☐	☐	☐
12) Παίζουν ελεύθερα	☐	☐	☐	☐
13) Συμμετέχουν σε δραστηριότητες που οργανώνει ο/η νηπιαγωγός	☐	☐	☐	☐
14) Εμπλέκονται σε παιγνιώδεις δραστηριότητες που έχουν επιλέξει τα ίδια τα παιδιά	☐	☐	☐	☐
15) Προβληματίζονται και συζητούν για ένα κοινωνικό θέμα (λ.χ. άτομα με ειδικές ανάγκες)	☐	☐	☐	☐
16) Κόβουν και χρωματίζουν προσχέδια	☐	☐	☐	☐
17) Διακόπτουν την αφήγηση μιας ιστορίας προκειμένου να σχολιάσουν όσα ακουσαν.	☐	☐	☐	☐

Γ1. Σημειώστε τον βαθμό που σας εκφράζει η κάθεμια από τις παρακάτω προτάσεις.

	Δεν συμφωνώ καθόλου ↓	Μάλλον δεν συμφωνώ ↓	Μάλλον Συμφωνώ ↓	Συμφωνώ απόλυτα ↓
1) Είμαι πεπεισμένος/η πώς οι παιδαγωγικές μου πρακτικές στο νηπιαγωγείο είναι κατάλληλες.	☐	☐	☐	☐
2) Οι γονείς των παιδιών με αποδέχονται ως παιδαγωγό.	☐	☐	☐	☐
3) Είμαι πεπεισμένος/η πώς οι πρακτικές μου συμβάλλουν στην ολόπλευρη ανάπτυξη και κοινωνικοποίηση των παιδιών.	☐	☐	☐	☐
4) Μπορώ να χειριστώ καλά τα προβλήματα στο νηπιαγωγείο.	☐	☐	☐	☐
5) Η δουλειά μου συμβάλλει καθοριστικά στην έγκαιρη παροχή βοήθειας και στήριξης των παιδιών που έχουν ανάγκη.	☐	☐	☐	☐

Γ2. Σημειώστε τον βαθμό που σας εκφράζει η κάθεμια από τις παρακάτω προτάσεις.

	Δεν συμφωνώ καθόλου ↓	Μάλλον δεν συμφωνώ ↓	Μάλλον Συμφωνώ ↓	Συμφωνώ απόλυτα ↓
1) Αποφασίζω μόνη μου για τις μεθόδους που χρησιμοποιώ στην παιδαγωγική πράξη.	☐	☐	☐	☐
2) Αποφασίζω και ορίζω μόνη μου τους στόχους της παιδαγωγικής εργασίας.	☐	☐	☐	☐
3) Αποφασίζω και ορίζω μόνη μου το περιεχόμενο της παιδαγωγικής πράξης.	☐	☐	☐	☐
4) Αποφασίζω μόνη μου τον τρόπο διαχείρισης των παιδαγωγικών προβλημάτων.	☐	☐	☐	☐
5) Δεν κάνουμε τίποτα που αντιτίθεται με τις επιθυμίες των γονέων.	☐	☐	☐	☐

Γ3. Σημειώστε τον βαθμό που σας εκφράζει η κάθεμια από τις παρακάτω προτάσεις.

	Δεν συμφωνώ καθόλου ↓	Μάλλον δεν συμφωνώ ↓	Μάλλον Συμφωνώ ↓	Συμφωνώ απόλυτα ↓
1) Είμαι ανεξάρτητη στο σχεδιασμό της παιδαγωγικής εργασίας.	☐	☐	☐	☐
2) Το πλαίσιο εργασίας είναι τέτοιο, ώστε σπάνια και με δυσκολία μπορώ να εφαρμόσω τις δικές μου ιδέες στην παιδαγωγική πράξη.	☐	☐	☐	☐
3) Η δουλειά μου είναι εξαιρετικά σημαντική για την ευημερία της οικογένειάς μου.	☐	☐	☐	☐
4) Η δομή και η οργάνωση του εκπαιδευτικού μας συστήματος είναι άκαμπτη και δεν μου επιτρέπει να διαχειριστώ ελεύθερα την παιδαγωγική διαδικασία.	☐	☐	☐	☐

Γ4. Σημειώστε τον βαθμό που σας εκφράζει η κάθεμια από τις παρακάτω προτάσεις.

	Δεν συμφωνώ καθόλου ↓	Μάλλον δεν συμφωνώ ↓	Μάλλον Συμφωνώ ↓	Συμφωνώ απόλυτα ↓
1) Ορισμένες φορές αμφιβάλλω για τον τρόπο που αντιμετωπίζω μια παιδαγωγική κατάσταση.	☐	☐	☐	☐
2) Η ατμόσφαιρα του νηπιαγωγείου είναι ευχάριστη και χαλαρή.	☐	☐	☐	☐
3) Συνεργάζομαι πάντα με τους γονείς των παιδιών.	☐	☐	☐	☐
4) Το πλαίσιο των δραστηριοτήτων για τα παιδιά καθορίζεται σε συνεργασία με τους γονείς.	☐	☐	☐	☐
5) Οι γονείς επηρεάζουν σημαντικά την εκπαιδευτική πράξη.	☐	☐	☐	☐
6) Οι γονείς με ενθαρρύνουν να οργανώνω δραστηριότητες που δίνουν έμφαση στα μαθηματικά.	☐	☐	☐	☐

181

Γ5. Σημειώστε τον βαθμό που σας εκφράζει η κάθεμια από τις παρακάτω προτάσεις.

	Δεν συμφωνώ καθόλου	Μάλλον δεν συμφωνώ	Μάλλον συμφωνώ	Συμφωνώ απόλυτα
Αν κάτι δεν πάει καλά (όπως θα έπρεπε) στην παιδαγωγική διαδικασία,....	↓	↓	↓	↓
1) φταίνε τα παιδιά.	□	□	□	□
2) είναι δική μου ευθύνη.	□	□	□	□
3) μου λείπουν οι μεθοδολογικές δεξιότητες για τον χειρισμό της κατάστασης.	□	□	□	□
4) ζητώ βοήθεια από έναν/μια συνάδελφο.	□	□	□	□
5) μπορώ εύκολα να διαχειριστώ δύσκολες καταστάσεις.	□	□	□	□
6) δεν έχω χρόνο να ασχοληθώ.	□	□	□	□

Δ1. Οικογενειακή Κατάσταση

Άγαμος □   Έγγαμος □   Διαζευγμένος □
Αριθμός τέκνων —

Δ2. Παρακαλώ περιγράψτε την επαγγελματική ιδιότητα του/της συζύγου

_____
_____
_____

Δ3. Προσδιορίστε την εκπαίδευση των γονέων σας:

	Μητέρα	Πατέρας
• Αναλφάβητος/η	□	□
• Απόφοιτος Δημοτικού	□	□
• Απόφοιτος Γυμνασίου	□	□
• Απόφοιτος Λυκείου	□	□
• Κάτοχος τίτλου Πανεπιστημιακής εκπαίδευσης	□	□
• Κάτοχος μεταπτυχιακού	□	□
• Κάτοχος Διδακτορικού	□	□

Δ4. Επιπρόσθετη επιμόρφωση

Συμμετείχατε σε κάποιου είδους επιπρόσθετης επιμόρφωσης κατά την διάρκεια του εργασιακού σας βιου (επιπλέον σπουδές);

NAI ☐   OXI ☐

ΑΝ ΝΑΙ, ΣΕ ΤΙ ΕΙΔΟΥΣ

_____

_____

_____

Δ5. Κατά την διάρκεια της εργασιακής σας εμπειρίας είχατε την ευκαιρία να συνεργαστείτε και να μοιραστείτε τις διδακτικές σας υποχρεώσεις με συναδέλφους;

NAI ☐   OXI ☐

Δ6. Είχατε την ευκαιρία να λάβετε μέρος σε μια ερευνητική διαδικασία;

NAI ☐   OXI ☐

Αν ναι, περιγράψτε την ερευνητική διαδικασία καθώς και τον ρόλο σας σε αυτήν:

_____

_____

_____

_____

Δ7. Παρακαλώ σταυρώστε για κάθε ένα από τα ακόλουθα την απάντηση που εκφράζει την δράση σας τον τελευταίο χρόνο.

- Έχω διαβάσει επιστημονικά άρθρα που σχετίζονται με την προσχολική αγωγή.

  NAI ☐   OXI ☐

- Έχω συμμετάσχει σε εκπαιδευτικά σεμινάρια που αφορούν την προσχολική αγωγή.

  NAI ☐   OXI ☐

- Έχω λάβει μέρος σε επιστημονικά Συνέδρια.

  NAI ☐   OXI ☐

- Στον ελεύθερό μου χρόνο έχω συμμετάσχει σε δραστηριότητες οργανώσεων που σχετίζονται είτε με την προσχολική αγωγή είτε με την παιδική ηλικία ευρύτερα (λ.χ. ΟΜΕΡ)

  NAI ☐   OXI ☐

Δ7. Παρακαλώ αναφέρετε το μάθημα που σας ενδιέφερε περισσότερο κατά την διάρκεια των σπουδών σας:

_____

_____

_____

Δ8. Παρακαλώ περιγράψτε την δομή του νηπιαγωγείου που εργαζόσασταν πριν την ένταξή σας στο Διδασκαλείο (περιοχή όπου βρισκόταν το νηπιαγωγείο, αριθμός παιδιών, αριθμός συναδέλφων, ύπαρξη ή όχι Διευθυντή/τριας και οι σχέσεις σας μαζί τους):

_____

_____

_____

_____

_____

_____

_____

This questionnaire is addressed to pre-primary teachers in order to explore their beliefs and practices in order to obtain significant information on their educational work. Completing this questionnaire is extremely important for the researcher and she is asking you to dedicate 30 minutes of your time for it. Be re-assured that the anonymity of participants will be assured and the answers given will be kept strictly confidential. Thank you very much for your cooperation.

A1. SEX
Male ☐
Female ☐

A2. UNIVERSITY EDUCATION
Yes ☐   No ☐
If Yes, at which university?

A3. SIMULATION
Yes ☐   No ☐

A4. STUDIES
Degree from an Academy ☐
Bachelor ☐
Master ☐
PhD ☐

A5. AGE
        20–30 ☐   31–40 ☐   over 41   ☐

A6. YEARS OF EXPERIENCE
        5 ☐   6–10 ☐   11–20☐   over 21   ☐

B1. Please fill in the sentences below by ticking the box that most reflects your personal beliefs.

	Not at all important ↓	Not that important ↓	Fairly important ↓	Extremely important ↓
1) It is _____ for the children to improve their mathematical skills.	☐	☐	☐	☐
2) It is _____ for the children to interact with the possible alternative solutions in a problem solving activity.	☐	☐	☐	☐
3) It is _____ for the children to develop the capacity to recognize familiar words in their environment and within texts.	☐	☐	☐	☐
4) It is _____ for the children to memorize very short texts in order to realize, progressively, elements of the language (e.g. syllables).	☐	☐	☐	☐
5) It is _____ for the children to have the freedom to determine the course of an activity.	☐	☐	☐	☐
6) It is _____ for the children to have the freedom to plan and organize their dramatic play.	☐	☐	☐	☐

Please select two of the above phrases that in your opinion are the most important. Enter the number representing them (1–6) in the following line.

a) _____

b) _____

	Not at all important ↓	Not that important ↓	Fairly important ↓	Extremely important ↓
7) It is _____ for children to enrich their knowledge through play.	☐	☐	☐	☐
8) It is _____ for children to participate in activities organized by the teacher.	☐	☐	☐	☐

	Not at all important ↓	Not that important ↓	Fairly important ↓	Extremely important ↓
9) It is _____ for children to have time for free play.	☐	☐	☐	☐
10) It is _____ for the children to take part in recreational activities.	☐	☐	☐	☐
11) It is _____ for playful activities to be based on children's interests.	☐	☐	☐	☐
12) It is _____ children's outdoors play to include organized activities.	☐	☐	☐	☐

Please select two of the above phrases that in your opinion are the most important. Enter the number representing them (7–12) in the following line.

a) _____

b) _____

	Not at all important ↓	Not that important ↓	Fairly important ↓	Extremely important ↓
13) It is _____ for children to participate in activities through which they can acquire experiences engaging all their senses.	☐	☐	☐	☐
14) It is _____ for children to learn through a lesson plan (even if they may not use all their senses).	☐	☐	☐	☐
15) It is _____ for children to have the freedom to use their imagination so as to define the course of an activity.	☐	☐	☐	☐
16) It is _____ for children to engage in previously organized activities so as to avoid unexpected consequences.	☐	☐	☐	☐

	Not at all important ↓	Not that important ↓	Fairly important ↓	Extremely important ↓
17) It is _____ to reinforce children's imagination as part of their learning abilities.	☐	☐	☐	☐
18) It is _____ for children to discuss with the pre-primary school teacher the emotional impact of an argument, fight, etc.	☐	☐	☐	☐

Please select two of the above phrases that in your opinion are the most important. Enter the number representing them (13–18) in the following line.

a) _____

b) _____

	Not at all important ↓	Not that important ↓	Fairly important ↓	Extremely important ↓
19) It is _____ for children to enrich their knowledge through peer interaction.	☐	☐	☐	☐
20) It is _____ for children to develop positive feelings towards learning.	☐	☐	☐	☐
21) It is _____ for children to become friends with their peers.	☐	☐	☐	☐
22) It is _____ for children to develop their communicative skills.	☐	☐	☐	☐
23) It is _____ for children to learn to cooperate.	☐	☐	☐	☐
24) It is _____ for children to learn the social rules that they have to follow when they take part in a discussion in the circle.	☐	☐	☐	☐

Please select two of the above phrases that in your opinion are the most important. Enter the number representing them (19–24) in the following line.

a)_____

b)_____

	Not at all important ↓	Not that important ↓	Fairly important ↓	Extremely important ↓
25) It is _____ for children to be encouraged to write in any way they can.	☐	☐	☐	☐
26) It is _____ for children to get used to memorizing, reciting poems, learning similes, word puns, etc.	☐	☐	☐	☐
27) It is _____ for children to recognize and compare different forms of written speech, e.g. a manuscript and printed text, the Greek language as well as others.	☐	☐	☐	☐
28) It is _____ for children to participate in team games, so as to broaden their knowledge through peer interaction.	☐	☐	☐	☐
29) It is _____ for children to be involved in role playing games.	☐	☐	☐	☐
30) It is _____ for children to use their imagination and narrate a fairy tale of their own.	☐	☐	☐	☐

Please select two of the above phrases that in your opinion are the most important. Enter the number representing them (25–30) in the following line.

a) _____

b) _____

	Not at all important ↓	Not that important ↓	Fairly important ↓	Extremely important ↓
31) It is _____ for children to imagine the outcome of a narrative.	☐	☐	☐	☐
32) It is _____ for children to share their fears and anxieties.	☐	☐	☐	☐
33) It is _____ to stimulate children's imagination and resourcefulness.	☐	☐	☐	☐

	Not at all important ↓	Not that important ↓	Fairly important ↓	Extremely important ↓
34) It is _____ for children to negotiate possible conflicts or tensions that may arise when they cooperate.	☐	☐	☐	☐
35) It is _____ for children to accept people from different linguistic, cultural, or religious backgrounds.	☐	☐	☐	☐
36) It is _____ for children to learn not to interrupt the course of an activity and wait until it is completed.	☐	☐	☐	☐
37) It is _____ for children to engage themselves as much as possible with computers.	☐	☐	☐	☐

Please select two of the above phrases that in your opinion are the most important. Enter the number representing them (31–37) in the following line.

a) _____

b) _____

	Not at all important ↓	Not that important ↓	Fairly important ↓	Extremely important ↓
38) It is _____ for children to experiment with the objects that can be found in the kindergarten school.	☐	☐	☐	☐
39) It is _____ for children to use their senses to explore the surrounding area.	☐	☐	☐	☐
40) It is _____ for children to choose and use creatively different materials.	☐	☐	☐	☐
41) It is _____ for children to involve themselves in writing activities through games.	☐	☐	☐	☐

	Not at all important	Not that important	Fairly important	Extremely important
	↓	↓	↓	↓
42) It is _____ for children to learn to control their feelings in the kindergarten school.	☐	☐	☐	☐
43) It is _____ for children to express their thoughts when listening to a narrative.	☐	☐	☐	☐
44) It is _____ for children to accept any rules and restrictions that apply in the kindergarten school.	☐	☐	☐	☐

Please select two of the above phrases that in your opinion are the most important. Enter the number representing them (38–44) in the following line.

a) _____

b) _____

B2. Please choose the extent to which you usually involve children in the following activities.

	Almost never	Rarely	Regularly	Very often
	↓	↓	↓	↓
1) Dramatic play	☐	☐	☐	☐
2) Puzzles and constructions	☐	☐	☐	☐
3) Activities that place emphasis on acquiring mathematical skills	☐	☐	☐	☐
4) Being asked to recognize familiar writing in their environment	☐	☐	☐	☐
5) Narrating stories	☐	☐	☐	☐
6) Writing their names	☐	☐	☐	☐
7) Painting	☐	☐	☐	☐
8) Singing	☐	☐	☐	☐
9) Counting	☐	☐	☐	☐
10) Memorizing texts	☐	☐	☐	☐
11) Defining the (evolution) outcome of an activity	☐	☐	☐	☐

	Almost never	Rarely	Regularly	Very often
	↓	↓	↓	↓
12) Playing freely	☐	☐	☐	☐
13) Participating in activities organized by the teacher	☐	☐	☐	☐
14) Being involved in playful activities that have been chosen by the children	☐	☐	☐	☐
15) Thinking about and discussing a social issue (e.g. people with special needs)	☐	☐	☐	☐
16) Cutting and painting outlines	☐	☐	☐	☐
17) Interrupting the narration of a story to comment on what they have heard	☐	☐	☐	☐

C1. Please note the extent to which each of these sentences expresses how you see yourself.

	I entirely disagree	I rather disagree	I rather agree	I entirely agree
	↓	↓	↓	↓
1) I am convinced that my educational practice in the pre-primary school is appropriate.	☐	☐	☐	☐
2) The children's parents accept me as a teacher.	☐	☐	☐	☐
3) I am convinced that my educational practice contributes to the child's development and socialization.	☐	☐	☐	☐
4) I can easily handle any problems in the pre-primary school.	☐	☐	☐	☐
5) My job contributes significantly to promptly providing help and support to children who need it.	☐	☐	☐	☐

C2. Please note the extent to which each of these sentences expresses how you see yourself.

	I entirely disagree ↓	I rather disagree ↓	I rather agree ↓	I entirely agree ↓
1) I decide which methods to use in my educational practice on my own.	☐	☐	☐	☐
2) I decide and define the aims of the educational practice on my own.	☐	☐	☐	☐
3) I decide and define the context of the educational practice on my own.	☐	☐	☐	☐
4) I decide the way of solving educational problems on my own.	☐	☐	☐	☐
5) I do not do anything to oppose the wishes of parents	☐	☐	☐	☐

C3. Please note the extent to which each of these sentences expresses how you see yourself.

	I entirely disagree ↓	I rather disagree ↓	I rather agree ↓	I entirely agree ↓
1) I am independent in designing (choosing) the educational practice.	☐	☐	☐	☐
2) The working framework is such that I can hardly apply my own ideas in my educational practice.	☐	☐	☐	☐
3) My job is especially important in my family's welfare.	☐	☐	☐	☐
4) The structure and the organization of the educational system are rigid and do not allow me to manage the educational process freely.	☐	☐	☐	☐

C4. Please note the extent to which each of these sentences expresses how you see yourself.

	I entirely disagree ↓	I rather disagree ↓	I rather agree ↓	I entirely agree ↓
1) Sometimes I have doubts about the way I handle a pedagogical situation.	☐	☐	☐	☐
2) The atmosphere in the pre-primary school is pleasant and relaxing.	☐	☐	☐	☐
3) I always cooperate with the parents.	☐	☐	☐	☐
4) The framework of activities for the children is defined in cooperation with the parents.	☐	☐	☐	☐
5) Parents influence the educational process significantly.	☐	☐	☐	☐
6) Parents encourage me to plan activities that place an emphasis on mathematics.	☐	☐	☐	☐

C5. Please note the extent to which you agree with each of these sentences.

	I entirely disagree ↓	I rather disagree ↓	I rather agree ↓	I entirely agree ↓
If something does not work (as it should be) in the educational process…				
1) it is the children's fault.	☐	☐	☐	☐
2) it is my responsibility.	☐	☐	☐	☐
3) I lack the methodological skills to handle the situation.	☐	☐	☐	☐
4) I ask for help from a colleague.	☐	☐	☐	☐
5) I can easily handle demanding situations.	☐	☐	☐	☐
6) I do not have the time to deal with it.	☐	☐	☐	☐

D1. Family Status

       Single ☐   Married ☐   Divorced ☐

       Number of children __

D2. Please describe your spouse's vocational capacity

_____

_____

_____

D3. Define your parents' education:

	Mother	Father
• Illiterate	☐	☐
• Elementary school	☐	☐
• Junior High school	☐	☐
• Senior High school	☐	☐
• University Degree	☐	☐
• Master's Degree	☐	☐
• PhD degree	☐	☐

D4. Additional Training

Have you taken part in any additional training programmes during your working life?

       YES ☐   NO ☐

       IF YES, WHAT KIND

_____

_____

_____

_____

D5. During your working experience, did you have the opportunity to cooperate and share your teaching obligations with your colleagues?

       YES ☐   NO ☐

D6. Have you had the opportunity to take part in a research project?

       YES ☐   NO ☐

If yes, describe the research project as well as the role you played in it:

_____

_____

_____

D7. Please tick the answer that corresponds most appropriately to your activity in the past year.

- I have read scientific articles regarding pre-school education.
  YES ☐   NO ☐
- I have taken part in seminars regarding pre-school education.
  YES ☐   NO ☐
- I have taken part in scientific conferences.
  YES ☐   NO ☐
- In my free time I have taken part in organizational activities concerning pre school education or childhood in general.
  YES ☐   NO ☐

Arbeit, Bildung & Gesellschaft
Labour, Education & Society

Herausgegeben von Prof. Dr. György Széll, Prof. Dr. Heinz Sünker,
Dr. Anne Inga Hilsen und Dr. Francesco Garibaldo

Bd. 1 György Széll (ed.): Corporate Social Responsibility in the EU & Japan. 2006.

Bd. 2 Katja Maar: Zum Nutzen und Nichtnutzen der Sozialen Arbeit am exemplarischen Feld der Wohnungslosenhilfe. Eine empirische Studie. 2006.

Bd. 3 Daniela De Ridder: Vom urbanen Sozialraum zur kommunikativen Stadtgesellschaft. 2007.

Bd. 4 Heinz Sünker / Ingrid Miethe (Hrsg.): Bildungspolitik und Bildungsforschung: Herausforderungen und Perspektiven für Gesellschaft und Gewerkschaften in Deutschland. 2007.

Bd. 5 Anja Bastigkeit: Bildungsbiographie und elementarpädagogische Bildungsarbeit. 2007.

Bd. 6 Antônio Inácio Andrioli: Biosoja versus Gensoja. Eine Studie über Technik und Familienlandwirtschaft im nordwestlichen Grenzgebiet des Bundeslandes Rio Grande do Sul (Brasilien). 2007.

Bd. 7 Russell Farnen / Daniel German / Henk Dekker / Christ'l De Landtsheer / Heinz Suenker (eds.): Political Culture, Socialization, Democracy, and Education. Interdisciplinary and Cross-National Perspectives for a New Century. 2008.

Bd. 8 Francesco Garibaldo / Volker Telljohann (eds.): New Forms of Work Organisation and Industrial Relations in Southern Europe. 2007.

Bd. 9 Anne Marie Berg / Olav Eikeland (eds.): Action Research and Organisation Theory. 2008.

Bd. 10 György Széll / Carl-Heinrich Bösling / Ute Széll (eds.): Education, Labour & Science. Perspectives for the 21st Century. 2008.

Bd. 11 Francesco Garibaldo / Philippe Morvannou / Jochen Tholen (eds.): Is China a Risk or an Opportunity for Europe? An Assessment of the Automobile, Steel and Shipbuilding Sectors. 2008.

Bd. 12 Yunus Dauda: Managing Technology Innovation. The Human Resource Management Perspective. 2009.

Bd. 13 Jarmo Lehtonen / Satu Kalliola (eds.): Dialogue in Working Life Research and Development in Finland. 2009.

Bd. 14 György Széll / Werner Kamppeter / Woosik Moon (eds.): European Social Integration – A Model for East Asia? 2009.

Bd. 15 Benedicte Brøgger / Olav Eikeland (eds.): Turning to Practice with Action Research. 2009.

Bd. 16 Till Johannes Hoffmann: Verschwendung. Philosophie, Soziologie und Ökonomie des Überflusses. 2009.

Bd. 17 Denis Harrisson / György Széll / Reynald Bourque (eds.): Social Innovation, the Social Economy and World Economic Development. 2009.

Bd. 18 Werner Weltgen: Total Quality Management als Strukturierungsaufgabe für nachhaltigen Unternehmenswandel. 2009.

Bd. 19 György Széll / Ute Széll (eds.): Quality of Life and Working Life in Comparison. 2009.

Bd. 20 Francesco Garibaldo / Volker Telljohann (eds.): The Ambivalent Character of Participation. New Tendencies in Worker Participation in Europe. 2010.

Bd. 21 Richard Ennals / Robert H. Salomon (eds.): Older Workers in a Sustainable Society. 2011.

Bd. 22 Christoph Sänger: Anna Siemsen – Bildung und Literatur. 2011.

Bd. 23 Nam-Kook Kim: Deliberative Multiculturalism in Britain. A Response to Devolution, European Integration, and Multicultural Challenges. 2011.

Bd. 24 Mirella Baglioni / Bernd Brandl (eds.): Changing Labour Relations. Between Path Dependency and Global Trends. 2011.

Bd. 25 Rüdiger Kühr: Japan`s Transnational Environmental Policies. The Case of Environmental Technology Transfer to Newly Industrializing Countries. 2011.

Bd. 26 Francesco Garibaldo / Dinghong Yi (eds.): Labour and Sustainable Development. North-South Perspectives. 2012.

Bd. 27 Francesco Garibaldo / Mirella Baglioni / Catherine Casey / Volker Telljohann (eds.): Workers, Citizens, Governance. Socio-Cultural Innovation at Work. 2012.

Bd. 28 Simone Selva: Supra-National Integration and Domestic Economic Growth. The United States and Italy in the Western Bloc Rearmament Programs 1945-1955. Translation by Filippo del Lucchese, revision by Simone Selva. 2012.

Band 29 György Széll / Roland Czada (Hrsg.): Fukushima. Die Katastrophe und ihre Folgen. 2013.

Band 30 Siqi Luo: Collective Bargaining and Changing Industrial Relations in China. Lessons from the U. S. and Germany. 2013.

Band 31 Litsa Nicolaou-Smokoviti / Heinz Sünker / Julia Rozanova / Victoria Pekka Economou (eds.): Citizenship and Social Development. Citizen Participation and Community Involvement in Social Welfare and Social Policy. 2013.

Band 32 Christ'l De Landtsheer / Russell F. Farnen / Daniel B. German / Henk Dekker / Heinz Sünker / Yingfa Song / Hongna Miao (eds.): E-Political Socialization, the Press and Politics. The Media and Government in the USA, Europe and China. 2014.

Band 33 Jukka M. Krisp / Michael Szurawitzki (eds.): Doctoral Experiences in Finland. 2014.

Band 34 Dimosthenis Daskalakis: Greek Labour Relations in Transition in a Global Context. 2015.

Band 35 Antoanneta Potsi: The Capability Approach and Early Childhood Education Curricula. An Investigation into Teachers' Beliefs and Practices. 2016.

www.peterlang.com